GOING INDIAN

JAMES HAMILL

# *Going Indian*

UNIVERSITY OF ILLINOIS PRESS

URBANA AND CHICAGO

© 2006 by the Board of Trustees
of the University of Illinois
All rights reserved
Manufactured in the United States of America
♾ This book is printed on acid-free paper.
I 2 3 4 5 C P 5 4 3 2 I

Library of Congress Cataloging-in-Publication Data
Hamill, James F. (James Francis), 1942–
Going Indian / James Hamill.
p.  cm.
Includes bibliographical references and index.
ISBN-13: 978-0-252-03032-1 (cloth : alk. paper)
ISBN-10: 0-252-03032-x (cloth : alk. paper)
ISBN-13: 978-0-252-07279-6 (pbk. : alk. paper)
ISBN-10: 0-252-07279-0 (pbk. : alk. paper) 1. Indians
of North America—Oklahoma—History. 2. Indians of
North America—Oklahoma—Government relations.
3. Indians of North America—Oklahoma—Politics
and government. I. Title.
E78.O45H295    2006
976.6004'97—dc22    2005022118

*To Bell*

# Contents

# Preface

I arrived in Norman, Oklahoma, in mid-May to begin the research project I had looked forward to for the past several years. I had chosen Norman as my base because it gave me easy access to the resources available at the University of Oklahoma, and my first job in setting up that base was to find a place to live. I was staying with my sister while I looked for permanent lodging, but I knew that the quicker I established a base the quicker I would be able to begin the research proper. I knew that I would be spending long hours at the University of Oklahoma's Western History Collections, and even more hours in front of my computer, so I looked for a place that would facilitate both. I was lucky enough to find a nice apartment over a garage less than a mile from campus. Its four hundred square feet easily accommodated my needs, and Monnet Hall was a quick bicycle ride from my door. The garage, the apartment, and the house associated with the garage where my landlord lived were beautifully kept, in a quiet neighborhood of similar homes shaded by large old trees. I felt many emotions as I went about the mundane chores of furnishing and supplying my research home for the next year. As I found a chair and a bed, turned on the phones and the lights, and stocked the kitchen with staples, I was at once elated with my privilege, challenged by the job I had set forward for myself, and frightened that I would not be up to the task.

That May I knew it was late in my career and that this would probably be my last opportunity to have this kind of an experience as an anthropologist. It had occurred to me that Oklahoma, unlike other places in the Indian country, was one place where there really were Indians.

My anthropological experience with Indian people had always been in a tribal context. The people I had worked with considered themselves Navajo, or Ute, or Ojibewa, and resisted the association with other Native American peoples that the idea "Indian" carried with it. When I began working as an anthropologist among Indian people in Oklahoma, those earlier experiences were challenged by new ones where people did consider themselves Indian, and their lives were filled with formal and informal institutions that reinforced peoples' Indianness. Indian professional groups, Powwows, Native American Church, sewing circles of Indian women, Indian research associations, and Indian social service agencies are parts of the everyday lives of Indian people throughout Oklahoma. This clash between my earlier reservation experiences and my experience in Oklahoma sparked my curiosity and led me to try to learn more, and that was when I first discovered the Indian Pioneer Papers and the Doris Duke Collection. In both of these collections, Indian people in Oklahoma were interviewed about their experiences as Indians. The interviews reported in the Indian Pioneer Papers were conducted in the late 1930s, and those transcribed in the Doris Duke project were taped between 1967 and 1970. I was sure these interviews could shed light on questions about Indian ethnicity. So I was excited about the opportunity to read the words, feelings, attitudes, and experiences of Indian people from the 1930s, the 1960s, and the end of the twentieth century. I hoped and believed that there was a story in all this that people would want to hear.

Part of the excitement that I felt certainly came from the selfish anticipation of the adventure I imagined myself having. I looked forward to the new experiences I thought I might have, the new people I hoped I would need to talk to, and the new things I wanted to learn. I also knew, however, that my time was short and that if I were to be successful I would have to conduct the research and make it available to the public more quickly than I had ever been able to do in the past. I wanted to do the research and write this book about it in less than three years (I made it in four). I also knew that my adventure was not free. I would spend more money maintaining a second residence, traveling back and forth between Oklahoma and Ohio, and purchasing the resources I would need to do my research. In addition to these expenses, the fact that my research year came with a substantial reduction in my pay added up to serious financial burdens. More important than the money, however, were the holes my absence created. My family, colleagues, and friends all had to fill in for me so I could have this adventure: I felt a keen sense of responsibility to them to make sure that I did it well and did it right.

Very soon after I began the formal process of collecting data, this sense of responsibility was reinforced by the very data I was collecting. The first time I visited the Western History Collections, I called up a microfiche containing some interviews taken in 1937 for the Indian Pioneer project. (Please refer to the appendix for a more complete discussion of these interviews.) As I brought up the first page of an interview with Mattie Bailey, the great-granddaughter of Cherokee Sells, a Creek woman, it occurred to me that Mattie wanted me to read her interview. She took time out of her life in January of 1937 to talk about her great-grandmother with Ella Robinson, the field worker who took the interview. Mattie Bailey knew what she was doing; she knew that her interview would be recorded for other people to read and to learn from at other times. She submitted herself to the interview so that her story could be known and be part of some larger story. I felt a debt to Mattie Bailey that, like my debt to my family, colleagues, and friends, required me take my adventure seriously and do the best I could with it.

This work is about identity, and that means that, other than Oklahoma itself, two important contexts define the landscape of this work: method (how I process what I observe), and theory (the ideas I use to understand what I observe). These issues are complex and slippery.

At its core, an identity appears simple, one of the many answers a person can give to the question, "Who am I?" (I am a father, brother, American, etc.) Just those multiple answers, however, reveal that identity is neither singular nor monolithic but has multiple dimensions (Fogelson 1998). An ethnic identity is a specialized case in which a group of people share an answer to the question along a political axis (I am Irish, Tajik, Navajo, etc.). We presume that the people in this group descend from ancestors who were also in the group; that they share certain cultural traits; that they deal with one another on a regular, perhaps primary, basis; and that they are part of a larger social system that has other similar groups. The classic cases of ethnic identity, on an individual level, and ethnic groups, on an organizational level, include once autonomous tribes who were brought under the umbrella of a central, often colonial, political authority, or who were immigrants ghettoized in large cities. While this approach is attractive, it cannot deal with changes in the cultural traits that make up the group or, as with Indian identity in Oklahoma, ethnic groups with no historical antecedents.

In recognition of this, Barth shifted the focus in anthropology away from the emphasis on observable histories and cultural traits to the boundaries between ethnic groups (Barth 1969: 10). Because these boundaries are constructed of symbols, attention turns, in this way of thinking, from the objective traits of the ethnic groups to the understanding of those things in the minds of members of the groups. In other words, the documentable histories of ethnic groups are not as important as the understandings of histories that members of the group construct. This approach is more intellectually satisfying for anthropologists because no amount of knowledge about the specific cultural traits of specific ethnic groups can illuminate the phenomenon of ethnicity itself, but it pays the price of turning away from the comfortable world of observable traits to the slippery world of subjective understandings and constructions (Jackson 2002: 6–10).

At some point, however, if these symbols are significant in maintaining the boundaries between ethnic groups, they must be acted out in public and, at least to the extent they are, become objective (Cohen 1996: 371–72). For Indian people, these constructions work out along political, historical, and cultural dimensions. Among the most eloquent voices exploring the political aspects of Indian identity, Ward Churchill attaches identity to sovereignty. He says, "defining for itself the composition of its membership (citizenry), in what ever terms and in accordance with what ever standards it freely chooses, is, of course, the very bedrock expression of self determination by any nation or people" (Churchill 1998). In other words, if Indian nations today are truly sovereigns, they have the right to say who is or who is not an Indian. Churchill develops this line to argue that Indian identity, especially as measured by tribal membership based on blood quantum, is racist and was imposed on Indian peoples by colonial powers. He advocates that tribes use more indigenous notions of group membership and identity, criteria that did not rely on blood. Rather, native people in North America maintained relatively high degrees of social cultural inclusiveness and consequent reproductive activity (interbreeding) among one another (Churchill 1998). Ward Churchill is no disembodied ivory tower scholar. The ideas and issues he expressed are current among Indian people in Oklahoma today, and a part of lively conversations around the state.

The politics of colonialism merge with constructions of history, especially in terms of forced removals from contact era homelands and policies of forced assimilation carried out through programs including allotment, education, and relocation. In the abstract, Indian people in Oklahoma share these histories in one way or another with other Indian peoples in the country. Historical disruptions and experiences of forced assimilation are central to Lumbee identity (Blu 1980), as they are to the urban Indians of the Riverton Indian community (Jackson 2002). Because of significant peculiarities in the Oklahoma brand of these experiences,

Indian people there are unique in contemporary Indian country. Where the reservation serves as a model and conceptual anchor for other Native American people, this is not true for Indian people in Oklahoma. Not only were most of the tribes in the state today removed by force to Indian territory, but the reservations they instituted there were obliterated by the process, especially that of allotment, that turned Indian Territory into Oklahoma.

Shared constructions of histories cannot, however, sustain an ethnic identity. These identities live in social interaction and require people to deal with one another in terms of those identities. Often the identities themselves are contested and negotiated in these interactions, and issues concerning legitimate claims to Indian identity sometimes rest on membership in a federally recognized tribe. Discussions orbiting around the feared identity of "wannabe" and the ideal identity of "full blood" (Fogelson 1998: 41) and positions on blood quantum and Indianness characterize many interactions among Indian people in Oklahoma. Those interactions often take place in religious contexts. Tribal religions, pantribal religious movements, and Christianity coexist on a complicated landscape that shifts between tolerance and intolerance, and inclusion and exclusion. Indian people in Oklahoma talk about religion, they bring their religions to their understanding of all things, and they understand that their relations with the supernatural embody the traditions that characterize their identity as Indians.

PART I

_Context_

# 1 Oklahomas Go Either Way

> "There's one Omaha Indian that lives at Vinita—
> Allen Dale—has been the chairman but he's not a
> state—natural-born state Indian. Not Oklahoma
> Indian."
>
> —Jess Rowlodge (Doris Duke Collection)

One day Leslie told me this story. Leslie is in her fifties now and a member of one of the smaller tribes in Oklahoma. She is active in her tribe, especially in its ritual life, and is regarded in her community as an important ritual leader. She is an accomplished artist, and sales of her work and honoraria from her guest teaching are an important part of her family's income. She devotes much of her energy to the preservation of her tribe's heritage and has had relations with various museums since her early twenties. It was one of those early museum experiences that was the source of the story she told me.

We were all students yet. I had Yakama roommates, they had come up with another group, had come up to the university, but they didn't stay. The Apache and the Yakama and I were roommates with the Musiology Program.

We would go down to town and spend weekends, play cards in a little park, out on the lawn, and see some sights, but there were various places in town where the kids would congregate, there were whole houses that were nothing but Indians. They would rent a three-story apartment house that there would be like fifty people living there, and they would all be from different tribes and they would have their own little groups of bars.

3

There were different degrees of what was going on there. There was one place that had a dance floor. There was a bottom floor and there was a balcony. Usually up in the balcony is where the southwestern kids sat—the Navajos, Hopis, and Pueblos—and down on the main floor is where all the Sioux kids and the Northern Plain tribes would congregate. There they were in the same building, they could use the dance floor, but they were separate entities.

When the Oklahoma kids went to the bar and asked to sit with one of the other groups they would say, 'Yeah, Oklahomas go either way.' We could either be with the Plains or could go with the southwest and pretty much the same with the Yakama kids. With so many different tribes in Oklahoma that you could fit in no matter where you go. With our upbringing where we have to depend on other tribal groups, we could go anywhere, go up here and tell jokes for a while and then go down there and play jokes awhile and have a few and just visit. There wasn't that division where all the Navajo kids had to stay in one spot or all the Northern Plains kids had to stay in one spot. So the Oklahoma kids you could find them either place; be in one group or the other group and switch back and forth and make the rounds because they had friends in both groups. So if there was a conflict they either tried to resolve the conflict or stand back and let it happen. So that's where we coined the term Oklahomas, because we were considered a different group altogether.

That phrase "Oklahomas go either way," and especially the word "Oklahomas," seemed to express a feeling that had been growing, unnamed, on me. At that time I was supervising a summer ethnographic field school in Oklahoma where I and my students encountered a situation at odds

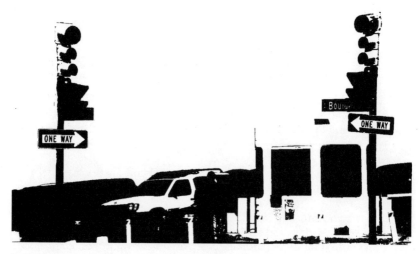

Intersection of Second and Boulder streets, Tulsa. Photo by the author.

with my professional experience elsewhere. When I began working with Indian people as an anthropologist, standard theory said that "Indian" was a misnomer and a manifestation of European colonialism. Indian scholars and anthropologists (Champagne 1994) alike pointed out that "Indian" has historical roots in Christopher Columbus's mistaken belief he was in Asia when he first made landfall in the Caribbean and referred to the people he met there as "Indians." This mistake was then compounded when European and American governments and peoples applied the term to all peoples in the hemisphere regardless of their cultural differences. My earlier research experiences, especially with Navajo people, confirmed this idea. My Navajo associates would correct me, sometime indignantly, when I referred to them as "Indian." I learned from these experiences that many of the Navajo people I worked with did not consider themselves Indians so much as they considered themselves Navajo. When I began supervising the summer field school, I made the mistake of presuming that the Navajo situation applied to Oklahoma. It did not, and it took a while for me to realize that. My new understanding started out as a sense of disorientation and confusion that began to crystallize when Leslie said: "Oklahomas go either way."

The syntax of the phrase struck me first. The place is named Oklahoma, and, in Standard English, "Oklahoman" refers to a person from that place. Leslie speaks Standard English very well, so this usage was not a mistake or an example of dialect variation. Rather "Oklahomas" was a noun that referred not to the place, not to people from the place, but to culture. Leslie used the word as a tribe name or a name of a people, much as she used Yakama or Navajo or the name of her tribe. "Oklahomas" thus refers to a culture identity that, since they go either way, is distinct from other Native American cultures. Because this identity emerged in a political and social context where Euro-Americans dominate the agenda, it can, at least structurally, be thought of as an ethnic identity. The use of "Oklahomas" to point to this ethnic group is, at least in my experience, rare. I have heard it only a handful of times, but this does not deny its existence. Euro-Americans and Native Americans alike throughout the state recognize the identity and the group that it forms and attribute various personal qualities and political stances to people in the group, as is common with ethnicities. The word that is usually used to point to it, however, is "Indian," not "Oklahomas." In other words, Oklahoma is a place where there really may be Indians.

This seemed odd to me. Usually we think of ethnic groups as emerging from some preexisting tribal or religious groups that come under the sway of a dominating central political authority, as in the former tribes of Afghanistan, but here there was no such precursor group. There was, and is, a Kiowa Tribe and a Choctaw Tribe and so on, but there was no "Indian" Tribe, so it seemed to me that Indianness and Indian ethnic identity had to emerge from someplace else. Wherever that was, it had to have the power to maintain symbolic boundaries that distinguish Indian from non-Indian. Those kinds of boundaries are often constructed from understandings of history and the reality of the world, and expressed in social institutions around which groups form. That is, these groups are formed and maintained through the ways people think about things and how they do things. I wanted to learn more about this, and the way to do that was to pay attention to what people do and say.

While I was conducting the field school, I sometimes used weekends to visit my family around the state. On my visits to my sister in Norman, I often looked around the University of Oklahoma for resources concerning Indian people in the state. On one of these trips I found the Indian Pioneer Papers and the Doris Duke Collection at the Western History Collections of the University's libraries. Both of these sets of materials report on interviews with Indian people; the Indian Pioneer interviews were conducted in the late 1930s and the Doris Duke interviews in the late 1960s and early 1970s. To me, these documents represent a source of knowledge that could open windows on how people thought about things in these two periods, so after I found them I spent large portions of my research time collecting a sample (about two thousand pages) of these interviews. (The appendix is a detailed description of these interview sets, the makeup of the sample I collected for use, and the means I used to analyze them.) I make heavy use of these interviews here, but that record is incomplete without the voice of Indian people in Oklahoma today.

To add that voice, I talked to Indian people around the state, and I asked some of the people I met if they would be interested in talking to me on a more formal basis. Nine people from nine different tribes around Oklahoma agreed to help me in this project. Four are women and five are men, and they range in age from their late twenties to their late seventies. They come from many walks of life: there are ceremonial specialists, lawyers, managers, health-care providers, and scientists in the group. They have all been aware of their Indian heritage, and have been active in Indian life and institutions for their entire lives. I tape recorded a series of interviews with those who agreed to help me, and I use much of that material here.

Among the things I agreed to do in return for their help was to protect their identities in any public use of their words. To accomplish this anonymity, when I use their words here I remove everything I can find that might help identify them. I never mention their tribal affiliations, where they live, or their professions—except where that information is significant in understanding what they are saying—for example, a consultant may speak from the point of view as a tribal administrator. I do my best to keep these exceptions to an absolute minimum. I do not use their names when I use their words; rather I use a pseudonym (see the following list). I do, however, use these names consistently; whenever I refer to Leslie, for example, I refer to the same person who told me how "Oklahomas go either way." This work rests on all of these contributions; my biases and the ways I understand things, the selected Indian Pioneer and Doris Duke interviews, my field notes, and the interviews completed in my fieldwork; and the understanding of Indian ethnicity that emerged as a result of my work.

*Consultant Pseudonyms*
Carol
Cory
Ed (in honor of Holly Hunter for her role in *Raising Arizona*)
Chris
Julian (in honor of Julian Steward)
Lee
Leslie (in honor of Leslie White)
Pat

This project also represents a kind of homecoming to me. I was born and raised in Oklahoma, and much of my family still lives there, as they have since before statehood. I hoped to find some of my family in the Indian Pioneer papers. My paternal grandfather and grandmother came to Indian Territory sometime in the late nineteenth or early twentieth century, before Oklahoma became a state in 1907. On my mother's side, my great-grandmother, Martha Marlow, was born in Choctaw, Mississippi, in 1827. She survived the forced removal, and sometime in the 1840s she married a man named Beals, a non-Indian, in north Texas, with whom she had thirteen or fourteen children. The last of those was my grandmother, Virginia Bell Beals, who we always referred to in the family as Bell; she was born in 1877.

When I was growing up in Oklahoma, these genealogical conditions entitled one to claim the mantle of being "part Indian," and my family did. That my grandmother was Choctaw, that she was on the rolls and had taken her allotment, and that her mother had come on the trail of tears was common conversation in our home and formed a part of how I and my siblings think about ourselves. Because Martha Beals died before my mother was born, the focus of our Indian connections was on Bell. She seems to become more important to me personally as I grow older.

Today these same genealogical conditions present me with conflict about labeling myself as Indian. On the one hand, my grandmother is very important to me, and in acknowledging her significance I must acknowledge her and my Choctaw heritage. On the other hand, a lot of people, in Oklahoma and elsewhere, live every day as Indians. They understand their world from Indian or tribal perspectives and they participate in their world through Indian points of view. Their families, their religions, their articulation to the Euro-American world, in short everything about them comes from their Indian heritage and community. I do not live that life; rather I live the life of a white university professor in a dominantly white community. For me to claim Indian identity in this context belittles those who live as Indian people. So when people ask me if I am Indian, I tell them about Bell.

Pointing to my grandmother Bell, however, does not answer the question; but if I use what I have learned in this work, the answer must be, "No, I am not an Indian." I was raised as a Catholic of Scottish and French-Canadian ancestry. I attended mass in the mainstream Christ the King Parish in Tulsa, and I was educated through high school in mainstream Tulsa Catholic schools. The fact that my great-grandmother, Martha Beal (nee Marlow), had come from Alabama to Choctaw Nation was all I ever heard of the trail of tears, and my one-thirty-second blood quantum was well below the one-fourth minimum to be considered Indian (a situation that was all right for my family). I have lived all my life as a white person in all-white or racially mixed groups on Euro-American cultural terms. I speak no North American Indian language, and I do not participate in Indian community activities, except on a professional basis as an anthropologist (a white endeavor if there ever was one). Indian people in Oklahoma are educated as Indians, they worship as Indians, and they engage their communities as Indians. They live being Indian every day of their lives.

My biases aside, I believe I did learn something about Indian ethnic identity in this process. Perhaps the most important thing I learned is merely that Indian ethnic identity is real. This is not "stop the presses" news; anybody who has spent very much time in Oklahoma knows this, to the point that no alternative is ever considered. Indian ethnicity is supported both through symbols such as clothing and jewelry and institutions like Indian professional associations. But the fact of Indian ethnicity means that there are at least two ways to be Native American: one can be Indian, or one can express a specific tribal identity. For the most part these two approaches coexist, because many people are as tribal as they are Indian, but it is not altogether a politically neutral situation. Many see Indian ethnicity as a threat to tribal ways and as a significant step on the road to total assimilation. This perception does more than merely confirm the reality of Indianness; it is part of the symbolic discourse that maintains Indian ethnicity.

I also learned that people like to talk about who they are. This too is not exactly big news, but very lucky for me, because it is mostly this talk that creates and maintains Indian, or any other, ethnic identity. Abstract meaning structures accomplish the creation and maintenance of ethnicity. These structures draw distinctions between groups, either directly, with statements like, "The other group did bad things to my group," or through implication, with statements like, "My group eats such-and-such" (implying the other group eats something else). These abstract structures are applied throughout all areas of life to one degree or another, but ethnic groups often focus on the past through understandings of history or constructions of the significance of ancestry. They also commonly emphasize the institutions that bring people together to express identity. I learned that Indian people in Oklahoma over the past century are no exception to these generalizations. It is easy to see in discussions of major historic events, such as the removals of the nineteenth century, or of central Indian institutions in peoples' lives, like the Powwow or Native American Church. In the next several chapters I will report what people said about these topics and how I believe their words reveal and define what it means to be Indian in Oklahoma today.

## 2   *The Lay of the Land*

When the Choctaws talk from the top of Rich Mountain, you have to go all the way to the panhandle to find anywhere in Oklahoma where anyone can do any taller talking. Rich Mountain is 2,660 feet high, whereas parts of the panhandle, and all the rest of Oklahoma, lie below 2,660 feet.

Once, the 4,438 feet northwestern corner boys tried to take the floor, figuring they had plenty enough feet over the Choctaws to have a taller talk. But the 4,973 foot obstruction of Black Mesa caused them to be poorly heard, and that, and the south wind blowing in favor of the Choctaws, caused the Choctaw talk to be more clearly heard over more of Oklahoma during the whole of the time that the 4,438 feet northwestern corner boys tried to hold the floor.

Once, the 1,558 feet southwestern corner boys tried to take the floor. But they came up 1,102 feet short.

Once, the 305 feet southeastern corner boys claimed that they had borrowed 2,356 feet from Black Mesa, and with that claim competed for the floor, claiming that Black Mesa had been reduced to 2,617 feet, thereby unobstructing much of the talk of the 4,438 feet northwestern corner boys, which was now giving the Choctaw talk enough competition from the northwestern corner to give the southeastern corner boys a say. But the northwestern corner boys continued to be poorly heard, and the south wind continued to blow in favor of the Choctaws, and the southeastern corner boys came up 2,355 feet short.

When the Choctaws talk from the 2,660 foot top of Rich Mountain, you have to go all the way to the panhandle to find anywhere in Oklahoma where anyone can do any taller talking.

—Don L. Birchfield, "Intermediate Choctology"

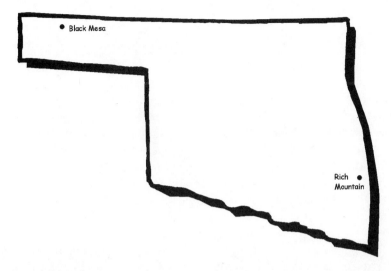

Map by the author.

We have evidence of people in Oklahoma, or what was to become Oklahoma, for about the past fifteen thousand years. I am not concerned here, however, with our distant cousins who roamed the territory living by their gathering and hunting skills, and perhaps helping to coax more than one species of megafauna into the dark night of extinction. I am concerned with Indian people in Oklahoma today and Indian identity over the last century or so. Most of those forty or so tribes in the state today started the twentieth century in what is now Oklahoma, but they did not start the nineteenth century in the territory. They all did, however, suffer extreme loss. Around 1800 they all lived near their precontact homelands, managed their own affairs under their own political systems, and enjoyed sovereignty over large areas of land. By the first decade of the twentieth century, most of the peoples had been forced out of their indigenous home environments to different environments in Oklahoma, lived under the complete domination of Euro-American local and national political systems, and were essentially landless. To have an understanding of Indian identity, it is important to know how today's Indian people in Oklahoma came to be there, and to have some understanding of the physical and political environments that have formed the context of Indian life in the state.

## Place

During the year I was in the field between 2000 and 2001, I set up accommodations in Norman, about twenty miles south of Oklahoma City. Norman was a good location for me because it gave me easy access to the resources at the University of Oklahoma while at the same time providing a good strategic location in almost the exact center of the state. If necessary, I could make a one-day trip to any part of the state, except the Panhandle, and be back home in the evening. I did this many times during the year. Sometimes I would travel west and south to Anadarko or Lawton. I followed Highway 9 west out of Norman through Blanchard, Chickasha, and Verdan. The road is almost straight; there are few curves, and those are gentle, but it probably appears straighter than it is because of the vast vistas provided on the southern plains. While this is not the treeless landscape of the high Plains in extreme western Oklahoma and eastern Colorado, it is also not the tangled forest just east of Norman.

A common route to the east might take me to Tulsa, Big Cabin, or Miami. That route took me east on Interstate 40 to a few miles west of Shawnee. From there I drove north on State Route 177 until it intersected Interstate 44 at Wellstone. Along that route all the way to Interstate 44, I passed mile after mile of widely spaced homes, sometimes half a mile apart, almost all carved out of a low, tangled hardwood forest. The trees are small: even the large ones probably do not exceed thirty feet in height, and the branches begin low to the ground. Where the hardwood forest has retreated, red cedar intrudes on the landscape. The erosions expose the bright red soil of central Oklahoma, which had given way to darker, richer soils by the time I got to Tulsa. Northeast of Tulsa toward Big Cabin and Miami, the scrub forest turns into open prairie. The forest shrinks to groves of trees, usually on hills, rising up from seas of grass. Herds of cattle graze in fenced pastures, and large rolls of hay, perhaps ten feet in diameter, dot the fields.

Sometimes I stayed overnight in Miami. From there I could drive south on State Highway 10 to Grove, Jay, and eventually to Tahlequah. That route goes through a beautiful oak and hickory forest characterized by tall straight trees and clear running streams that have been dammed up in the twentieth century to provide drinking water and recreation. Further south from Talequah into the southeastern quarter of the state, around Hugo and Idabel, the oak and hickory forest is replaced by a mixed forest of oak and pine. My route to this forest did not go south along the Arkansas border, however; rather I would go south from Norman on Interstate 35 almost to Texas before I turned east on U.S. Route 70. That route took me south over the gently rolling Arbuckle Mountains, past Turner Falls (a favorite summer playground in central Oklahoma), and then east past Ardmore, Madill, and Durant and sometimes on to Hugo in the hot, humid environment of the Red River Valley. Map 1, "Well-Traveled Roads," shows some of the routes I drove and the places I visited in my year in the field. If I had not known it before, the trips I took around the state in the course of my research would have clearly demonstrated the diverse environments within the state. They also showed me that if I hoped to come to an understanding of Indian identity in Oklahoma, I needed some basic understanding of the physical environments the various cultural heritages in the state adapted to.

Like Norman, Oklahoma is in the middle. While it is located in the southern half of the forty-eight contiguous states, its northern order is about as far north as the border between Tennessee and Kentucky. It is west of the Mississippi, but it's about equally far from Oklahoma City to Washington, D.C., as to San Francisco. On its east, Oklahoma is bordered by Arkansas and Missouri, on its north by Kansas and Colorado, and in the west and south by New Mexico and Texas (see map 2, "Homelands of Some Oklahoma Peoples"). It is larger than almost all the states east of the Mississippi but smaller than almost all the states to its west. It is situated in a transition zone between the relatively lush eastern United States and the dry west (Morris 1986: map 1). This transitional quality

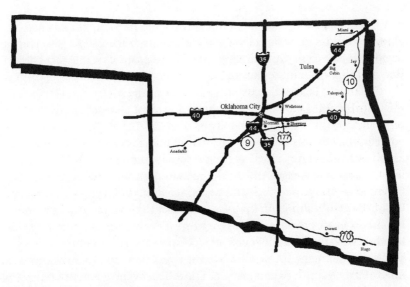

Map 1. Well-traveled roads. Map by the author.

Map 2. Homelands of some Oklahoma peoples. From Carl Waldman, *Atlas of the North American Indian*, rev. ed., with illustrations by Molly Braun. Copyright © 2000 by Carl Waldman and Molly Braun. Reprinted by permission of Facts on File, Inc.

manifests itself in many ways: its elevations, its geological zones, its climate, and its environments, among the other things. For as long as people have lived in the area they have had to adapt to its physical diversity, and that diversity emerges in culture.

Oklahoma is also about halfway between the Mississippi River and the Continental Divide. This produces a general slope of the state from highlands in the west to lowlands in the east. Black Mesa, the highest point in the state, is nearly five thousand feet above sea level. The lowest point in the state, a little bit under three hundred feet in elevation, is found in the southeast. Among the major cities and towns in the state, Guymon in the far west is a little over three thousand feet above sea level; Oklahoma City, almost in the exact center of the state, is at about twelve hundred feet elevation; and Muskogee, near the Arkansas border, is at six hundred feet above sea level (Morris, Goins, & McReynolds 1986: map 3). The decrease in elevation from northwest to southeast Oklahoma is mirrored by a similar gradient in climate. The average January temperature in the Panhandle is below freezing, whereas in the southeast corner of the state it's in the mid-forties (Morris, Goins, & McReynolds 1986: map 7). The geological conditions of elevation and the climactic conditions of average temperature and rainfall produce various vegetation zones throughout the state. The western half of the state is dominated by grassland. In the high, cool, and dry Panhandle, the short grass prairie is almost completely devoid of trees, and grasses seldom grow beyond the height of six to eight inches. From the state's western border with Texas through most of the rest of the western half of the state, the open plain features these western short grass varieties where it is dry. In wetter areas, plants more characteristic of the third grassland type in Oklahoma, the tall grass prairie, are more common (Risser 1980: 97–99).

The eastern half of the state is dominated by forest. From the northern border with Kansas south along the Missouri and Arkansas lines all the way to Texas, extensive forests of oak, hickory, and pine cover about the eastern fifth of the state. A large post oak and blackjack oak (the most abundant trees in Oklahoma) woodland called the Cross Timbers takes up much of the central portion of the state. Parts of it extend from the extreme eastern border at Fort Smith almost all the way to Texas, and from the southern border into Kansas on the north (Risser 1980: 99–100). In the Cross Timbers, these trees grow so closely together that it is almost impossible to get through the forest on foot or on horseback. Its large size made the state's two major river systems (the Arkansas and the Red) important factors in moving around the state prior to the introduction of railroads after the Civil War (Wright 1930). Washington Irving traveled through Indian Territory in the 1830s and said of the Cross Timbers: "I shall not easily forget the mortal toil, and the vexations of flesh and spirit, that we underwent occasionally, in our wanderings through the Cross Timber. It was like struggling through forests of cast iron" (Irving 1956 [1835]: 125). While map 2 captures the geographic centrality of Oklahoma in the United States, it also demonstrates how Oklahoma is not so much central, as terminal, to Indian people in Oklahoma. Most obviously, Oklahoma (Indian Territory) is at the end of the trails of tears that brought most of the ancestors of the Native peoples in Oklahoma today to the territory in the nineteenth century.

## Indian Territory

Many Indian people in Oklahoma, and many non-Indians who are familiar with Indian life, break the forty or so tribes in the state into three larger groups: the Five Civilized Tribes, the Small Tribes (almost all of whom suffered not one but two removals), and the Western Tribes. These labels are names rather than descriptions. The name "Five Civilized Tribes," for instance, is an artifact of nineteenth-century racism rather than any current claim that members of these peoples are more civilized than members of other tribes. While most of the Western Tribes can be found in the western half of the state, some tribes there are not considered Western Tribes, while other tribes in the eastern part of the state are. Many of the Small Tribes are larger than some of the Western Tribes and even some of the cultural communities within the Five Tribes. For this reason I think the name "small" is misleading, and I prefer to think about this group as the "twice-removed" peoples, because almost all of them were removed from their homelands, usually in the eastern United States, to "permanent" reservation in what was to become Kansas, and then a few years later to other "permanent," but almost always smaller, reservations in Indian Territory. Here I will use both terms interchangeably. These larger groupings are often used to capture commonalities in individual attitudes or tribal policies, but they also capture significant similarities in tribal history and culture, especially in how they came to be in Indian Territory.

## WESTERN TRIBES

The work in this study is built in part on information from eight of the Western Tribes (see the list that follows). Around the beginning of the nineteenth century, these peoples represented almost all the Indian people in Indian Territory, or what was to become Oklahoma. They lived in their traditional homelands and by their traditional ways. Caddoan-speaking peoples farmed and hunted outside the southeastern border of the area where Oklahoma, Arkansas, Louisiana, and Texas now come together. In the west the Comanche, Kiowa, Plains Apache, Wichita, and Lipan had by this time acquired horses and used them to exploit the southern plains. In the north, Siouan-speaking peoples such as the Osage, Otoe, and Missouri exploited the tall grass prairie and fertile soils. By the end of the century, that had changed more than anybody could ever have imagined at the time. For the most part, those changes came about because of increasing control of the Unites States government over the area, which in 1800 was the uneasy border with the Spanish colony of Mexico, and by 1900 all but the final steps had been taken to make it a state.

*Western Tribes in the Study*

Arapaho
Cheyenne
Comanche

Kiowa
Osage
Wichita
(The first four of these tribes signed the Treaty of
Medicine Lodge in 1867.)

At the start of the eighteenth century, the Wichita lived between the
Arkansas River in Oklahoma south along the Red River to the Brazos in
Texas. Around 1805 the Kiowa moved from their lands in the northern
plains, perhaps in response to pressure from the Cheyenne and Dakota,
and established themselves near the headwaters of the Cimarron. In this
era, they and the Comanche hunted much of what is now western Oklahoma (Wright 1986). Between 1800 and 1810 the Cheyenne and the Plains
Apache encountered the Lewis and Clark Expedition in the Black Hills of
South Dakota, and many Osage people settled on the Arkansas River, in
what is now Rogers county in the north central part of Oklahoma (Wright
1986). At this period in their history the Cheyenne were, like the Kiowa,
Comanche, and Plains Apache, nomadic hunters making a livelihood from
the vast herds of bison on the plains. The Siouan-speaking Osage practiced
a mixed economy, living in permanent villages and cultivating gardens
but making periodic hunting expeditions to the west for bison. On these
expeditions they encountered most of the other Western peoples.

In the early nineteenth century, the Western Tribes began the process of making treaties with the United States government. In 1808 the
Osage ceded vast lands in what are now Missouri and Arkansas to the
United States in a treaty signed at Fort Osage (Kappler 1904: 95). The
Cheyenne Nation signed its first treaty with the United States in 1825
on the Teton River (232), and the Comanche, with the Cheyenne, signed
their first treaty with the United States in 1835 (435).

For five of the Western Tribes, the 1867 Medicine Lodge Treaty signed
in Kansas marked a significant turning point in their relations with the
United States, other peoples, and the land. In what had to be one of the
most memorable and colorful gatherings of Indians in this region, the
Comanche, Kiowa, Oklahoma Apache, Arapaho, and Cheyenne agreed to
settle on reservations in Indian Territory (Kappler 1904: 982). The Kiowa,
Comanche, and Oklahoma Apache reservation extended west from the
ninety-eighth meridian between the Washita River on the north and the
Red River on the south. The Cheyenne and Arapaho reservation extended
west from the Arkansas River and north of the Cimarron River to the
Kansas border. On these reservations, the Indian people were supposed
to become farmers and not bison hunters, to live in permanent com-

munities with other peoples and not move through the territory, and to accept the authority of the United States.

The most striking thing exposed by this litany of treaties is that these Western Tribes are left pretty much where they were when the whole process started. The reservations created by the treaties at Medicine Lodge are a very small part of the territories these peoples exploited at the turn of the nineteenth century. The story of the treaties speaks only indirectly, however, to the massive cultural changes these peoples endured during the period. They went from the autonomous life of nomadic herders to a sedentary and subjugated life on reservations in a very brief time. The Kiowa, for example, went from the first treaty signed in 1837 to confinement on the reservation in just thirty years. They stand in stark contrast to the experiences of other peoples in Oklahoma who were removed by force to the state, where, with varying degrees of success, they were able to reestablish many of the life ways of their homeland.

## FIVE TRIBES

Most of the information collected for use here comes from people in one of the Five Tribes, and that is probably as it should be. The Five Tribes' membership outnumbers all of the other tribes in the state and has since their removal to Indian Territory. The list "Five Tribes" requires a brief aside, however, as eight tribes are on it. Individuals in the study were assigned a tribal category based on self-identification: that is, if someone said she or he was a Choctaw in an interview, she or he was put into the Choctaw category; those who self-identified themselves as Miami were numbered among the Miami; and so on. The Keetoowah in the Five Tribes list are Cherokee who now constitute a recognized Cherokee band. They are listed because people in the interviews identified themselves as Keetoowah. The Yuchi are a distinct cultural community within the Creek Nation, and many interviewees identified themselves as Yuchi. On the other hand, people in the Seminole and Creek tribes referred to themselves as Muskogee, so that is also listed in the "Five Tribes" list.

*Five Tribes*
Cherokee
Chickasaw
Choctaw
Creek
Keetoowah
Muskogee
Seminole
Yuchi

All the Five Tribes had relations made through treaties with other powers before there was a United States. The Cherokee made treaties with the British during the French and Indian War (Wright 1986: 59), as did the Creek after the allied Indian nations were defeated by the English in the Yamassee War in 1715 (131). In 1765, the Choctaw and Chickasaw nations negotiated treaties with the English that opened trade and established the nations' eastern borders (102).

Soon after the United States was established, the Five Tribes began making treaties and opening formal relations with the new country. The Cherokee signed a treaty at Hopewell, North Carolina, in 1785 (Kappler 1904: 8), and the next year the Choctaw and Chickasaw signed treaties at the same location (9). The Seminole did not come under the jurisdiction of the United States until Spain ceded Florida in 1819, but in 1823 tribal leaders signed a treaty with the United States reserving land for the nation in the interior of Florida east of Tampa Bay (Wright 1986: 229–30).

The 1820s also saw the United States begin a new round of treaty-making with the Five Tribes; these agreements sought to remove the nations from their homelands in the southeast. These treaties were the start of a process that produced trails of tears and five republics in what Rennard Strickland calls the "bright autumn of Indian nationhood" (Strickland 1980: 1–31). The best known of these stories is that of the Cherokee, who were forcibly removed by the terms of the 1835 Treaty of New Echota (Kappler 1904: 439). Most of the Cherokee people followed John Ross and opposed removal; however, a substantial minority believed that resistance was dangerous and futile. The leaders of this faction, including Major Ridge, his son John, and his nephews Elias Boudinot and Stand Watie, signed the Treaty of New Echota with twenty-two other prominent Cherokees in December 1835 (Wright 1986: 65).

The removal itself was delayed for two years, as most Cherokees refused to go, but about two thousand Treaty Party followers departed for Indian Territory soon after the treaty was signed. Finally, after the federal government began to use force at gunpoint, the Cherokee leadership agreed to conduct the removal themselves. Detachments of about one thousand Cherokee, many on foot, made the eight-hundred-mile journey to Indian Territory together. Before leaving their eastern homelands, the General Council declared the sovereignty of the Cherokee Nation and adopted its constitution. About four thousand people died along the way, but most of the survivors arrived in Cherokee Nation by the spring of 1839 (Wright 1986: 65–67).

The Choctaw and Chickasaw experienced much of the removal process together, or as interested parties in the same event, as did the Creek and Seminole. The United States made treaties with each of these pairs as a unit in some cases and also facilitated negotiations between nations in each pair. Each of these pairs has deep linguistic and cultural ties. The languages are closely related. While they are all Muskogian, Seminole and Creek are much more closely related to each other than they are to other languages in the family, as are Choctaw and Chickasaw. The same can be said of many other facets of culture such as family organization, political structures, myth, ritual, and general orientation to the supernatural. These close ties with one another are reflected in their respective histories with the United States and their removal to Indian Territory.

Both the Choctaw and Chickasaw opened relations with the United States in 1786, when each signed treaties at Hopewell. After this the treaty histories of the two nations diverges for a time but later come back together in a new structure, with removal. The Choctaw were the first to feel the pressure to move to Indian Territory and the first to agree. In 1820, three Choctaw chiefs—Pushmataha, Apuckshenubbee, and Mosholatubbee—negotiated with a government commission headed by General Andrew Jackson and signed a treaty at Doak's Stand in Mississippi. The terms of the treaty were not carried out (Wright 1986: 104), but the Treaty of Dancing Rabbit Creek in 1830 finally ceded all Choctaw lands in the East for land in Indian Territory and provided for the removal of the Choctaw people to Choctaw Nation in Indian Territory. In the treaty the United States recognized and agreed that the Choctaw Nation was sovereign, had jurisdiction over all the persons and property within its borders, and that no part of the of the Nation would ever be a territory or state (Kappler 1904: 310). The Chickasaw agreed to removal to Indian Territory two years later in 1832 with the Treaty of Pontotoc Creek. Many Chickasaw people were dissatisfied with some important provisions of the treaty, and it was renegotiated in treaties signed in 1832 and 1834. The United Stated government could find no suitable land west of the Mississippi for the Chickasaw people, so the Chickasaw and the Choctaw were again put together (Wright 1986: 88). In 1837 the Chickasaw and the Choctaw nations agreed to reunite in the Treaty of Doaksville (Kappler 1904: 486–87). The treaty formed a Chickasaw government in the form of a commission to oversee tribal funds.

While the forced removal of the Cherokee along their trail of tears is better known to the general public, the Choctaw forced removal and trail of tears was the first for the Five Tribes. The 1830 Treaty of Dancing Rabbit Creek forced the removal, which began in 1831 and ended (at least the first wave) in 1833 (Debo 1972 [1934]: 55–56).

Most of the Choctaw people made the journey on foot, walking the 350 miles from their homelands in Mississippi and Alabama to the Choctaw Nation in Oklahoma Indian Territory. In the first winter of the removal (1831 to 1832) the Choctaw endured one of the worst blizzards on record, and in the following summer (1832) they were beset by a cholera epidemic that killed many. These disasters were exacerbated by inadequate provisions and incompetent administration by the federal government (Debo 1972 [1934]: 56). Estimates of the number of people who made the journey and the number who died along the way are unreliable, but a census taken by the United States government in 1831 listed almost twenty thousand Choctaw people in Mississippi. A fairly good census conducted by the Choctaw Nation a little over ten years later counted about twelve thousand people. In the decades that followed the earliest removals, Choctaw people from Mississippi migrated to Choctaw Nation either voluntarily or in response to pressure from the United States government. Between 1845 and 1847, about four thousand additional Choctaws made the trip; in the 1850s a few hundred more followed as a result of specific United States government programs (69–70).

Compared to the brutal and tragic debacle of the Choctaw removal seven years earlier and the Cherokee removal of the same year, the Chickasaw removal was "tranquil and orderly" (Gibson 1981: 191). The removal itself did not began until five years after the 1832 Treaty of Pontotoc Creek was signed. During that time, tribal leaders toured the western part of Indian Territory and finally settled on suitable land in the western half of the Choctaw Nation, and a plan was developed to accomplish the removal with a minimum of hardship. The trip itself, while not as easy as the planners had envisioned, was accomplished in several waves and modifications of the original plan (84). By 1838 the largest of the Chickasaw removals had been completed, but Chickasaw people continued to migrate from the Mississippi homelands to the Chickasaw Nation for decades to come (186–88).

The Creek and Seminoles have much in common with others of the Five Tribes, but they also exhibit significant differences. Before contact with Europeans, the people who were to become the Seminoles and the Creek were a number of culturally related peoples occupying what are now Georgia, Alabama, and Florida. These peoples shared the land, many features of social and political organization, and a religious life, but they were also distinguished from one another along the same lines, as well as in the languages they spoke. While most of these peoples, including the Cowetas, Kasihtas, and Abihkas, spoke Muskogian languages, others, including the Hitchitis, and Yuchis, spoke non-Muskogian languages (Wright 1986: 1–5). During the precontact era, these peoples had close relations with one another and commonly intermarried.

Soon after the intrusion of Europeans into Creek territory, they found themselves surrounded by three of Europe's superpowers: the French to the west, the Spanish to the south, and the English in the east and north, along with the powerful and centrally organized Choctaw and Chickasaw in the west. While Creek and Seminoles' strategic position gave them common cause, the Europeans dealt with them as a single entity, which also forced a common identity. The European treatment of all Indians alike in some ways produced the Creek as a unified political entity, whereas before they had been a culturally related collection of autonomous towns in British-controlled Georgia and Alabama (Wright 1990). The Seminole in Spanish-dominated Florida emerged in the context of Spanish colonial rule whose relatively loose control made northern Florida a refuge for black free men and women and escaped African slaves from English- and then American-controlled Georgia, Alabama, and Mississippi. By the seventeenth century, Creek and Seminole peoples had developed separate cultural identities. They occupied medium to large permanent villages, subsisting on intensive agriculture supplemented by fishing and hunting. By the early eighteenth century, both peoples were involved in the deerskin trade with the Europeans and had adopted domesticated cattle into their subsistence pattern (Sattler 1998: 79).

After the Revolutionary War, the Creek chief Alexander McGillivary successfully sought trade and alliances with both the United States and Spain, but his greatest accomplishment was the unification of the Creek Nation. He spent much of his political life pursuing the goal of maintaining the Creek Nation boundaries as they were before the Revolutionary War, but white lust for the Creeks' Georgia land and the tense, often hostile, Indian-white relations it produced doomed that dream to failure in the early nineteenth century (Wright 1986: 132).

These tensions between Anglo-American Georgians and Indians eventually led to the Red Stick War between the United States and isolationist Creeks. The Creek warriors were finally defeated by Andrew Jackson in 1814 at the Battle of the Horseshoe Bend, where nearly one thousand Creek people were slaughtered (Debo 1987: 76–83). As a result of their defeat, the Creeks ceded their Georgia land through a series of negotiations and treaties that culminated in a treaty signed in Washington, D.C., in 1826 (88–91). Later Chief William McIntosh and his associates who had signed the treaty were executed for violating a Creek tribal council law that made it a crime punishable by death for any chief to cede Creek lands. The 1826 treaty signed in Washington did more, however, than cede the Creek lands in Georgia and produce near civil war among the Creek. It also introduced the idea of a Creek Nation west of the Mississippi and provided for the removal of the McIntosh faction to Indian Territory (91).

By 1832 the Creeks had lost all their land in Georgia and were confined to their eastern Alabama territories, and they signed a treaty agreeing to removal to Indian Territory. One provision of this treaty allowed individual Creeks who agreed to put themselves under the control of state and federal law to remain in Alabama. So many Creek people opted for this provision that the United States backed away. This eventually led to the second Creek war in 1836 and the forced removal of the Creeks to Indian Territory (Green 1982: 174).

In the meantime, the Seminole had no dealings with the United States until 1819, when Spain ceded Florida (Wright 1986: 229). Open hostilities between the United States and the Seminoles erupted after that, ending, for a while, in a peace treaty signed at Camp Moultrie, Florida, in 1823. This treaty ceded much of the Seminoles' prime land in Florida to the United States and confined them to a reservation in swampland east of Tampa Bay, but the government found it impossible to enforce the treaty or even to define the boundaries of the reservation. As a result, tensions between Indians and non-Indians remained high. When Andrew Jackson signed the Indian Removal Act into law in 1830, the federal government began pressing the Seminoles for a removal treaty (Howard 1990: 9).

Representatives of the Seminole signed that treaty at Payne's Landing, Florida, in 1832, but in a dispute over when the treaty was to be implemented, the Seminole leadership renounced it and refused to move to Indian Territory. As a result, the Seminoles and the United States fought a bloody war from 1835 until 1842. About fifteen hundred American soldiers lost their lives in this war, but Seminole losses were even more drastic. In the end, nearly forty-five hundred Seminole people were captured and deported to Indian Territory. By 1837, only about five hundred Seminole people remained in Florida (Howard 1990: 12).

Large numbers of Creek and Seminole people were removed to Indian Territory in 1836. In that year fourteen thousand Creeks made the journey, joined by large numbers of Seminoles. The majority of those traveled by one of two main routes: one over land, and the other by water. Creeks who took the water route started at Montgomery and traveled on barges, steamboats, and ocean-going ships that took them westward to Fort Gibson in Indian Territory. The trip was long and arduous, and many Indian people died of disease spread by the overcrowded conditions on the boats. In another tragedy, more than three hundred Indians died when their riverboat was rammed by another and sank (Wright 1990: 284–85).

The land route to the West was usually taken by the upper Creeks, those who lived above the Coosa and Tallapoosa forks of the Alabama River (Wright 1986: 3). Large parties, sometimes numbering two or three thousand, traveled the overland route starting in Alabama. Most of these people walked alongside overburdened wagons across Alabama and Mississippi to Memphis, Tennessee, where they were transported across the Mississippi. From there they followed the Arkansas River upstream to Fort Gibson (Wright 1990: 286). As many as 10 percent of the Indians died en route, including many prominent tribal leaders (287).

## Second Wave

The historical processes that brought the Five Tribes to Indian Territory share much in common with one another, but at the same time contrast sharply with the processes that put the Western Tribes in the area. The Five Tribes all come from about the same place, what is now the southeastern United States. By the time of their removal, many had shared histories with each other and with Europeans that spanned centuries. At removal, all of the Five Tribes were participating in the money economy of the United States, and many individuals were very wealthy. Each of the Five Tribes was also dealing with the federal government on a nation-to-nation basis. For each people, the removal process resulted in an autonomous republic in Indian Territory, but the process itself was contentious and deadly. Like the Five Tribes, the Western Tribes all come from about the same place. But the Five Tribes were forced to come to Indian Territory, while the Western Tribes were confined to reservations in Indian Territory that were within or near their precontact homelands. In addition, the Western Tribes had experienced relatively brief official relations with the United States or other Europeans. Many of the Western Tribes were signing their earliest treaties at a time when the Five Tribes already had long official relations with Europeans and were being pressured to sign removal treaties.

The historical processes that brought the Small Tribes to Oklahoma are yet again distinct from the Western Tribes and the Five Tribes, but they share similarities with each process. Well over half of the forty tribes in Oklahoma today fall into this category. Their experiences as a group in coming to Oklahoma during the nineteenth century are far more heterogeneous than those of the Western Tribes or the Five Tribes.

Even in that diversity, they share experiences that bring them together. The final corpus of data for this work included information from representatives of thirteen of those twenty or so peoples. (See the list that follows.) It is striking that of the thirteen small nations in the data, eight (the Delaware, Kaskaskia, Miami, Ottawa, Potawatomi, Shawnee, Sac, and Wyandotte) signed the Treaty of Greenville in 1795 (Kappler 1904: 39). It may be even more surprising that of the twelve peoples who signed the Treaty of Greenville (the aforementioned eight plus the Chippewa, Wea, Eel River, and Pankishaw) only one, the Chippewa, do not now have tribal headquarters in Oklahoma. Soon after signing the Treaty of Greenville, the Wea, Eel River, Pankishaw, and Kaskaskia were merged into the Miami and Peoria nations.

*Small Tribes in This Study*

Caddo
Delaware
Kaskaskia
Miami
Oto Missouri
Ottawa
Peoria
Potawatomi
Quapaw
Sac and Fox
Seneca
Shawnee
Wyandotte

The Treaty of Greenville was a peace treaty negotiated by General Anthony Wayne with representatives of the twelve nations in Greenville, Ohio. It established peace between the United States and the signatory nations and exchanged prisoners of war. It defined boundaries between the United States and Indian land and relinquished all United States claims to that land. In the treaty these Indian peoples retained for themselves much of northern Ohio and the land west of the current Ohio-Indiana border north of the Ohio River to the Mississippi River. The Indian nations ceded all their claims to southern Ohio and lands east (Wilson 1894: 81–90).

The terms of the Treaty of Greenville notwithstanding, the United States government began pressing these Indian peoples for land concessions soon after it was signed. The Sac signed a treaty in 1804 that ceded some hunting rights within their territory in Wisconsin, Illinois, and Missouri, but Anthony Wayne interpreted the treaty as an outright cession of land. Tribal outrage over this fraud eventually led to the Black-hawk War of 1831 and 1832. Soon after this treaty, in 1805, some of the nations who signed the treaty had ceded more land to the United States (Kappler 1904: 170), and it was apparent that the United States sought to solve its "Indian problem" (that is, Indians had land that white citizens of the United States wanted) through removal.

That policy was perhaps first publicly articulated in the 1817 Treaty of St. Mary's. This treaty gave the Delaware reservation land in what is now Missouri, but pressure for removal extended even that far west by the 1830s. In 1829 the Delaware in Missouri signed treaties that ceded their land in Ohio once and for all and removed them to a reservation in what is now eastern Kansas (Goddard 1978: 224). In 1828 as the Delaware were being removed to eastern Kansas, the Eel River were merged with the Miami (Kappler 1904: 286) and the Kaskaskia with the Peoria. The Ottawa ceded their lands in Ohio for a Kansas reservation in 1831, the Potawatomi in 1837, the Sac and Fox in a series of treaties beginning in the 1840s and lasting nearly twenty years, the Miami in 1840, and the Wyandotte in 1842. This flurry of treaties and land concessions in the second quarter of the nineteenth century removed almost all the peoples in what we now call the upper Midwest to reservation lands in eastern Kansas.

New pressure from white settlers in Kansas in the 1850s resulted in either severe contraction or the outright obliteration of the Kansas reservations. In 1854 a treaty with the Miami, who had been in Kansas less than eight years, provided for the allotment of reservation land to individual Miamis and the sale of so-called surplus land to non-Indians. In the same year the Shawnee Wyandotte and the Delawares on the reservation in Kansas suffered the same fate (Kappler 1904: 618). By the end of the Civil War, these eastern Kansas reservations had been reduced to small parcels of commonly owned tribal land, and individual tribal members had been allotted up to two hundred acres each. Even these concessions were not enough for the white settlers. The Omnibus Treaty of 1867 began the process of removing these peoples once again to new lands in Indian Territory (960).

Almost all of the peoples in this removal were confined to reservations (usually much smaller than their Kansas land), but others, particularly some Shawnee and Delaware, were not. These Shawnees and Delawares were removed from Kansas into Cherokee Nation, but rather than Cherokee Nation ceding any land to them for their own reservations, they were made citizens of Cherokee Nation. The federal government recognized the tribal status of these Delaware in 1997 and the Shawnee in 2001 (thus making two Delaware and three Shawnee tribes in Oklahoma).

The Small Tribes share many things in common with the Western Tribes and the Five Tribes, but they also share histories among themselves that distinguish them from both other groups. Like the Five Tribes, and unlike the Western Tribes, all the Small Tribes suffered removal. While the numbers of people who died on their trails of tears do not approach the thousands lost by the Cherokee, the Creek, or the Choctaw, their losses were proportionally large. Like the Five Tribes, they were removed from one environment in their homelands into very different environments in Indian Territory. Like the Western Tribes, however, almost all of the Small Tribes experienced reservations. Their lands in Indian Territory were federal protectorates under the control of the United States government in the person of an Indian agent. The federal government controlled the agenda of the official tribe and appointed the official tribal leaderships. On the other hand, citizens of the Five Tribes lived in republics under elected leadership and an Indian-controlled agenda.

The Small Tribes were removed into the Indian Territory in the decade or so following the Civil War. By the late 1870s and early 1880s, all the tribes in the state today were in place, and Indian Territory took up almost all of what is now Oklahoma (see map 3, "Indian Territory 1866–89"). In this era, the lands in the five republics and reservations of

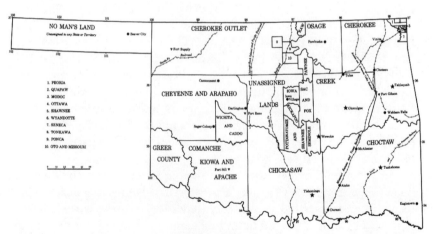

Map 3. Indian Territory, 1866–89. From John W, Morris, Charles R. Goins, and Edwin C. McReynolds, *Historical Atlas of Oklahoma*, 3rd ed. Copyright © 1965, 1976, 1986 by the University of Oklahoma Press. Reprinted by permission.

Oklahoma made up the vast majority of what would be Oklahoma in a few years. The push by whites for statehood began as early as the 1870s, and by 1900 the steps toward Oklahoma statehood were, for the most part, complete. Europeans, rather than Native Americans, had control of the political, economic, and legal institutions and were enforcing policies aimed at the destruction of native ways of life.

## AMERICANS

In the 1880s, Indian Territory was in one way or another in the control of Indian people. Indian agents, white men appointed by the federal government, supervised the reservations, but these lands were reserved for exclusive Indian use. In the eastern part of the state, the Five Republics had Indian people in control of their own destiny, but the pressure to open Indian Territory to white settlement was well underway. This would quickly eliminate any Indian control in the state. From the earliest part of the nineteenth century there had been Euro-Americans in the Territory, mostly garrisons of soldiers and their families, merchants and traders, and white people who had married into the various peoples. At that time, local political control and cultural articulation to white America was clearly in the hands of Indian people. Official moves to open Indian Territory to white settlement began soon after the Civil War and continued to their logical end with statehood in 1907. Between the mid-1860s and the late 1870s, bills were commonly introduced in the United States Congress that would open Indian Territory for white settlement. One of these, introduced by Senator Benjamin F. Rice of Arkansas in 1870, also introduced the name "Oklahoma." These bills met opposition, not only from the Five Tribes but also from powerful cattle interests that held lease arrangements for pasturage in the Western part of the state. Other powerful economic interests, however, maintained the pressure for settlement. Railroad companies, bankers, and farm machine manufacturers all wanted to see homesteaders in Oklahoma. They pursued their goals both in the halls of Congress and through the pages of major newspapers (Gibson 1981: 173).

In 1879 the *Chicago Times* published in article written by Elias C. Boudinot, a prominent Cherokee attorney, that claimed that nearly fourteen million acres in Indian Territory were available to be settled. Boudinot was one of many hired by railroad and other interests to promote the settlement of Indian Territory by white people. These professional promoters, called "boomers," extolled the richness and beauty of Indian Territory and encouraged people to colonize the Indian lands. Colonies of common folk were organized along the Indian Territory's northern and southern borders in the early 1880s. These potential settlers made raids into Indian Territory throughout the 1880s, attempting to establish their homesteads by squatters' rights (Gibson 1981: 174–76). Finally, in 1889, leaders of the Seminole and Creek nations agreed to relinquish any claim they had to the so-called unassigned territories (see map 3). The first land run followed in April of that year (176).

The land run of 1889 ranks as one of those epic events—like the Gold Rush in California or the Alamo in Texas—that mark the founding of a state for many Oklahomans. In March 1889, Congress approved a rider to the Indian appropriations bill, called the Springer amendment, that provided for the opening of the unassigned lands, also called the Oklahoma District. President Benjamin Harrison set the date for the opening on April 22 of that year. On the assigned day, as many as forty to fifty thousand people congregated on the borders of the Oklahoma District ready to run on foot or ride on horseback to stake their claim to a homestead. Some came into the district prior to its opening, hid in the brush and woods until the appointed hour, and used their illegal head start to stake their preferred claim. These homesteaders became known as "sooners." This founding myth is referred to today in the title of the University of Oklahoma's fight song, "Boomer Sooner" (Green 1989: 116–123).

The final push to statehood did not begin with the opening of the unassigned territories in 1889, but two years earlier with the passage of the General Allotment Act in 1887 (Gibson 1987: 229). The General Allotment Act is more widely known as the Dawes Act, after Senator Henry L. Dawes of Massachusetts, its principal supporter in the United States Senate. The Act authorized the president of the United States to survey each Indian reservation and nation, prepare tribal rolls, allot tribal land to each person on the rolls according to a formula, and dispose of "surplus" land by allowing eagerly awaiting Euro-American boomers to homestead. The Act exempted the five eastern republics as well as the tribes in the Quapaw agency in the extreme northeast corner of Indian Territory. The boomers, of course, supported the legislation, as did the corporate interests that backed them up, but support also came from the left wing of American politics. "The friends of the Indians" were late nineteenth-century liberals who believed the only hope for Indian people was in the destruction of Indian cultures. In the words or their motto, they sought to "save the man by killing the Indian," and allotment was just one of the programs they supported to this end.

The Allotment Act was intended to change the basis of Indian economic systems, therefore wiping out the cultures those systems supported. Prior to allotment, tribes owned all Indian lands, whether on reservations or in one of the Five Republics, thereby controlling its use. The Allotment Act eliminated tribal ownership of land and instituted a system of private ownership. Along with the shift in ownership patterns came a political shift that took control of the land away from the tribes and put it in the hands of white Euro-Americans. After the Seminoles and Creeks relinquished any of their claims on the unassigned territory, of course, there was no allotment there, but the opening of the lands paved the way for the Oklahoma Organic Act, passed by Congress in 1890. This act established a government in the Oklahoma Territory, in the former "unassigned lands," including an appointed governor, a court system, a local legislature, and a representative to the United States Congress. It also stipulated that as reservation lands in the West were allotted and "surplus" land became available for settlers, it was to be incorporated into the Oklahoma Territory (Gibson 1981: 176–78).

In 1889, by provision of the Springer amendment, President Harrison appointed a commission authorized to negotiate with those nations confined to reservations in the western half of Indian Territory. This commission, called the Cherokee Commission or Jerome Commission, after its chairman David H. Jerome, was charged with making agreements with the nations for the allotment of their land and the opening of "surplus land" to non-Indians. The first of these agreements was made with nations on reservations in the central part of Indian Territory: the Sac and Fox, Potawatomi, and Shawnee. Their lands were allotted and opened to settlement in 1891. In 1892 the Cheyenne-Arapaho Reservation was opened for homesteading. Although the Jerome Commission experienced difficulties negotiating with the Cherokee Nation, they were able to come to agreement on the Cherokee Outlet, a wide strip along the border with Kansas extending from the Cherokee Nation to the Panhandle. The Outlet had been reserved for the Cherokee Nation by the Treaty of New Echota, but was claimed by the United States. The Jerome Commission agreement with the Cherokee Nation resulted in the great land run of 1893 (Gibson 1981: 180–81). The Cherokee Outlet, more commonly known as the Cherokee strip, was opened for homesteading in September 1893. More than one hundred thousand settlers raced across the starting line for the forty thousand claims available in the outlet (Blochowiak 1993: 116). In the five years from 1889 to 1894, the Jerome Commission supervised the transfer of the western half of Oklahoma from Indian reservation land to privately owned land. Most of the private owners were Euro-Americans.

While the General Allotment Act of 1887 provided exemptions for the Five Republics and other tribes in the eastern part of the Indian Territory, the United States always assumed that these lands would also be transferred to private ownership. The Five Republics resisted the transfer, and a frustrated Congress amended the Act in 1893, removing those exemptions and establishing the Dawes Commission to implement the enrollment and allotment. The Five Republics still resisted, until in 1897 Congress passed the Curtis Act, which abolished tribal governments and required tribal members to submit to allotment (Gibson 1987: 238–39). The Act extended suffrage to non-Indians, authorized the establishment of a public school system, and abolished tribal courts. At this point the federal government took over the task of surveying the land in the Five Republics, which amounted to over twenty million acres, enrolling the citizens of the republics for eventual allotment, and finally the allotment of land to each citizen. The remnants of the Choctaw and Chickasaw governments submitted to allotment in 1897, the Seminole Nation in 1898, and finally the Cherokee and Creek Nations in 1901 (Gibson 1981: 194). By 1905 the commission's work was done, and the commission was terminated by Congress. The legislation making Oklahoma a state was signed into law in 1906. A constitutional convention was appointed and began work soon after. Elections were held to adopt the constitution and to elect state and local office holders in 1907. Oklahoma officially joined the United States in November of that year.

# PART II

# Assimilation

# 3  *Betrayals of Tears*

The Indians in their old homes in the eastern country were contented. They had their own hunting grounds. They could go wherever they chose and could visit with their kinsmen and friends with no interference from anyone.

Just as soon as the white men began to increase in number in the eastern Indian country, there began to be evidence of the beginning of discord between these two classes, the whites and Indians. It didn't seem possible that the Indians were forced to leave the homes that they loved for an unknown country, but when they had arrived in the Indian Territory, the leaders and some of the older prophets of those times talked of their heavy "sa-bo-gas," saying that this would not be the last time they would have to take them up and carry them away.

"Sa-bo-ga" is a Creek and Muskogee word meaning a bundle or a load of anything which is easily carried. The word used in this case would mean the hardships that the Indians had been through as they were being brought to the new country which was to be their homes. Many of those early day Indians had been through sickness, loss of all the few possessions they had and the starvations as well as the deaths that occurred without number.

When the first settlements were completed for the Indians, the weary Indians without knowing whether they would be permitted to stay always in the Indian Territory are said to have remarked, "We place our sa-bo-gas here for we will need to take them up again."

The Indians then began to make their homes and getting accustomed to their new country. The older Indians did not forget their "Trail of Tears" soon, and time went on until the Civil War period.

Again, some of the "sa-bo-gas" were taken as some of the Indians under able leaders left the Indian Territory to seek safety from a cause in which they had one [sic] wish

to be made a part. These flights did not take place with
no loss of lives but many lives were lost, with starvations
and deaths from sickness. Some of the leaders with their
faithful followers took their groups to Kansas or south to
Texas. Even when the destinations were reached, the men
folks had to sacrifice their lives protecting the women
and children. Some enlisted in the army.

After the war, the Indians reentered the Indian Territory and made efforts to establish homes. Things seemed
to be going well with the few would-be-Indian-leaders
stirring up feelings and causing uprisings. In this unrest,
some of the Indians were again forced to take up their
sa-bo-gas and seek safety from these hostile feelings.

It was a feeling, even after the uprisings were stopped,
that their "sa-bo-gas" could not be permanently placed.
Then there began the talk of "eka-na te-wath-ka." This
is used in reference to the talk regarding the laying off of
lands into allotments for individuals. The older Indians
had prophesied such a thing and it was not until these
allotments were made that the Indians are believed
to have placed their "sa-bo-gas" in a permanent place
on their allotments which were then protected by the
government.

Some old Indians are said to have prophesied that this
allotment could not always exist, but that the "sa-bo-gas"
would be taken up again.

—Amos Green (Indian Pioneer Papers)

Ethnicity is interesting to anthropologists because it seems
to arise only in certain cultural conditions. In other words, people do
not have ethnic identities, and there are not ethnic groups, because of
the cultural norms and values of peoples; rather, ethnic identities arise
because people find themselves relatively powerless in a centralized
political structure that we call a state. Because these groups originate
in a wide variety of cultural and historical contexts, the phenomenon
seems to expose something basic about us as human beings and arouses
anthropological curiosity. To me this is also part of the appeal of Barth's
idea that it is the boundaries between the groups that anthropologists
need to be interested in, and not so much the cultural content within
the boundaries (Barth 1969: 15–16).

The classic model of what are now ethnic groups—formerly autonomous villages, tribes, and other communities that in recent times have
been absorbed into a state—applies to many of the classic cases of ethnic

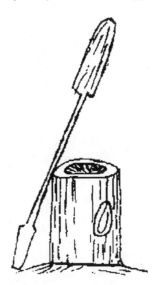

"Mortar and Pestle," by Meagher. Drawing. Indian Pioneer Papers, Western History Collections, University of Oklahoma, Norman, Oklahoma, 30:20.

identity (Cohen 1996: 370–71). This model remains, however, a mere icon of the phenomenon, and ethnic groups emerge through other historical processes as well. In the case of Oklahoma Indian identity, there was no previous tribe or village of Indians. There were Kiowas, and Choctaws, and Modocs, and so on, but there were no Indians. From the start, Europeans dealt with these peoples simply as Indians, but these relations did not amalgamate these various tribal identities until relatively recently. Yet Indian identity did arise in Oklahoma, so this is not a case of the old tribe becoming an ethnic group; rather it is a new ethnicity that emerged from the colonial situation. Indian ethnicity and identity did not emerge in a cultural or historic vacuum. Rather, Indian people constructed it from their cultural traditions and common historical experiences.

The cultural traditions come from everywhere. The tribes in Oklahoma today were originally in almost every area of the country, including the southern plains of Oklahoma, and elements of those different cultural traditions make up much of the boundaries that distinguish Indian ethnicity. On the other hand, these people share significant historical experiences that almost all come from Euro-American policies to eliminate Native American cultures. White Americans saw Indian people as a problem that they tried to solve by getting rid of Indians: they tried warfare, they tried moving Indians away, and they tried to force Indians to assimilate. This chapter and the next will look at how Indian people in Oklahoma talked about those experiences. This chapter will concentrate on what Indian people said about land: the removals and allotment. The next will deal with Indian education and how it was used as a tool of assimilation.

## Removal

Nannie Lee Burns talked to Mrs. Irene Shafer, a Quapaw, at her home in Baxter Springs, Kansas, for the Indian Pioneer project. Mrs. Shafer was sixty-two years old at the time, and she related how her grandfather came to Indian Territory:

> My grandfather had continued to live here (Pine Bluff Arkansas) after his kinsmen and tribesmen had left Pine Bluff for the Indian country but of course Grandfather heard from his family and they had always visited him and he knew where they were and how they were doing. Grandfather had refused to consider leaving and it was not until in the early '90's at the time that they were living in the Quapaw Nation, that the tribe sent some of their people from here to their kinsmen who were living in the Osage Nation and to Pine Bluff to try to get these people to come to the Indian country so that they could share in the land in this new country. It was at this time that Father and some of our people decided to come here. The Quapaw wanted to increase the size of their tribe. They had been in danger of losing their homes because so many of the Quapaws had left the Quapaw Nation. (Shafer 1938: 30–32)

As a removal story, this is unusual. The Quapaw had been removed to what is now Ottawa County, Oklahoma (the northeasternmost county in the state) in the early 1830s from their homelands in southern Arkansas, so this story is about the decision of an individual to join his tribe, rather than a story about the hardships encountered on the trails of tears, or about the fundamental injustice of the forced removals perpetrated through the military might of a colonizing power. Even at that, however, it does expose, if only by contrast, these two themes that the forced removals contributed to the symbolic construction of Indian identity. It also directly expresses a third theme that is common in these interviews, that of Indian people exercising what control they can over their lives. Like almost all the references to forced removals, the story is contextualized in terms of family and tribe, and the politics of colonialization ultimately motivates the move. These themes can be seen in the family stories from Indian people in Oklahoma, but the Five Tribes emphasize hardship and injustice, where the tribes that were confined to small reservations after the Civil War tend to emphasize the agency that Indian people take in creating their communities.

FIVE TRIBES

Amos Green, a Creek, was fifty-seven years old when he told Billie Byrd, a fieldworker for the Indian Pioneer project in 1937, about "sa-bo-gas" in the passage that starts this chapter. This particular passage stands out among all the removal stories in the data because it looks more like an origin myth than a family history. In this passage, the Indians were autonomous and content in the homelands (previous world), but corruption disrupted the peace and they were forced, with much hardship, to move to the Indian Territory (the next world), where they again established autonomy. They gained wisdom from their experience in the knowledge that they would have to take up their burdens again, which they do first because of internal strife, and finally because of allotment. Almost all the other stories in the data are family history narratives. People report on the experiences of a grandmother, or uncle, or some other close relative, who survived (or didn't survive) the trail of tears. Those stories that are not cast as family history are related as tribal history. "My tribe signed this treaty here, and were moved to there and so on . . ." Its unusual structure notwithstanding, however, Amos Green's story expresses all the main threads found in the rest of the interviews. He talks about the injustice at the heart of the forced removals, the hardships of the forced march that too often resulted in death, and the reestablishment of control over their lives in their new home.

About the same time Amos Green was talking to Billie Byrd, Jackson Miashintubbee told fieldworker Johnson H. Hampton about his grandfather's and grandmother's experiences on the Choctaw trail of tears:

> A good many of the Choctaws were banded together and when they started to move, they were under the command of a white man, who was bringing them through in wagons and horse back. They left there sometime in the fall, and before they got very far, winter overtook them; it was a severe winter; they did not have sufficient clothes to keep them warm, and some of them froze to death. There were a good many Indians died from exposure, and it seems that they did not have food to keep them from starving along the road. They, some of them, said that this white man in command did not care for them at all; he did not care if all died on the road coming over here. They finally landed here, and they began to build their log houses. (Miashintubbee 1938: 3–4)

Jackson Miashintubbee's family history expresses the same themes that Amos Green talked about. The Indians were forced to move by whites; they suffered great hardship and even death on the way, which their white masters cared little about; and finally, they came to their destination and established their new homes. These major structural elements, hardship and injustice, are resolved at the end of the story when control passes from white to Indian hands; whites force the move, but Indians build their own homes.

Mrs. Mary Payne's family history relates almost exactly the same ideas. Mrs. Payne was a Cherokee and seventy-seven years old when Ella Robinson interviewed her in 1937. Both of her parents were infants who survived the removal, but her aunt, who also survived the journey, was a teenager at the time and later told Mrs. Payne the family story.

> My father was David Israel, a full blood Cherokee and my mother was Martha Jane Miller Israel, a quarter Cherokee. They were born in Georgia. My mother in 1836 and my father in 1837. They were brought to Indian Territory by their parents over the 'Trail of Tears' when the Indians were driven from their eastern homes by the United States Troops. They were too young to know of the tragedies and sorrows of that terrible event. My aunt, who was 15 years old at the time, told me of the awful suffering along the journey. Almost everyone had to walk as the conveyances they had were inadequate for transporting what few possessions they had and their meager supply of food. Only the old people and little children were allowed to ride. They died by the hundreds and were buried by the roadside. As they were not allowed to remove any of their household goods, they arrived at their destination with nothing with which to start housekeeping. My grandparents located in Going Snake District on Spring Creek where the village of Oaks is now located. (Payne 1938: 72–73)

Jackson Miashintubbee and Mrs. Payne detail the hardships and injustice of the removal, and in doing that emphasize their Indian ethnicity. Indians were forced to walk, Indians had little food, and hundreds of Indians died along the way and were improperly buried. These hardships were compounded by unjust brutality. Indians were deprived of their rightful possessions, and they were driven by white, United States soldiers. It is interesting to me that Mrs. Payne talks about her grandparents' destination in Cherokee political terms, Going Snake District, and not in terms of white, Oklahoma, political divisions where she lived in 1937. Her use of the image of Indians being driven by whites on the trail of tears is also interesting because of how frequently it is used in these family histories. Almost the same details dominate Isaac Batt's story.

> His grandfather was Walter Adair, father of John Batt. Batt is the Cherokee way of speaking Adair. Grandfather Walter Adair was born in Georgia, date unknown, and came from Georgia on what was known as the Trail of Tears. This grandfather told him when they left Georgia they

drove the Indians like driving cattle for the first day or two and if any of them got sick and died on the road, they would just bury them there and go on and leave them. They would have a lot of bread at a place on ahead and would drive these Indians there before camp and the soldiers would sit up all night and guard these Indians, afraid they would turn back. (Batt 1938: 49–50)

The soldiers drove the Indians like cattle, and they used scarce food to force the Indians ahead on the trail. Ida Mae Hughes also evokes the image of being driven by force. She related her family history about her grandfather, Alfred Miller, and his experience of the removal.

[He] was born in Georgia in 1812 and came to Oklahoma with the Cherokees over the Trail of Tears. I have heard him talk of his journey here. He said they walked part of the way, came on steamboat part of the way and had to suffer great hardships. They were driven like slaves by the masters of the expedition. The weather was cold and the Cherokees suffered, many of them died on the way. (Hughes 1938: 219)

These passages all emphasize the force the United States government used to remove Indian people from their eastern homelands, and they all mention death as a result of that abuse. These references to death on the trail also all carry an ethnic theme. The white soldiers who were forcing them to move did not even care if Indian people died, and they would not allow the Indians to respect and mourn the deaths of their loved ones and observe the proper rituals. In these narratives, whites totally controlled Indian lives, but Indian people regained control with their arrival in Indian Territory and the establishment of their homes. This theme was common, like the discourses on injustice and hardship in these family histories, and almost always couched in terms of making a home and community. A good example of this is J. W. Brewer's family story of how his father and mother survived the trail of tears. Mr. Brewer was a Cherokee and in his late sixties when he was interviewed for the Indian Pioneer project.

His father died when he was seven years old, his mother when he was a very young boy. He lived with his uncle and aunt until he became a grown man. They told him about the trip of his father and mother when they came from Georgia and were driven here in what was called "The Trail of Tears." He said they told him there were ten thousand when they left Georgia; but when they arrived at Evansville, Arkansas, there were only five thousand. When they were driving them here, he said they fed them only very little. Some would get sick and some died on the road. Whenever anyone got sick or died they were just left. They were guarded at night; afraid they would go back.

> When they first arrived here they would clear up a piece of land, would hoe one man's crop out, until every man had his crop worked. They farmed mostly with hoes. (Brewer 1938: 109)

Themes of hardship and injustice constitute the bulk of this story, but it ends with both a new home and community. Sickness, death, and subjugation make up the journey itself: Indians were driven, they were abandoned if they fell behind because of sickness, and half of them died on the way. After this chaos, stability is established upon arrival at the new home. A crop is planted, with the community hoeing one person's land at a time until all had their crop in. Eliza Palmer's family history is expressed in much the same way. She first details the deprivations of the Creeks' forced removal and ends with a brief description of the new community in Creek Nation.

> Food and water were very scarce on the way here. Her brother who didn't want to come caused trouble and was shot and killed by one of the soldiers. When they got to this country the relatives were all scattered and to this day they do not know what became of some and there may be relatives scattered around that they don't know about. They were lonesome for the loved ones when they got here and worried about what had happened to them. They were some of the first to come over under McIntosh and settled on the Verdigris River near Muskogee. They had to cook outside where they had been used to cooking indoors at their old home. Some had to do without furniture as they didn't know how to make it. Others were handy and made their furniture. The old persons knew the herbs that were used for medicine and found some of them in the woods here. They had to go to Fort Gibson for their supplies and some had to walk. (Palmer 1938: 70–71)

As a result of the removal, her brother is killed by soldiers and her family is dispersed in the new Creek Nation. But after enduring these hardships, the story ends on an optimistic note as people take control and begin building new communities from the diverse talents among the survivors. This optimism is more characteristic of the removal stories told by members of the smaller tribes to Indian Territory after the Civil War.

## SMALL RESERVATIONS

The United States used its military might to force Indian people of the Five Tribes out of their homelands and into Indian Territory. The descendants of those who suffered on these trails of tears maintained the experiences in their family histories, which detailed how Indian people were driven like cattle in mass movements over very long distances. The interviews commonly relate those histories in terms of hardship, subjugation, and death. In contrast, other Indian people, often members of tribes removed from the eastern United States in the 1840s, came into Oklahoma over the relatively short distances from their Kansas reservations, and were often allowed much more individual say in determining the details of their moves. Often members of the tribes were encouraged to stay on their land in Kansas as part of the United States policy of forced assimilation. These differences are reflected in the family removal stories that members of these twice-removed tribes recorded in the Indian Pioneer and Doris Duke collections.

The split in the tribes between these two groups, those who retain their Kansas land and those who stay with the tribe on new lands in Indian Territory, is reflected in much of this family lore. Willis McNaughton, who had been chief of the Peoria Tribe, is a good example of this. He was in his late eighties when Peggy Dycus interviewed him in 1969 for the Doris Duke project, and he talked about how his grandfather had chosen to come to Indian Territory.

> My grandfather Perry came to this country, the first one among the first that came. Well, he, ah, and East Peorias and that bunch came down here from what is now Miami County, Kansas. Paola is county seat. They came down here, I believe, in '70, if I'm not mistaken, in '76. Came down here and looked this country over and then they bought, they bought up their reservation. I have forgotten the exact number of acres, but however, it wound up that we were allotted two hundred acres a piece, 153 of them came down here. And they, a bunch of them stayed in Kansas. They were paid off up there, and they are still up there. (McNaughton 1972: 5)

The contrast between this and the family histories from the Five Tribes is striking. Willis McNaughton does not talk about the journey that brought grandfather Perry from Paola to Indian Territory, so there is no mention of being driven like slaves, or death on the trail, or abuse of power. There is only oblique reference to the injustice of removal with phrases like "they were paid off," and even the discussion of Indian control in Indian communities is distinct from the way that theme is expressed in the Five Tribes interviews. The whole point of this passage is that the tribe was able to exert some control over the process: they surveyed and purchased their reservation in Indian Territory, and individuals decided for themselves whether or not they would make the move. In the Five Tribes, by contrast, Indian people retake control of their lives only at the end of the journey with the establishment of Indian nations and new homes. Both the Five Tribes and the smaller tribe narratives, however, relate that Indian people started feeling in control of their own destiny in Indian Territory.

Eunice Bluejacket Wilson, interviewed by J. W. Tyner for the Doris Duke project in 1969, develops these ideas in her discussion of the removal of the Shawnee to Cherokee Nation. She contextualizes the removal in terms of family, and the choice her grandfather and grandmother were given: to stay in Kansas and live as white people in a white community or move to Indian Territory. Her story also describes the journey to Cherokee Nation and even mentions hardship and injustice.

> J. W. Tyner: That wouldn't have been long after the Delawares come here. Would it?
> Eunice Bluejacket Wilson: No the Delawares come here the same time the Shawnees did.
> Tyner: 1867?
> Wilson: I think—yes—I think that it was '69 maybe when Grandad, Grandmother came. They didn't come to start with. They—oh—they didn't know what to do. They had two hundred acres on the Shawnee reservation. Those that wanted to accept allotments and then carry the responsibility for those allotments. And Grandad had his two hundred acres. Had a deed to it and they parleyed about it. And he left it up to Grandma. He said, "Now that's up to you. You've got these little children." See, they had four. And he said, "If you want to go down to the Cherokee Nation. We will." Well, you know, after they, well, weeks and weeks passed so they finally decided to come.
>   Summertime, nice time to travel. And I said oh, what a pitiful thing. Just see those Indians, had to gather up what they could haul in a wagon. Leave their homes and start out cross the country to a new home and not knowing anything about it. But, of course, the Cherokee Nation at that time was a wonderful place to be in. 'Course they told 'em, said, "Oh, there's lots of fish, lots of game." Oh, that's a happy thought, isn't it? To look a person in the face, well, you can live on wild game as far as we're concerned. (Wilson 1972: 7)

The story moves from a family crisis, through hardship, and ends in a "wonderful place." It is a story about the value placed on family—Grandad leaves the decision up to Grandma because she has the four children—and how the family takes control of the situation in their decision not to take the two-hundred-acre allotment in Kansas, and in their selection of the time to make the move. Eunice Bluejacket Wilson acknowledges the hardships and injustice of forced removal, but only in passing, with the reference of the pitiful sight of Indians with all their possessions in a wagon. The happy ending comes when the family reaches its final destination, a paradise teeming with fish and game. The story also contains a kind of ethnic direction that is absent from the Five Tribes narratives. Eunice Bluejacket Wilson's family moved from a white context in Kansas to an Indian context in the Cherokee Nation.

Much the same structure is evident thirty years earlier in Elizabeth Lindsey Palmer's family story of the removal. Mrs. Palmer, a Miami born in 1860 on the Miami Reservation in Kansas, occupies an interesting place in time. Her mother, Mary Pesawah, survived the removal of the Miami from their homelands in Indiana and, like her mother, Mrs. Palmer experienced the removal of the Miami Tribe to Indian Territory as a young mother in 1882. Her family story is about both removals.

> My grandmother and mother came from Peru, Ind., with a party of Miamis when they moved from that country to Kansas near the year of 1846. This party traveled by boat down the canal to the Ohio, through the Mississippi and up the Missouri to Kansas City where the boats were left and traveled over land to Marysville, Kansas.
>
> As this party made their way slowly down the river on large flat boats, those from the banks could see some of them sleeping, some smoking, others gathered together solemnly talking with children gathered near and some of the women cooking and doing the various tasks.
>
> Mary Pesawah was eleven or twelve years of age at this time and could not understand why she and her mother should leave their home and relatives (some by the name of Aveline still living there) and take this strange journey. (Palmer 1938: 78)

Elizabeth Palmer, like Eunice Wilson, evokes the hardships of the forced removal through the sight of the people on their journey, but she puts the condemnation of the injustice of the removal in the voice of her mother, who was then twelve years old, thus adding symbolic force to the indictment. While it picks up the themes of hardship and injustice, this part of the story involves no Indian control of the process, does not comment about moving into an Indian social environment, and does not have a happy ending. The Miamis are simply brought to undefined Kansas land without any comment. A few pages on in the interview, however, Mrs. Palmer finishes her family's removal story with her experiences in the removal from Kansas to Oklahoma. The themes absent in the first part are emphasized in the second.

> Chief Richardville had previous to this arranged and bought for the Miamis sufficient land from the Peorias for each of the tribe living in Kansas to have 200 acres each. The land laying west and south of the Quapaws and west of the Peorias.

Mrs. Palmer tells me that all of the Miamis did not come at one time but came a family or several families at a time over a period of several years and that all of them never came which resulted in a surplus of land. The land that they owned in Kansas they sold as it was theirs individually and they sold as opportunity presented itself. Chief Richardville owned a large two-story, eight-room house and several hundred acres of land. Their houses were well furnished and they had plenty and [sic] good stock around. Mr. Palmer's brother's wife now lives on this place which is one mile south of Fontana, Ka.

Chief Richardville and family came in 1882 and settled three miles west of Commerce, Oklahoma and improved the place that is now the Robinson-Mainess Dairy and here true to form he built a large two-story house and large barns. Mr. and Mrs. Palmer came in the early spring of 1884. She and her son, Harley, came by train to Baxter Springs and bringing what Mr. Palmer could not bring through in a wagon. He drove a large pair of dappled grey mares and brought his stock with him. He came directly to her land, and her son's, which is three miles due north of Miami, and immediately began ploughing and preparing to make a home; while she and her son remained in Baxter, seeing him only on weekends. When the warm weather came she insisted on living with him, so their home for the summer was a large tent and a large cook shed that he erected by placing posts in the ground and a support through the middle from which the boards sloped each way. (Palmer 1938: 80–81)

The Indian control over the removal, absent from the first part of Mrs. Palmer's story, dominates the second. Her recollection of the Miamis' removal from Kansas to Indian Territory is a story of people controlling their fate. The tribe, through its chief, controlled the acquisition of its new reservation, individual members of the tribe controlled whether they would stay in Kansas or sell their land there and relocate to Indian communities in Indian Territory, and those who moved exerted control over when and how to make the move. The story ends with new ground plowed and the family united in their new home.

Mrs. Palmer and Mrs. Jane Baptiste may have known each other, and may have even been friends. Both lived in the same small, tribally diverse Indian community in Miami, Oklahoma. They were about the same age, and members of closely related tribes: Mrs. Palmer a Miami, and Mrs. Baptiste a Peoria. Whether they knew each other or not, however, their family stories of removal contain many of the same elements.

When I was fourteen, in the year of 1875, the folk decided that they would bring me to the Indian country and they could live on my land that I would get here. They loaded our things into wagons and, driving a herd of Hereford cattle, they set out. It rained every day and we were a week on the road. We finally reached our old friends and neighbors,

some of whom were living around Peoria. We stayed for a few days with
the Peter Labadie family. We stayed here until my step-father could rent
a place. He rented from Ed Black, then the Second Chief of the Peoria
Tribe. (Baptiste 1938: 2)

Mrs. Baptiste talks about hardship on the trail, caused by weather
rather than by armed force. She makes no reference to the injustice of
the removals, but, on the other hand, she frames her family story in the
control her family takes in making the move. Her family decides to move
her to an Indian community and successfully establishes a new home
in that community. These decisions on both ends of the frame are made
in terms of Indian community. The family moves in the first place to
live with other Indian people, and in the end, the family is integrated
into that community. In a way, these Indian communities were the goal
of the various removals for the United States. The idea was to separate
Indian people from whites into their own permanent, but distant, communities. The United States wanted to solve its "Indian problem" by
removing the Indian people from the land it wanted to have clear control
over. In doing this, the government promised Indian peoples new lands
that would forever be Indian, but that was not to be.

## Allotment

The General Allotment Act of 1887 was the legislative beginning of
the end for Indian Territory. For white society, it was no more than an
expression of popular opinion that had been building for some time. Euro-
Americans saw Oklahoma as the last of the western frontier, and the last
chance to homestead and civilize the wilderness. To the Indian people
in Indian Territory, however, it was not a frontier, it was home. A series
of treaties, agreements, and legislative acts had put them there either
on reservations (for the Western Tribes and the those removed to Indian
Territory after the Civil War) or in Indian nations (for the Five Tribes) and
guaranteed their continued existence. While there was resistance to the
allotment program, ultimately Indian people and their tribes were powerless to stop it, and individual Indian people and their families had to
cope with this program, which many whites hoped would be the end of
Indian cultures. For Indian people confined to reservations, dealing with
allotment often meant protecting the integrity of their families, while
for citizens of the Five Tribes it meant political resistance that was often
violent and sometimes fatal. These traumatic events became part of the
consciousness of Indian people, usually in family histories, and part of
the construction of Indian identity.

## RESERVATIONS

A series of spectacular land runs in the late nineteenth century opened Oklahoma Territory to white settlement and eventual statehood. Thousands of people on foot, on horseback, or in horse-drawn wagons lined up across miles of prairie and, when the starting gun was fired, raced to be first to claim their parcel of land. But the land was not empty, and some of those who had, until then, lived on the land watched as the hopeful Boomers rushed to make their claims, sometimes only to find that a cheating Sooner had beaten them to the land office. Jess Rowlodge was about eight years old when he watched the run that opened the Cheyenne and Arapaho Reservation. He said:

> Well, the rolls of the allotments that had been completed were closed May 2, 1892, but however after the allotments were completed they made that run April 19, 1892. But the final rolls of the selection of allotments were closed for the records. I remember the day of the run. Annie (Pedro) and I were still just kids. They took a hayrack—load of us kids up there where the German Prison Camp is, north of the Fort Reno Reformatory. They took us and unloaded us over there. We was waiting for the start of the run, which started at noon. You could see a whole line of people. When the gun started it you could see the smoke and they all started that run. To choose their lands, and file on them, and prove their claims on them. (Rowlodge 1972a: 19)

Because they were confined to reservations in Indian Territory, both the Western Tribes and the tribes who were removed to Indian Territory after the Civil War share much of the experience of allotment. One significant aspect of their common experience is that the tribes and their people had little to say about whether allotment would be done. The United States government enacted the General Allotment Act in 1887, the Jerome Commission quickly worked out details of the process with each reservation, and the land was allotted. There were few paths and little opportunity to resist the policy, so most of the mention of allotment from these tribes emphasized how Indian people dealt with their land rather than what they felt about the idea itself. While the land as an economic resource is important in this discourse, the land as a means of maintaining family cohesion is more central, and the passages commonly mention how people selected their allotment based on family considerations. The passages do expose some small differences between the Western Tribes and those tribes confined to smaller reservations in the eastern part of the Territory, especially in terms of their histories with allotment and how they approached the ownership of land itself.

One important area where the eastern reservation tribes were differ-ent from the Western Tribes was in the relation to the land itself. In the Doris Duke and Indian Pioneer interviews, where people from the res-ervations in eastern Indian Territory talk about allotment, they express a familiarity with private ownership of land that often includes private land ownership before allotment. Perhaps because these eastern tribes had, by the time the General Allotment Act was passed, been in contact with European concepts of land ownership for nearly two hundred years, the members of these tribes saw nothing remarkable about the idea. The Western Tribes, on the other hand, were just signing their first treaties with the United States in the 1830s when the Five Tribes were being removed to their republics in eastern Indian Territory, and had no expe-rience with private ownership. Jess Rowlodge, an Arapaho, expressed it this way in one of his Doris Duke interviews with Julia Jordan:

> At Medicine Lodge there's one instinct of the tribe at that time that I sense more than anything else. That I learned thereafter. That was that ordinarily the Plains Indians didn't know that land could be sold. Our mother earth. For them—especially under the Act of 1887, when allotment was being made, and several times to be paid for it, it even became stronger in the minds of people that to sell land—their native country—their loved country—the soil that they fed on—to be sold in material value. That was a thing that the Indians never had in their mind. Because they never sold no land. They was supposed to own the land but they claimed their land to be forever theirs. But when it comes to being informed that they could sell land—dispose of it and then remove from it—that was a pretty strong feeling over that. (Rowlodge 1972c: 11–12)

Jess Rowlodge refers here to cultural constructions of space held by the bison-hunting pastoralists who roamed the Great Plains before they were confined to reservations in 1867, only twenty years before the passage of the General Allotment Act. In these cultural traditions, land was not a commodity that could be exchanged for anything; rather it was more like the commons, there for all to use. The whole idea behind allotment, therefore, clashed with the way Jess's father, Row of Lodges, and his contemporaries understood the world around them. It also clashed with the promise, which the United States made with the Treaty of Medicine Lodge, of a permanent reservation home in exchange for peace. Andrew Perdasophy, a Comanche born in 1882, had his first experience of allotment with the surveyors who were mapping the land in anticipation of white homesteading: "When the country was first to be opened for the white people's homes, white men came here survey-ing it. The Indians would go where the surveyors were working and talk with them; we couldn't understand much they said only that on our land was to be white people's homes. We didn't care too much for this" (Perdasophy 1938: 7).

Andrew Perdasophy's experience with the surveyors introduced him to allotment and a society where land can be owned, but the common experience among members of the eastern reservation tribes by the late nineteenth century was one of repeated episodes of allotment and ownership. Dickson Duncan (Na-Ma-Quo) talked about Sac and Fox movement and allotment with Lenna M. Rushing in 1937 for the Indian Pioneer project:

> My parents belonged to the Mo-ko-ho-ko band of the Sac and Fox tribe. It was this band that stayed in Kansas after the majority of the Sac and Foxes had come on to Oklahoma.
> When the Keokuk band split from the Blackhawk band, they came to Iowa. And lived among the Mesquake Indians who are also a branch of the Sac and Foxes. After a number of years the Indians were brought to Oklahoma, and as I stated before, the Mo-ko-ho-ko and the Mesquake bands stayed in Iowa. But the Mo-ko-ho-ko band soon moved to Nebraska. Here they lived until their land was ceded to the Omahas and the Winnebagos. Their next move was to Kansas where they were given allotments. The government believed at that time that their permanent home would be in Kansas. Later their land became taxable, and most of the Indians sold their allotments. When their land was all gone, they had nowhere to go or stay, so they came on to Oklahoma just at the time when the allotments were being made down here. The chiefs got together and decided to give these late Indians allotments also. (Duncan 1938: 185)

Members of the Mo-ko-ho-ko band of the Sac and Fox were like other Indian people in Kansas after the Civil War. As the United States sought to open their reservations to white homesteading, members of the Miami, Ottawa, Peoria, Potawatomi, and other tribes were offered allotments if they wished to remain in Kansas and assimilate into white society. Unfortunately, as Dickson Duncan pointed out, this allotted land was often transferred to white control, and the Indian people were left with nothing but the opportunity to move to Indian Territory. For many of these Indian people, on the other hand, that move offered its own appeal. Many Indian people preferred to live in Indian communities, even when, as with Delaware and Shawnee people, that meant they would have to give up their tribal identities and become official Cherokees. Eunice Bluejacket Wilson was referring to this situation when she described her grandparents' decision to give up their two-hundred-acre allotment in Kansas and move to Indian Territory.

They did decide to come to Cherokee Nation, which Eunice Blue-jacket Wilson goes on to describe as a wonderful place full of game and fish. One of the striking things about this and many of the other passages concerning allotment is the emphasis on family they exhibit. Here the decision to give up private property in order to live in an Indian community is based on family values, but all aspects of the allotment process were to some extent constructed in terms of family. The use of family as an organizing principle in allotment often began when people selected their allotments. Jess Rowlodge described his family's allotments in some detail. When Julia Jordan asked him who picked out the allotments, he replied:

> My father, fact, they got in bunches. Like my father, he had an aunt that had three daughters and they were unmarried—they were widowed, I think—and he brought them in there and he allot them along with our area. And their son. Nephew or whatever it was. In the family. He allot them with us. Just so the family stays together. . . .
>
> We were allotted north of Geary, here—across the river. My mother happened—she had an allotment that had a little timber on it—about forty acres was just bearing timber. That was enough for wood. The rest of her place was pasture and farmland—eighty acres. She took eighty. And she took another eighty where there was heavy timber, further north a mile. And my father took his allotment by hers, because that was hay land—eighty acres. And then they allotted me right beside my father. And my land turned out to be nothing but alkali. Stock wouldn't eat that. I told my father, "You must have thought I wasn't going to live—you gave me that old alkali." He said, "No, son, I wanted you right close to me." I said, "That didn't help me. You gave me bad land. You gave your sister and your aunt and her children good land." "Oh," he said, "I didn't want you, too far away. I want you right along side of me." . . .
>
> My brother's allotment was right south of me. And my cousin was right west of my brother's. And right northwest of me was one of my father's grandsons by his daughter. But we always took eighties. . . .
>
> One family had a section of land, and if there was more, there was more than a section, but however, they, were in eighties, and the other eighties were further north—further east or further west—depending on where the timber was and where the river was. (Rowlodge 1972c: 13–15)

There is a kind of sweet irony here. According to Jess, his father, Row of Lodges, (and, I suspect, many other Indian people) appropriated the white program that was intended to break up Indian communities and used it to keep his extended Arapaho family together. Fred Bigman described much the same thing when William Bittle asked how Fred's family chose the land. Fred replied:

You see, I heard when they first started, when they allotted these lands, they hunted. My daddy, they hunted. They don't see any place out there (in the country) like I got here (in Anadarko). Well, he went down there and picked that land out, you know. My mother's lot . . . together. Then he went there and picked his out at the river bottom. Rachel owns it now . . . across the track down there. It's divided, eighty acres apiece. Eighty down on the bottom and eighty on the hill and that there was his pick. That's what he got. . . .

You know where that Wetseling Mission is? Well, that quarter section there. It's supposed to be eighty acres there and he got that and then back up north, toward the river. That's where he got them two. Then they went ahead and got mine down there by Broxton, then my sister's (Connie Mae Bigman) and Clarence Starr, and my mother. They got right there in one section. (Bigman 1972: 1–2)

The emphasis on family in the allotment discourse in the Twice-Removed Tribes and Western Tribes should not be taken to mean that allotment met no resistance. Perhaps the most significant expression of that resistance was a lawsuit filed by Lone Wolf, a Kiowa, asking the court to stop Ethan Allen Hitchcock, the secretary of the interior, from opening the Kiowa, Comanche, and Apache Reservation to homesteading. Lone Wolf lost his suit at the Supreme Court, and the case today remains one of the core cases in Indian law (Clark 1999). Jess Rowlodge commented on how Lone Wolf's family may have weakened the case:

They sued Secretary Hitchcock, Secretary of Interior Hitchcock for the contention of the value of their lands along the Deep Red River. And the Kiowa chief, Lone Wolf, his son had graduated from Carlisle and he was instrumental in that case. . . . But the Old man condone that case himself—Lone Wolf. They didn't want no allotments. They wanted the value of their land, known as the Big Pasture. But during—after they won that case the Court of Claims—there was an appeal to the Court of Appeals—and at that time, as far as I can remember, Old Man Lone Wolf must have had two or three wives. Anyhow, it wasn't the mother of this Lone Wolf that interpreted for his father, DeLos Lone Wolf, that was instrumental in this. But it was Lone Wolf and another wife and a daughter by this other wife, that suddenly wanted to take their allotments right west of Anadarko, just adjacent to the city now. He should have been bucking against any allotment, but he wanted to take allotment there. So that weakened his case. (Rowlodge 1972a: 19)

Of course, resistance to allotment could have also taken political form, and that is what makes Henry Armstrong's recollections about the allotment process interesting. Henry Armstrong was a Delaware; his tribe suffered removal first to a reservation in Kansas and, after the Civil War, to Indian Territory, but not to a reservation. Rather, the Delaware people were officially made citizens of the Cherokee Nation. He recalls:

> My father was a member of the Cherokee Council and when the Indians wanted the land allotted he opposed it. I remember we were at the Fourth of July picnic on the Joe Parker place on Brush creek, north of Dewey and the question of the allotment was discussed. My father was asked his views and he discarded his coat and tie, climbed upon a wagon and made a wonderful speech. He told them the restriction would be lifted in a few years, and the Indians would soon sell their land and in a few years they would be penniless. He spoke of the future for the younger generation and his predictions have come true. In conclusion of his speech, he told them if they still wanted the land allotted, he would help them. The land was sectionized and each given his allotment. Out of the eight hundred Delawares who received allotments, there are only about two hundred who have their homes now. The registered Delaware Indians had the same rights as the native born Cherokees. (Armstrong 1938a: 89–90)

In the Cherokee Nation, and in the other four republics in eastern Indian Territory, resistance to allotment was expressed in their internal politics.

## INDIAN REPUBLICS

Unlike either the Western Tribes or the tribes confined to smaller reservations in eastern Indian Territory, the Five Tribes had enough political clout to resist allotment. The United States recognized this and exempted the tribes in eastern Indian Territory from the provisions of the General Allotment of 1887: the Jerome Commission was only authorized to carry our the allotment of Indian land in the west. Congress authorized the president to appoint a commission charged with negotiating the terms of allotment with the Five Tribes, but the Five Tribes resisted and snubbed the Commission, headed by former Senator Henry Dawes. They were able to drag their feet over the issue because they had popular support to resist. A large portion, if not most, of the citizens of the Five Republics opposed allotment, while a substantial minority favored it, along with statehood for Oklahoma. Allotment was a contentious issue for Choctaw, Chickasaw, Cherokee, Creek, and Seminole people in the decades leading up to statehood, and members of the Five Tribes talked about this sometimes violent political era in the Indian Pioneer and Doris Duke interviews.

When Mrs. Mary Freeman talked to Jerome M. Emmons for the Indian Pioneer project, she said: "I never cared whether the land was held in common or not. I just got it for myself and children" (Freeman 1938: 257). Mrs. Freeman's attempt to avoid taking sides on allotment exposes an understanding of the issue and, in this small way, acknowledges its significance to her Creek community. Because of this significance, Mrs. Freeman shared, with many others in her community, a clear opinion about the issue. Her idea was to avoid it, where others often were either for or against it. Many of the passages in the Doris Duke and Indian Pioneer Papers refer to allotment with a simple statement of position. J. W. Brewer, for example, said simply: "The Brewers was all against allotment of land; they wanted it to remain as it was" (Brewer 1938: 109). Others, like Tom Devine, gave a brief justification for their stand on the issue. "My family was in favor of the allotment. There were many acres of land claimed by full bloods who would not use it to their advantage, and many Cherokees that would make a showing did not have any at all. For this reason we were in favor of the allotment" (Devine 1938: 197–98).

It is interesting that both J. W. Brewer and Tom Devine state their positions on allotment in terms of their families. That structure, this idea that it is a family position, comes right out of the assimilationists' construction of race and culture. In that way of looking at the world, the two—race and culture—were very closely tied together. The more white a person was, the more civilized he or she would be, so it was natural that opinions on these issues would be attached to families. Tom Devine's justification of his position gives more detail to this broad outline. Those who opposed allotment were full-bloods, thus less assimilated and less "civilized."

The polarized political atmosphere that the allotment program generated in the Five Republics produced formal organizations or groups that took one position or another. It should not be surprising that sometimes these groups crossed tribal boundaries, because all the tribes faced the same problem. Adam Folsom told Peter W. Cole about one of these groups that was formed to oppose allotment:

> After the enrollment of the Five Civilized Tribes of Indians, particularly Choctaws in this case, to be allotted lands to them by the United States Government, there were few Choctaws who opposed this movement, as well as those who were against Indian Territory to become as a state. Being opposed to the movement of what the Government is to do, there was an organization or party formed by these people who declared themselves, as against the allotment of lands to the Indians and declared themselves 'A Band of Snake Indians' or 'Ishki Oshta Clan,' and would not yield to the allotment of lands. They were in favor of the land to be held in common, not to be owned by any one individual, firm or corporation,

that one may move on any certain piece of land to make improvements and live on as his home. If he desired to move to some new location, he had the privilege of selling the improvement, but that he was required to dispose of the land.

This was some of the ideas that these parties or clans had written in their constitution they had adopted; hence they did not care to be interfered with by the government. It was at this time when the government allotted Willis Tobly, a full-blood Choctaw Indian, one hundred fifty acres of homestead land where he finally lived and made this his home until he died.

Mr Tobly was a Methodist minister and a leader of the band of Snake Indian Clan, who finally settled down on this tract of land that the Department had set aside for him. After settling down, he held several Snake Clan Meetings where Creeks, Seminoles and Cherokees participated in holding of these meetings. (Folsom 1938: 12–14)

Given that this group was formed to oppose allotment, its choices of name, organizational principles, and membership reveal significant features in the construction of Indian identity. The members of the group called themselves the Band of Snake Indians, or the Snake Clan, a name that evokes Native American traditions. They could have called themselves anything they wanted—a committee, an association, and so on—but they chose to be a band or a clan because they took the Indian side in the dispute. On the other hand, they recognized that the idea they opposed came from the white world, from the United States government, and gave themselves legitimacy in that political arena with a constitution. Most interesting of all, to me, is that the Snake Clan was a pan-Indian organization, including Choctaws, Cherokees, Creeks, and Seminoles.

Even though the issue of allotment confronted all Five Republics collectively, it was played out in the politics of each one individually. There were opportunities for the citizens of the Five Republics to express their opinions about allotment by voting, especially in tribal leadership elections, and the established political parties of the republics took stands on the issue. In 1938 David Wade remembered his participation in the Choctaw debate on allotment: "I belonged to the National Party; they did not want allotments. The other Party was the Progressive Party. Two of the leaders of the National Party were Ben Smallwood, a half breed Choctaw Indian who was Congressman; the other, Jacob Jackson, a full blood" (Wade 1938: 40).

The names of these parties themselves index the basic conflict between the assimilationist-white and the nationalist-Indian positions. The progressives took the white side, whereas the nationalists took the Indian side. This was a contentious issue, and the politics turned dangerous and violent. Gomer Gower reported Nancy Whistler's recollection of the intensity of feelings on both sides of the issue:

> The last clash between the National and Progressive Parties occurred in 1892, when the issue of whether or not the land which had been held in common by the Choctaw Tribe should be partitioned. The Progressive Party favored the partition while the Nationalists sought to prevent it, and thereby prevent the dissolution of tribal existence. Wilson Jones and Jacob Jackson were contenders for the office of Principal Chief, Jones for the Progressives and Jackson for the Nationals. Green McCurtain, a former Principal Chief and a pronounced Progressive, took the field in support of Jones. The campaign became so heated that a display of armed support appeared in the interest of both contenders. The husband of the subject of this sketch, Martin Whistler, was a participant in these armed forces in support of Jacob Jackson who was his step-father, and who lived in the same general locality west of Shady Point. However, it is said no group killings resulted from the campaign and after the election Jones was declared elected as principal Chief. (Whistler 1938: 74–75)

While Nancy Whistler did not report any fatalities from the conflict, she talks clearly about the symbolic divide between white ways and Indian ways. This divide is embodied in the clash between the National and Progressive parties, each raising an armed camp to help pursue its political ends. She understands each side's platform (Progressives favored partition, while Nationalists tried to prevent it), and she knows what it means to her (the continued existence of the Choctaw tribe). In some cases, however, these conflicts did end in death. Columbus Wm. Ervin recalled the murder of a Choctaw man named Joe Hoklotubbe in the heat of the campaign:

> When I was about nine years old, while still living on the place I have just described, something happened that I want to tell you about. Probably you remember the story of Silan Lewis and how he was the last man executed legally under the Choctaw Government's jurisdiction. Well, I knew him; he was a friend of my father's and he came to our house in the Fall of 1894. . . .
> The way I heard it is that this Joe Hoklotubbe was on one side of a political fence and Silan Lewis was on the other side. One faction was called Progressives and the other side Nationalists and the former wanted to open up the Choctaw Nation to settlement by whites, while the latter faction wanted to keep the whites out as much as possible and retain the Choctaw Nation exclusively for Indians. There had been a lot of hard feeling over an election recently and Hoklotubbe was the leader of the Progressives in this neighborhood while Lewis was a sort of leader of the other faction. (Ervin 1938: 175)

Despite the violence, elections were held, and eventually the Choc-taw Nation, along with the other four Indian Territory republics, were dissolved and their lands allotted. In other words, the dispute was resolved by carrying out the policy, but these actions did little to change peoples' minds. Those in favor of allotment naturally participated by putting their names on the tribal rolls and taking their allotments, but many of those who opposed allotment refused to be enrolled. Sometimes these people were enrolled despite their stand on the issue. Winey Lewis described her family's experience in the Creek allotment to Grace Kelley:

> When they allotted us, our parents had to go and file for themselves and also for us. They had already made homes and improvements which they wanted so they went and asked for land they had so improved. Some-times another Indian beat them to it and he would have to move off to another place. We were lucky and got the home place where we were all born. Father was born one mile north of here but he filed on the place a quarter west, where he and mother lived. It was just like a race, the first ones there got what they wanted.
>
> My husband's people didn't allot for they didn't know that it would be better for them than the way they were living. The Government allotted them.
>
> When a family or neighbor who knew a family real well went to allot, they were asked all about this neighbor, and if one wouldn't allot, this person who knew them so well, told all about the family and they were allotted anyway. Some were left out but not many. (Lewis 1938: 13–14)

"Some were left out" echoes today, not as it concerns allotted land but rather as it concerns the legitimacy of Indian identity. For exam-ple, I talked to a Cherokee man one hot summer evening at a Powwow. His great-uncles and grandfather had been Eastern Cherokee and had migrated to Indian Territory in the early twentieth century for the pur-pose of getting an allotment. This was apparently not uncommon. Gar-field Shoals talked about the Mississippi Choctaws who were allotted near his allotment (Shoals 1972: 3), and Mack McDonald remembered moving to Indian Territory at the age of twelve in 1904 so his family would get their Choctaw allotment (McDonald 1938: 64). The problem my acquaintance at the Powwow had was that, while his great-uncles had enrolled and been allotted, his grandfather had missed the deadline to enroll, so he did not get an allotment. His grandson could never, there-fore, be an official member of the Cherokee tribe. This is a relatively rare story, however, and most of those members of the Five Tribes who were left out of allotment were among the most traditional members of the tribe. As a result, today there are Indian people in Oklahoma who have only Indian ancestors, who speak their tribal language, and who play significant roles in Indian community life but who cannot be members of their tribe.

Like the unpopular incumbent politician whom no one can remember voting for, by the time of the Indian Pioneer project, support for the allotment program was rarely voiced. The internal political disputes over the issue in the Five Tribes faded in significance, and many, like Charles W. Loftin, believed that more Choctaws would have resisted the programs had it not been for the lure of a possible liberal cash payment from the sale of their lands, because they seemed to realize and regret that allotment meant a dissolution of their tribe (Loftin 1938: 86). Along the same lines, Joseph Jefferson McElroy acknowledged the hardship and suffering in the transition from tribal to individual ownership of the land; he also recognized the "identity of his beloved Choctaw Tribe of Indians [being] forever blotted out from among the living Nations of the earth" (McElroy 1938: 105). Where Lofton and McElroy pointed to the tragic political results of allotment—the dissolution of their nation—Nancy Whistler's account concentrated on the economic effects.

> Despite all the wealth which had been placed in the laps of the Choctaws through the inheritance of the Choctaw Nation with its wealth of natural resources, this poor old full-blood Choctaw woman finds herself in her advanced age with nothing but one hundred and sixty acres of land which she can neither sell nor eat, nor can she find a properly equipped farmer to whom she can rent it with the view of making it productive of a living for her. She . . . wonders if after all, it would not have been better had the Nationals had their way. (Whistler 1938: 76)

Whether resistance to allotment was through litigation or political action, however, it failed, and in the twenty years between the 1887 General Allotment Act and 1907, when Oklahoma became a state, virtually the entire state was transferred from Indian control to white control. At least this aspect of allotment was successful from the point of view of the United States government, which forced the program on the tribes and governments of Indian Territory. The assimilationists' ideals, however, which generated much of the white support for the program, were not, and probably could not, have been achieved. The Indian peoples of Indian Territory did not assimilate into white society; rather the allotment program itself became one of the elements of the boundaries that maintain Indian identity.

## *Allotment Now*

At a simplistic and fundamental level, allotment defined the legal bound-aries between the land that one person owned and the land his or her neighbors owned. Because almost all the allotted land has been trans-ferred to white ownership over the past century, those legal boundaries are relatively unimportant, but the boundaries that allotment helps to maintain between Indian people and white society remain significant. In terms of Indian identity, allotment still plays a role in the official docu-mentation of tribal membership, and on a symbolic level it takes on an ambiguous quality, referring in some contexts to white abuse of Indian people but in others to Indian solidarity.

The process that led to allotment required that official lists of tribal members, rolls, be drawn up so that all those on the roll got their allot-ment. Today, while the requirements of tribal membership vary from tribe to tribe, all the tribes require that members be on the allotment rolls or be a direct descendant of someone on them. So in important ways today the allotment program defines who can and who cannot claim Indian identity. This is an imperfect measure, however, not so much because of the non-Indians who were put on these rolls but because of the strong opponents of allotment, in all the tribes, who refused to participate and did not go on the rolls. The conversation with Carol got around to this topic one April morning when we talked in her office.

> A lot of families did not sign up on the rolls. . . . One of the interesting things, I know there are full-blood Cherokees who are not on the rolls who still speak Cherokee, not English, and they cannot vote with any tribe. I don't know to what extent that's true of some of the other larger tribes, I would guess it is, so again the ongoing question is who is Indian? When I was going through the Dawes rolls years ago, I was interested that lots of people were one-three hundred twentieth at the beginning of the rolls—what does that make them now?

Carol recognizes the contradiction that to some extent non-Indians are deciding on who can and cannot call themselves Indian. The allotment rolls are official documents, created by the government of the United States for its own uses, but they form the basis for tribal membership with no regard to cultural heritage. This situation is often constructed as United States government meddling in internal tribal affairs, which the tribes are powerless to combat. Other constructions approach allotment on a more global level, numbering it among a list of United States gov-ernment programs designed to carry out a policy of divide and conquer.

Leslie talked about allotment this way one winter morning when I met her at an arts fair. She said: "It was a government policy to divide and conquer, that's what allotment was equated to. You don't have a localized group anymore, you are not in common. You don't have this community situation because everybody is here and there that you aren't real anymore." A little later she went on to say: "But you're supposed to have your own little apartment or just like here, allotment. It's the same thing. Take them away from the family group, put them in boarding schools, put them on relocation or put them on a homestead and live or die."

Leslie puts allotment on a list of programs with education and the 1950s relocation program. She understands these programs to flow from the principle that breaking up Indian communities is good. Because this principle is held by white society, and its policy realizations are implemented by the United States government, it emerges as a central symbolic cluster that distinguishes Indian people from whites. This theme comes up in many ways. Chris describes how the inheritance of allotment property divides even Indian families:

> Allotments, as far as allotments are concerned, that is being eroded as well. Because allotments, let's say the original allotment was eighty acres or a hundred and twenty acres or whatever—well, that original allotee passes away, and that allotment gets divided among six kids, and then that one-sixth gets passed down to two children, and so forth, that it gets so fractionated that the government has come in, and I guess in my rebellious thinking, I maintain it is an unauthorized taking, their coming in and just reverting that back to the federal government. Some of them, yeah, I think, with some compensation. But if it is so fractionated [that] there are some heirs that are struggling with, "Okay, which one of us is going to buy out the others so that this can be with one owner rather than twelve of us?" And to sell your property if you're wanting to sell it, that is another nightmare because you have to go through the Bureau of Indian Affairs.

If the allotment program is constructed in terms of a divide-and-conquer policy, the allotments themselves are sometimes seen as symbols of Indian resurgence. People praise those in their communities who still live on their family's allotment, and they strive to regain allotments that were lost. Ed talked proudly about how, soon after she was married, her family was able to buy one of her tribe's original allotments from its white owner. She saw this as a small part of the recent strides her tribe had made in revitalizing its language and culture. So despite its original intention to force Indian people to assimilate into white society, the residue of the allotment program works in two ways to reinforce the boundaries that protect Indian ethnicity. The program is seen as an example of white disrespect and abuse of Indian culture, while at the same time, allotments in Indian hands today are seen as strengths in Indian communities.

Allotment and removal are both about land. In the removals, Indian people were taken away from their homelands and forced to new lands far away from their origins. The allotment program officially took control over Indian lands away from Indian people and put it under the political control of Euro-Americans. Allotment and removal also shared a common goal: to relieve whites from the need to deal with Indians. The removals tried to accomplish this goal by taking Indian people away from the places where whites wanted to live and by controlling the economic resources that land represents. The allotment program tried to do it by eliminating tribal culture and forcing Indian people to assimilate into white society. It does not take a lot of thought to understand that these were major historical traumas to Indian people, and it should come as no surprise that they contribute to the construction of Indian ethnic identity. They were not, however, the only nineteenth-century attempts to solve the "Indian problem." Indian education was a third movement to eradicate Indian culture, but it did not attack the physical world; rather it tried to change people's minds.

# 4  *The Great Wisdom*

When this was finished they went and prophesized to
the people the marvels that had been seen. And one was
that man would someday fly in the air and another was
that the tracks of the Cherokee would someday lead
west to the valley of the Mississippi, never to return.
And another was that there would be a school to teach
knowledge to all the people. But a fourth prophesy said
that in after times young people would return from the
school and point really to the old men of the tribe and say
"they were of no account because they knew nothing."
The people considered this a long time, and wondered
what the great wisdom might be taught in these schools
that the children should point to the old people and talk
in this way.

—Sam Hair (Doris Duke Collection)

It was two steps from the end of a long day. I had already driven
over a hundred miles and taped two interviews along the way. I had made
an appointment earlier in the week to see Ed for my last interview of
the day, after which I faced a long drive back to Norman. I would not be
home until well after dark on this late spring day, but the opportunity
to talk to Ed was well worth the effort. She had agreed to meet me in
her office at the end of her day, so we were both tired, but that did not
seem to slow her down at all. I, as an anthropologist should, started with
Ed's genealogy, but the topic got around to education, and her mother's
experience in a nearby rural public school:

It was difficult for them because in looks it was impossible for them to
escape the fact that people could look at them and tell they were Native.
When Mom was very small, she tells this story: she didn't go to board-

ing school, she didn't go to the Indian school—my mother is eighty-two now, she went to a little bitty school . . . and when they would call roll for all the Indian children they were not allowed to answer their name, they would answer their roll number, because the school would get a nickel for each Indian child in attendance. That's her early memories of what it meant to be Indian is that the school got a nickel.

To me there are two themes embedded in what Ed says here: the first is that school is an incurably white institution, and the second is that it does not serve Indians as Indians. These two themes recur over and over again throughout the data. In these interviews people talk about their experiences with school from the 1850s on to the present; even people who did not go to school report on what school meant in their lives. They talk about many kinds of schools—subscription schools, Indian national schools, agency schools, mission schools, and public schools. They relate their experiences as Indian people in grade school, high school, college, and postgraduate work. They talk about their experiences in schools that punished them for acting Indian, and they report on how they used schools to help remain Indian in a white world. From all of this emerges a story of persistence, of how Indian identity survived extreme pressure to assimilate, and of appropriation, how they used the white schools to strengthen Indian communities and identity.

Seminary Hall, Northeastern State University, Tahlequah. Photo by the author.

## Indian Schools

> When my parents settled in the Indian Territory there were no schools in this part of the Territory. In 1875 my father built the first school house, located one-half mile north of the present County Farm, on Coon Creek. This building was of native lumber, and there were about fifteen white, Indian and Negro children enrolled. This was a subscription school and the parents paid one dollar a month for each child. The first teacher was Mrs Frank Bellows whose husband was postmaster at the Bartles store. (Armstrong 1938a: 80)

The subscription school Henry Armstrong describes here represents one of the common school experiences for people in the data set from the late nineteenth century. Other kinds of schools that people talk about include the various schools run by the Five Republics in eastern Indian Territory, mission schools, United States–operated boarding schools, and public schools. The subscription schools themselves, however, had many features that distinguished them from other schooling alternatives people describe in the interviews. The mixed-race student body is unique in the data. Race is a thread that comes up in several places aside from this reference, but the races are almost always separate in the Indian Pioneer and Doris Duke papers. All the other schools mentioned in the interviews were backed by relatively large institutional interests like church hierarchies or government bureaucracies, whereas the subscription schools appear to have been private businesses (Mayes 1972: 2). They were generally very small, often one room (Killebrew 1938: 41; Mayes 1972: 1–2) and sometimes outdoors (Harkins 1938: 21). The curriculum was basic—reading, writing, and arithmetic—and the regimentation characteristic of the other educational alternatives in Indian Territory was absent from the subscription schools.

Until statehood in 1907, the Five Republics in eastern Indian Territory operated school systems for their citizens. These systems included different kinds of schools, and in some cases the schools themselves survived into statehood after the Curtis Act of 1896 dissolved the republics. Indian people in the Doris Duke and Indian Pioneer collections relate their school experiences at the Cherokee Male and Female Seminaries at Tahlequah (Brewer 1938: 125; Butler 1938: 171; Sanders 1938: 106; Scott 1938: 4), the Cherokee Orphan Asylum at Selina (Butler 1938: 167; Duncan 1938: 223), the Spencer, Wheelock (Bacon 1938: 18), Jones (Ervin 1938: 176), and Goodland (Cross 1938: 80) academies in the Choctaw Nation, and Creek National School at Fishertown (Scott 1938: 14–15).

The Cherokee Female Seminary became the core campus for Northeastern Oklahoma State University.

The curriculum in these schools emphasized the basic literacy and computational skills, along with training in work skills. Sallie (Johnson) Butler, who attended the Cherokee Orphan Asylum about 1875, said "they hired women in the neighborhood to come there and do the washing; the school girls would do the ironing, and the boys did the farm work" (Butler 1938: 68–69). Students in these schools were often regimented along military lines. Lindsey Mayes attended the Cherokee Male Seminary between 1904 and 1908. He reported that "it was a wonderful school. It's a cheap school you know, good school. School where they learn you about everything. Learn how to be a man. . . . Learn—you, how to drill and all that stuff" (Mayes 1972: 9). The vocational approach to the curriculum and the military regimentation were common in Indian schools of the late nineteenth century, mission schools on the reservations, and institutions administered by the Bureau of Indian Affairs.

A connection between education and Christianity emerges very early in the data set and continues through the interviews conducted in the last year or so. The Five Republics in eastern Indian Territory often put their national schools in the hands of one of the Christian denominations. For example, the Reverend W. A. Duncan served as superintendent of the Cherokee Orphan Asylum in the late 1870s (Butler 1938: 169), and the Choctaw schools at Goodwater, Goodland, and Skulleyville were operated by missionaries (Oakes 1938: 17). The pattern of the official school as a Christian institution was also common for those Indian people in Indian Territory who were confined to reservations. The Kaw School (Burnett 1972: 11), the Sac and Fox School (Duncan 1938: 155–156), the Seneca School (Long 1972: 4), and the Quapaw School (Shafer 1938: 32) were all in the hands of priests, ministers, or nuns. In addition to these official connections, however, many denominations opened and maintained schools independently. These were sometimes small day schools and sometimes larger boarding schools. They were often named for the minister who ran them, as in the Faits Mission near Anadarko (Jones 1938: 148) and the Levering Mission in the Creek Nation (Lowe 1938: 18).

All these Christian schools in the early data, whether they were agency schools or national schools, were missions from the point of view of the ministers running them. They were bringing the civilizing influence of the white man's religion to Christian and non-Christian Indians alike. That pattern does not hold in the recent data. While there are several passages where Christian education is discussed, most of those refer to denominational private schools or Christian academies that serve a mostly white clientele. They are not Indian schools. These schools do not intend to convert Indian people to Christianity but to provide their version of Christian education to students in their area.

Indian people in what would become Oklahoma were subject to the same whims of policy and program as Indian people elsewhere in the United States, and this was no less true in the area of education. In the mid-1880s, the United States government began to pursue its assimilation policy with a program to remove Indian children from their homes and educate them at distant boarding schools. The idea of these schools was to take Indian children away from their tribal cultures and immerse them in white culture so that they would give up their Indian ways and merge into white society. The schools were multitribal—to make it more difficult for students to cling to tribal ways—and, at least in their early years, brutally intolerant of tribal languages, customs, and beliefs. Several of these schools opened in the late nineteenth and early twentieth centuries, including the schools at Carlisle, Pennsylvania; Riverside, California; the Haskell School in Lawrence, Kansas; and Chilocco in northwest Oklahoma. The remnants of that system, although much changed, remain with us today. Haskell, for example, is now a college for Indian students.

The early boarding schools shared their curriculum and military school organization (Rowlodge 1972a: 29), with the national and mission schools. Like the mission schools, and some national schools, they were also Christian; Sunday church was required at Haskell (Rowlodge 1972a: 29–30), and Riverside was a Catholic school. Many of the people whose interviews I use here went to one of these schools or had a close relative—mother, father, brother, or sister—who attended one of the schools. In some cases, where two siblings were in the boarding school system, they were split up and went to different schools. Their experiences with the boarding schools appear in all three of the interview sets beginning in the Indian Pioneer Papers, through the Doris Duke interviews, and into my recent interviews.

In the aftermath of Oklahoma statehood in 1907, the Indian education systems that had evolved withered, so that little remained by the mid-1930s. Because the people who were interviewed for both the Doris Duke and Indian Pioneer collections were elders, they went to school when the Indian systems were still strong and generally had much of their education in those Indian systems. On the other hand, almost all the people I talked to attended public schools with white and, after 1954,

African American classmates. There are a few passages in the Doris Duke and Indian Pioneer data that refer to public schools, but they are rare. Discussions of public school come up often in the interviews I conducted for this project, and they describe a wide variety of experiences. The people who talked to me attended urban and rural schools, and experienced traditional and experimental teaching methods. Sometimes their Indian identity was officially recognized, and sometimes it was ignored. When they started in the public school system, some were just barely aware of their Indian heritage, while others spoke no English when they arrived at school.

These different kinds of schools—subscription, national, Christian, boarding, and public—do not in any way exhaust the educational experiences reported in the interviews. Many of the people finished high school in one of these systems and went on to Indian colleges like Bacone or Henry Kendall College in Muskogee; still others attended white business schools, seminaries, or colleges. They took associate, bachelor, and postgraduate degrees, and sometimes became teachers, physicians, lawyers, or scholars. The experiences Indian people in Oklahoma had with these different kinds of schools are significant to Indian identity in many ways. They represent, if nothing else, a large investment in time and wealth for both individuals and tribes. For many it was also a central experience in their lives that became a major component of how they defined themselves, and it was often an oddly Indian experience. With the exception of the public schools and the rare subscription school, all the students in these schools were Indian people. It is an odd Indian experience, because even if all the students are Indian, school is a white institution. Often school was an institutionalized Indian experience of whiteness. Recognition of this is common in the experiences and attitudes expressed about school throughout the data, and is not lost even on those who had little or no formal education.

## White Schools

In the summer of 1937, David Wade talked to Marvin G. Rowley for the Indian Pioneer project. David was born to Choctaw parents in Atoka County in 1861. He was a Choctaw Nationalist who opposed allotment, and he said: "I did not go to school because there were none at that time. I can remember the time there was not a white man in Atoka County" (Wade 1938: 40). In this David expresses the basic fundamental fact about education that permeates everything in the interviews. That is, that education—school—is a white institution. The people in the interviews construct multiple ways to understand and deal with this fact. Many accept the absence of school as one of the defining deficiencies of Indian culture, others view white education as a resource that can be deployed to achieve Indian goals, and still others would like school to become more Indian; but the essential whiteness of school is always central. Perhaps the most striking expressions of this awareness come from the Indian people who had little or no schooling.

The interviews contain few examples of people who describe having little or no experience with school. Out of the entire data set, I coded fewer than thirty passages that expressed this theme, all coming from the Indian Pioneer set. Some of this bias, no doubt, comes from the way that people were selected for interviews and from the cultural ideals of the time. People may have avoided talking about having no education because the ideology of the day denigrated that condition. I believe, however, that part of this absence also comes from the relatively common availability of schools in Indian Territory from the latter half of the nineteenth century on. The passages that do appear share some common features that point to the recognition of school as a white institution.

The people who were interviewed in the late 1930s had lived all their lives in an ideological environment that took cultural hierarchy for granted. Some cultures, notably the white Anglo-European culture of the United States, were considered better, superior, to others—Choctaw culture, Kiowa culture, and so on. All these people probably had direct experience with this belief on a daily basis, and certainly felt it in government programs, like allotment, that used the hierarchy to justify the policy. Not only were they in that environment but they often accepted the belief. As a result, these passages about having little white education are almost confessions. These interviewees almost always try to explain why they had little education; they are often painfully self-denigrating. Ollie England, for example, was over ninety years old when W. J. B. Bigby interviewed her. She said that "she grew to womanhood just as many other Indian children, and did not attend school on account of poverty, and the Civil War" (England 1938: 94). And in another similar passage, Jancy Bell (over seventy years old) said: "I never attended school during my life. At that time there was no school which I could attend. The schools started in later years but I was too big to go to school, so I did not go at all" (Bell 1938: 21). Needing these excuses for not going to school points to the cultural hierarchy and places school firmly on the upper (white) rung of the ladder: Albert W. Keith makes the equation explicit by saying: "My grandmother spoke just a few words of English.

My mother was an educated Indian and dressed like the white people" (Keith 1938: 97).

Albert W. Keith not only expressed the dominant ideology of the day—placing Euro-American culture higher on the scale than Indian cultures—but also picks up another theme, that of language, that is common in these passages. Language, and various language skills, also participates in the hierarchy. Literacy skills, reading and writing, are more valued than speaking skills, and English is more valued than North American Indian languages. In both cases the white side comes out on top of the cultural pyramid. Nancy Miashintubbee put all this together with school when she said to Johnson H. Hampton, "I am a full blood Indian and never went to school so I am not able to speak nor read nor write English, and I am not able to read nor write in my own language, and I am too old now to try to learn to speak English" (Miashintubbee 1938: 15).

This insidious cultural hierarchy sometimes penetrated very deeply into the minds of people who belittled themselves and their knowledge in the face of this ideology. One striking example of this appears in an interview with Lottie Choate, who said:

> I am a full blood Choctaw Indian and all of my people were Fullbloods. They never had any education at all; they could not speak English so we children did not attend school. I am unable to speak English and I can't read it. I don't understand English at all and can't read in my own language, having been raised in the mountains and I never had the opportunity for school nor anything else, so I am just blank in anything. (Choate 1938: 25–26)

It is unclear how these interviews, and others like them where the interviewee did not speak English, were conducted—whether the interviewer was a speaker of Choctaw or used an interpreter, or what. It is clear that all Lottie Choate knew and learned in her sixty-five years added up in her mind, at least as she wished to express it to the fieldworker Johnson H. Hampton, to "just a blank in anything," because she "lacked" a white education, could not speak English, and could not read or write. This attitude persists, sometimes, even in the face of remarkable academic accomplishments. For example James Carnes, a Choctaw who was also interviewed by Johnson H. Hampton, said of his schooling:

> I did not attend school much. I went to the Academy but did not learn much. I can speak a little English and read and write a little, but I don't understand all of it, that is to get up and make a speech or anything of the kind but can speak enough to make trades with a white man. I can speak and write in my own language pretty well. I did not go to school

> very long at that time; we had to get the consent from the County Judge
> as to how long we could go; so I, being up in years, did not get but a term
> or two, and that is all the schooling I got. (Carnes 1938: 64–65)

And Eastman Ward, who was in his midforties when he was interviewed
for the Indian Pioneer project, said:

> My father was a full blood Indian and also my mother, they did not
> attend any school during their lifetime and of course my mother and
> father could not speak any English at all. My father learned to write in
> Choctaw and could read it but mother did not learn how to read nor
> write in either language.
>
> I went to school for about two or three months is all the schooling I
> had, but I can read English pretty well and write it pretty good. (Ward
> 1938: 129)

Neither Choctaw nor any other native American language was part
of the curriculum in the schools these men and women attended. When
they learned to read and write in their native languages, it was on their
own initiative. James Carnes taught himself to read and write Choctaw,
as did Eastman Ward's father, William Garland. And Eastman Ward could
read and write English "pretty good" after only a few months of schooling. These are intellectual feats to be proud of, but the ideological web
that they were caught in prevented Eastman Ward, Lottie Choate, and all
the others from acknowledging their value. Their experiences are Indian,
therefore inferior in this belief system, and the benefit of school was to
make Indians white.

## Kill the Indian

The goal of education to force Indian people to assimilate into white
society was not lost on the Indian people who were students in the
schools. One day I was talking to Leslie at a community event near his
home. When the discussion got around to school and white attitudes
and policies toward Indian education, he said it was "that kind of the
Indian policy. Save the man, kill the Indian, cut his hair, dress him in a
uniform, make him conform. . . . Show him what a good life it is to be
a domestic worker or pump gas. And this carried on through relocation
policies. You couldn't think about being upper level. You were doing good
if you were a secretary or mechanic." In 1969 Agnes Burnett expressed
the same theme of education as a tool of white assimilation policies but
from a very different point of view. She said: "I remember a Kaw family,
Barkley Delano, he's full-blood but he was educated at Haskell had good

education. But he come back and went back to the old Indian ways" (Burnett 1972: 9). Still earlier, Dr. Isabelle Cobb expressed the theme in terms of the teachers that the Cherokee Nation wanted to hire for its flagship Male and Female Seminaries in Tahlequah. She gives credit, that through Chief Lewis Downing's influence, "eastern teachers were brought here and taught in the Seminaries—the Miss Noyes of Mt. Holyoke among them" (Cobb 1938: 32).

While all three individuals acknowledge the assimilationist goals of white education, they approach that fact in different ways. Dr. Isabelle Cobb and Agnes Burnett both accept these goals as appropriate, but they accept them in different ways. Agnes Burnett looks at education in utilitarian terms, so Barkley Delano, in her opinion, wasted his good education for an Indian life. Dr. Cobb takes a less limited view of education and assimilation. The teachers from the prestigious, elite, eastern white colleges are the best for Cherokee students because they represent the best of white ways. The function of education is not to learn how to do useful things; rather it is to learn to be white. Leslie, in contrast, sees limits that white society puts on assimilation and hypocrisy in white educational ideology. All three experienced Indian education and, to some extent, the principal tactics Indian education used to achieve this assimilationist agenda. Those tactics included the suppression of North American Indian languages in favor of English and an emphasis on work, discipline, and Christianity.

Over and over again in the data, English emerges as a central icon of white society, associated so closely with it that the language comes to stand for the society. This association was reinforced by almost all interactions that Indian peoples had with white society and was a central assumption of those who used education as a tool of forced assimilation. These assimilationists sought to replace North American Indian languages with English, and for a period most Indian schools were taught only in English. Often this meant that children had experiences like that Fred Bigman related to William Bittle in a 1967 Doris Duke interview:

> Fred Bigman: And boy I had a hard time. I didn't know a word of English.
> William Bittle: How old were you then?
> Bigman: Oh, I don't remember. About eight or nine years old. And I didn't know nothing about English that time, I had a hard time, when I first start school over there. I had to ask what they say. Ask somebody that knows English alright. And I always ask what they say. When they talking English I don't know what they talking about. And when I went to school in class I met that teacher,

told me to come up to him come up to blackboard, write something on it. I didn't know what to write. I didn't know what he
said. So I ask a guy, Robert Clarence, what'd he say. What that
lady, he said. She said for you to run out. Boy I jumped up and
grabbed, my cap and away I went. I went plumb back to our boy's
building. She come down there and got me. They punished him.
(Bigman 1972: 24)

Inside the story of Robert Clarence's prank on Fred Bigman is another
story of the boundaries that build ethnic identity. There may be a more
stark contrast of cultures to an eight- or nine-year-old boy than what
Fred Bigman experienced, but I can not think of one. He is talking about
his first day of school. It was boarding school, so he had just been taken
away from the family he had always lived with, and in the first class on
the first day he had to respond to a language he neither spoke nor understood. White culture and the white society's cultural institution of school
used only English and did not even acknowledge Plains Apache, the only
language Fred Bigman knew when he started at the Cache Creek Mission
school.

Not all Indian children going to boarding school for the first time
had to deal with this situation. Many, no doubt, were English speakers
before they arrived, but others got help in other ways. Mamie Turkey
Long had sisters and brothers who had gone to boarding school before
her, and she learned from them:

Velma Neiberding: Did you have any language difficulty when you
    went to school?
Mamie Turkey Long: Well, I didn't have it so bad as my sisters, and
    brothers—sisters and brothers did, because we all talked Indian
    when we were home. And, of course they went to school ahead of
    me, and of course I learned from them.
Neiberding: Oh, you learned English from them.
Long: I learned from them.
Neiberding: I believe Laura told me she took an interpreter with her—
    is that true?
Long: Well, I don't. know. She could have. (Long 1972: 5)

Nor was the ethnic divide always as severe as in Fred Bigman's
experience. In many of the national schools, for example, English and
the national North American Indian language coexisted, sometimes in
the context of Christianity. In 1937 Leister Reed talked to Nettie Cain
about her experience in the Creek Nation schools in the late 1860s and
early1870s. Cain reported:

Mrs Reed attended school at what was known as the Lilley school, John Ramsey was her teacher. This was a mixed school for Indian and negro children but it was financed by the United States Government. . . .

John Ramsey married one of the Lilley daughters at the time he was teaching. The Reverend Mr Ramsey would preach to the Indians and would sing in the Creek language; sometimes he would preach in English and an uncle of Mrs Reed's, Doniee McGuirt, would interpret in Creek. When Mr McGuirt died John Ramsey preached his funeral sermon in the Creek language. The Reverend Mr Ramsey and family would come to Mrs Reed's house on Wednesday night and they would have religious services.

Mrs Reed's mother would sew and make clothes for the children who were attending the Indian school. (Reed 1938: 66–67)

But many were like Fred Goodbear and had to pick up the new language cold, as Clara Winona Goodbear related to David Jones:

David Jones: Did the teachers of the school talk Cheyenne?
Clara Winona Goodbear: No.
Jones: How did you get along?
Goodbear: We start going and I guess we start caught on. They were white people, they didn't talk Indian. Long time, I guess it used to be pretty hard for Indian kids to start going to school. Cause you don't understand and they talk that English. But now it easy for them—for our grandchildren. They already talk English and they already understand. But long time, we didn't used to understand them. Used to have hard times thinking up. (Goodbear 1972: 2)

Clara Winona Goodbear had to struggle because her teachers did not speak Cheyenne, but she caught on and got through. It is interesting that she establishes the ethnic boundary—white people do not talk Indian—but goes on to say that her grandchildren speak English and did not have to pick it up on the fly in school. The replacement of Cheyenne with English in her family, at least to the extent that her grandchildren spoke English, if not Cheyenne, represents a success in the eyes of the assimilationists. But because of this, the symbolic function of English as an ethnic marker may have changed. It is a bitter irony that so many of the goals of the assimilationists were achieved with respect to North American Indian languages—today most of the languages that were spoken here five hundred years ago are no longer spoken, and many of those are only spoken by a handful of people (Silver and Miller 1997)—but the language they promoted has become the language of Indian ethnicity in Oklahoma.

If the identification of white society with English and school draws a strong distinction between white and Indian cultures, then the military regimentation of students at boarding schools draws an almost equally powerful distinction. When these students went to school they took off their home clothing and put on uniforms modeled after the United States military. At the same time, they were taken out of their home's social organization and put into military organizations that emphasized hierarchy, command, and control. Albert W. Keith was thirteen or fourteen years old when he first experienced Indian school regimentation near the end of the nineteenth century: "In 1897 my folks sent me to school at Haskell Institute at Lawrence, Kansas. I stayed at this school for three years. At this time Haskell had an enrollment of nearly eight hundred, and every tribe in the United States was represented there. We were placed in companies according to our size; we went to school three hours each day, and each was taught a trade" (Keith 1938: 102–3). The Quapaw Mission school that J. W. Barbee attended was smaller than Haskell and run by Catholic nuns, but it also followed the military school model:

> I was sent to the Quapaw Mission to the boarding school east of Quapaw and this was out on the prairie and we had to stay here and some of us grew homesick and decided to run away and go home. We were middle-sized boys and they dressed us in brown duck trimmed with brass buttons. The larger boys had blue clothes with a red strip down the outside of the leg of the trousers which were made something like the uniforms worn by the soldiers who had been stationed near there. (Barbee 1938: 165)

The military dress and organization that characterized these schools was part of life for students of both sexes. The organization defined the classes students took, and therefore their classmates, the work all students did, and even where each student ate and with whom. Mamie Turkey Long went to the Seneca Indian School in the first two decades of the twentieth century and remembered both of these features in her Doris Duke interview:

> Velma Neiberding: Could you tell me how the school was? I understand, it was quite different than it did . . .
> Mamie Turkey Long: Oh, my, different—I think so!
> Neiberding: Tell me about it.
> Long: Well, it just so different, it's pitiful is all I know. Well, any way, we had to march. Everywhere we went—we marched to school, we marched to the dining room and we had roll call. And we was—we wasn't allowed to chase all over the place to get on the grass or anything. When we went to the school house, we

marched—we marched back. And then, we'd even have to march with the boys down in the ball diamond after—before school was out. We had to pass the review just like the boys did.

Neiberding: Kind of a military.

Long: Yes, it was.

Neiberding: Did you wear a—I mean a uniform?

Long: We wore uniforms, our Sunday uniforms.

Neiberding: What did they look like?

Long: Oh, they were blue serge, rough and scratchy. (Long 1972: 5)

A little later she goes on to say:

Long: Well, I know we just marched into the dining room. We each had a—knew where our table—places were at the table. And before we sat down we sang Grace. And we sat down, and we had our meal. (Long 1972: 6)

Here the United States government school dresses and organizes its students along white military lines and attaches school and military to Christianity by marching to meals and then singing grace. This close association of Christianity, military discipline, and English with white schools for Native Americans adds to the list of boundary symbols that maintain Indian ethnicity. Sometimes this distinction was especially striking because, from the student's point of view, Christianity was a new religion. Joe Creeping Bear was an Arapaho who was born in Wyoming in 1885. He and his family moved south to Indian Territory, where he lived the rest of his life, and he started school in 1891. He said: "We settled here in Colony and got ready for school. Mr Seger had a log cabin in which he taught school until the new school was built in 1892. We had old time slates and pencils to do our writing with and the picture of Jesus was the first one I had ever seen and I had never heard of Jesus until I came to Colony" (Creeping Bear 1938: 443).

In the mission schools, of course, Christianity was a central aspect of the curriculum. After all, the missionaries were there to convert the Indian people, and the students were aware of this. Andrew Perdasophy, a Comanche Indian, recalled, "At my first schools each morning we were taught to pray, each night before we went to bed we must say our prayers" (Perdasophy 1938: 6). And Fred Bigman said of the Cache Creek school: "It is mission alright. Boy, they is real missionaries. Sort of like Baptist" (Bigman 1972: 24). There were, however, some differences between schools. Later in the same interview Fred Bigman contrasted the "sort of Baptists" at the Cache Creek school with the nuns at the local Catholic school near Anadarko that he attended for two years.

William Bittle: Was there much religious teaching at the Catholic
    School?
Fred Bigman: Well, no. We had teachers, they call them sisters. Any-
    more, before go into breakfast we go into chapel. A priest down
    there, call him father, we get down there, get on our knees about
    an hour. Boy, I get tired. Priest get up there, preaching, oh, we
    have to stay on our knees behind our desk, you know. Oh, about
    an hour I guess, by the time he gets through knees, they hurting.
Bittle: What did he talk about?
Bigman: About the Bible. The church rules, just like the rest of them.
Bittle: Why didn't you become a Catholic out there?
Bigman: I just didn't want to.
Bittle: Did many of the Indian kids become Catholics?
Bigman: Yea. They try to get me to join that Catholic, but no.
Bittle: How did they treat you at all of those schools? Was the disci-
    pline pretty hard?
Bigman: No, not here. That place, down yonder, Cache Creek Mis-
    sion. They won't let us play on Sunday. No. Not supposed to play
    on Sunday. Got to go to church, Sunday School. When Sunday
    School was through, we go to dinner. After dinner, they go to our
    building our matron she puts us to bed. She don't want the boys
    playing. Till it's time to go to church then she wake us boys up.
    She say alright boys you boys clean up get ready to go to church.
    There we were, Wash up like when we get up in the morning.
    Clean up, change clothes, put our church clothes on. There we
    go. March down the church. From one o'clock till about four. Had
    a preacher down there. There's some Indians come down there
    some Comanches. Come down there go to church. All those kids
    down there, school kids, we go to church down there. Yea, they
    won't let us play on Sunday. (Bigman 1972: 26–27)

Along with this Christian environment, instruction in English, and
military organization, the mission schools, boarding schools, and national
schools all shared a commitment to work in their assimilationist philosophy. Sometimes labor was included as a part of the formal curriculum,
sometimes it was an important part of the school's economic base, and
sometimes it was merely work for work's sake. Work was always, however, white. The curricular and economic functions of student work for
schools often merged. Students worked because it was part of the training they received, but the fruits of that labor were added, in one way or
another, to the school's coffers.

George French described his experience at the Cherokee Orphan Asylum in the 1870s and 1880s: "We had our own cows and hogs. We also
had our own milk and butter and meat. The boys were taught to farm and
truck. The girls were taught to cook and sew. They washed, ironed and

took care of the milk and butter. We had Saturday evening to ourselves" (French 1938: 280). Mrs. I. V. Jones attended the Faits Mission school in the late 1890s and early 1900s and described a similar situation to the Indian Pioneer project fieldworker, Thad Smith, Jr. "The Mission had a cook employed, but the older girls helped set the table and wash the dishes, and at the same time learned to cook. The girls were also taught to sew and mend. They did most of the laundry work" (Jones 1938: 149). Mamie Turkey Long reported much the same thing when she talked about the curriculum at the Seneca Indian School:

> Velma Neiberding: Yes, well, that's interesting. The—how was the food in those days—didn't they raise a lot of it?
> Mamie Turkey Long: Oh yes, they raised their own food. They had their own chickens and cows and they raised their hogs. They just raised practically everything. We raised our own gardens.
> Neiberding: The children worked?
> Long: Uh-huh, we worked. We eat—
> Neiberding: Oh, you had to work, uh-huh.
> Long: We each one had a garden. We raised a garden in the spring and we—they furnished our seed, and we—we had to tend it. We go down, oh, once a week or in the afternoons and go down. It depended on what—what day—you see, we went to school every other—every day, a half day. Sometimes we go in the morning, and maybe we go this morning, why we go the next afternoon. And then, it'd be the next morning then. That's the way we went.
> Neiberding: The—lessons were half a day?
> Long: We just have—
> Neiberding: And the other half, you worked.
> Long: And the other half day, we worked. We worked in the laundries, sewing room in the house and in the kitchen, dining room. (Long 1972: 6–7)

Fred Bigman's experience at the Rainy Mountain School also shows this confluence of vocational training and benefit to the school's bottom line.

> William Bittle: Did you like the government schools or the public schools better?
> Fred Bigman: Well, I like the public schools better than the boarding schools. Boy they work the life out of you at the government schools. When I first went to Rainy Mountain Indian School they put you a certain kind of work. They got a dairy barn, I didn't know how to milk too. Shoot, I had to milk two cows. I think there was twelve of us boys. In the morning. Gaah, it was cold too. We didn't have no fire in that dairy barn, you know, Cold in

the morning. We get up at four o'clock in the morning . . . winter time. I was about fourteen, fifteen years old then. We got there yea, they got twelve of us boys they put us in things like there, and on farm. See, I know about that before I went to that school. I know all about farming. They put me out there, on that farm. Get out there and work. Wheat ground, you know, it'd be all plowed up, all you had to do was harrow it down before they put the wheat. They put me out there, but in the morning in the winter time when we was getting up, it was cold. We didn't have no kind of heat down there in the dairy barn. Sit around down there and it was cold. We go to milking till them cows started breathing that heat, you know, kind of warm things up by the time you get through. Pretty cold, our hands, our hands, you know, but them bags, they warm. Put our hands over them bags.

Bittle: What did they teach you at Rainy Mountain school?

Bigman: They teach us . . . books. Like any other school.

Bittle: Did they, you ever get taught about farming in any of those schools?

Bigman: I learned that from my job down there at Rainy Mountain. Course, I already knowed it you know. Through my dad . . . farming. No, they didn't teach me no kind, down there. Well we had, a principal who was an Indian . . . Caddo Indian. Name of Henry Inkinish. He was our principal. He worked us boys on the farm. He worked with us. Show us how to do this work. One thing and another. Don't tell me much about it . . . already know it. One day he ask me, say, me telling you how to do it, to work, you know it already. Well I said, I did it at home I said. Oh he said. But some of them boys don't know how. Don't even know how to set a plow. I learn it when I was a young fellow. I watched my dad, you know. Setting plows. I set it. (Bigman 1972: 28–29)

Often, however, the curriculum was not apparent in either the kind of work done or in when and how often it was done. The goods and services the students in these schools produced clearly had more importance in the school's budget than in the lessons the work taught. Sarah Longbone, for example, talked about what she learned at the Wyandotte Mission school. "After we came here, grandmother took me to the Wyandotte Mission and placed me there. We learned to scrub, had to get on our hands and knees and scrub with brush. They didn't give us much to eat, either. Sundays we had breakfast, no dinner, and for supper we got two pieces of light bread with or without molasses" (Longbone 1938: 197).

To the people who ran these schools, work clearly had value beyond its role in the production of wealth. Labor was one of the ways that Indian children would be assimilated into Euro-American society, so it was divided along gender lines. Because of its purported power to transform Indian children into white adults, school administrators included manual labor in the school experience without regard to its economic meaning. Alex Lowe attended the Levering Wetumka Mission school in the 1880s and 1890s and talked about some of the school work he did:

> When I went to school they called it the Levering Mission. It was named for the first missionary who was there. That was in 1889 and there were somewhere about fifty boys and fifty girls at this mission. That is not exactly the number but it is near it. The boys had to work so many hours every morning and every evening but from nine A.M. till four P.M. we studied. . . . I never could understand why they had us do the work that we did in the mornings and evenings but they were very strict and insisted that we should work hard and do just as the teachers told us. We cut brush in the river bottom. As I was small I gathered this brush and put it into a pile. The cleared space was not used for a garden nor for anything. The brush was just allowed to rot instead of being burned and the place grew up again into more brush. Once in a while the better pieces were used for wood but we were not getting wood, we were just working. (Lowe 1938: 18–19)

Indian students worked in Indian schools, and whether this work was done for its own sake or to contribute to the school's budget or as part of a vocational curriculum, it was always viewed as one of the pillars of the assimilation policy. The white society's values and the educational philosophy that controlled these schools sought assimilation only on narrow grounds. These schools did not exist to train junior scholars and develop their critical thinking capacities; rather they were to train laborers, farmers, homemakers, and domestic servants. This imposes a distinction between white and Indian culture that helps form the foundation of Indian ethnicity.

## Indian Education

The Indian schools gave many young Indian students an intense and common experience of white society, and consequently gave these students, and their friends and families, one of the themes around which Indian identity is constructed. These schools were an extension of white culture and an embodiment of the idea replacing tribal or Indian ways with Euro-American culture. The fact that the vocational portions of the experience emphasized labor force skills were not because the curriculum planners wished to provide practical options to their students but because that was the best the planners thought Indian people could do. Indian people, on the other hand, often take the position that school has utility, that it is a resource that can be used for a person's own ends, and that school should respond to Indian people's needs. This approach to school coexists with assimilationist approaches that emphasized English and Christianity, and was sometimes even the position taken by tribal leaders. For example, Osmond Franklin reported that when he was a boy in the 1880s and 1890s, the Sac and Fox chiefs "wanted the young people to attend school. They said, 'Go to school, later you will be handicapped in meeting and dealing with whites if you do not learn their ways'" (Franklin 1938: 29).

In this construction, education has utility in whatever arena a person chooses. It could be applied to personal goals or to broader Indian agendas. Jess Rowlodge made reference to both, first mentioning an early county treasurer in Wetonga who was a "full-blood Indian. Educated at Haskell, Kansas. Then there was an Indian that had attended Carlisle who was a pretty good blacksmith." A little later, Jess brought up *Lone Wolf v. Hitchcock* and the role Lone Wolfe's son, a Carlisle graduate, played in the case as interpreter for his father (Rowlodge 1972a: 18–21). The county treasurer and the blacksmith had used their Indian school educations to pursue careers in the white world. Lone Wolf's son applied his Carlisle education to help his father try to stop the allotment of Kiowa lands.

Jess Rowlodge himself lived an example of school having both personal and cultural significance. After he finished the eighth grade at a local Indian school in Darlington, he worked for a period as a clerk in a local store and in the Kiowa exhibit at the St. Louis World's Fair. These experiences led him to believe he needed more education. He said: "I made up my mind that there was lot of things I ought to know that I didn't know, and only way I could know was to go to school. . . . My folks didn't want me to go off to school. But I told my folks, 'You're getting old. You need more help as you get older.' Well, my father died that fall. So I put my mother under the care of my oldest brother and I went off to school then" (Rowlodge 1972a: 24). And later he made it clear that he went to Haskell so he could get a better job. When Coach Warner invited him to play football at Carlisle, he said: "'No, I come to go to school. I didn't come to play football.' I just played it on the side, you know. So I didn't go. So when I finished in 1910 I went on and took—I finished the academic, and then I went on and took the two year business—complete business course. Except telegraphy. I passed Civil Service" (Rowlodge 1972a: 25).

Jess Rowlodge's father, Row of Lodges, had been an influential intermediary chief of the Arapaho in the late nineteenth century (Fowler 2002: 37), and soon the tribe called upon Jess Rowlodge for help.

When I come home, they organized a Council. And they knew I was pretty well versed on legal matters—contracts, and all those things—so they just planned to keep me. I told them I was all ready to go to a good law school. Well, they just kept after me. So my cousins and my brother, they just insist I stay with the tribe. I says, "All right. But if I get any job brochure, I'll always be here, but I'm going to try to get a job." (Rowlodge 1972a: 25)

Jess Rowlodge applied his school experiences to Arapaho political, legal, religious, and ritual affairs for the rest of his life. While his story is one of education applied to Indian life in Oklahoma, in other stories education is applied to career goals. Angie Barnes is a good example of the strength this idea had among Indian people in the late 1960s. She was in her early forties when she described to Katherine Maker in a Doris Duke interview the process she went through to become a licensed practical nurse. She said:

I felt the urge to do something that I had always wanted to do since childhood. I had always wanted to be a nurse. The opportunity came for me to do this and I thought first I would be—I always wanted to be a nurse. So I went back to where I—to see if I still wanted to do this and I took the Nurse Aide course in Tulsa at Hillcrest Hospital. I commuted 60 miles each day for four weeks to complete this course. And at the end of this course I was hired at Hillcrest to work on the medical floor. (Barnes 1972: 3)

After a period of work as a nurse's aide she was encouraged to continue her education.

[They] pushed me to do things that I was not licensed to do and really didn't have any business doing. But they felt that I was capable of doing these things and allowed me to do them under their supervision. So I began to think that if they had this confidence in me that I was capable of doing a little bit higher level work. So I put my application in at a licensed practical nursing school and I asked the doctors if I could give them as recommendations and the supervisor and they gave me very fine letters of recommendation. . . . So I went to Bartlesville, Oklahoma. They have a school at Jane Phillips Hospital there and I placed my application there and was interviewed and again sent recommendations. And I was accepted there. So I got a leave of absence from my work at the hospital for a year to attend this school. And I also had to commute each day to and from Bartlesville, which was added expense and a hardship at times. And I also worked at the local hospital on Saturdays and Sundays during this year, which was against the rules of the hospital at Bartlesville. But they did not know this and my local employer did not tell them. He said what they didn't know wouldn't hurt. And we would keep it under our own hats. So I was—I was really busy that year. But since my children were all grown; had one girl in college that year, and one boy and an eleven year old girl at home. And all helped me very much all through the year. Had it not been for them and, my husband I would not have been able to finish or fulfill this desire. And I finished—completed my schooling in September, a year ago. And since that time I come back to Hominy and I have been employed here as a licensed practical nurse for the last year. (Barnes 1972: 3–5)

Angie Barnes worked very hard just to have the opportunity to go to school in Bartlesville, and it is a measure of her belief in the utility of school that she would put forth the effort that she did. Her personal motivation to use school to become a nurse's aide did not in any way diminish her participation in her community. She went to school and became a nurse's aide while she and her family participated in Indian life. In other words, she did not have to chose between Indian and white—within her the two worlds could coexist.

The Indian people that I talked to also approached and participated in school on these utilitarian grounds. They went to school themselves, and they encourage others to go to school so they can do better. They believe that education will help Indian students get better jobs and bring important expertise to Indian communities. Pat said: "A severe automobile accident that led me to say, 'I'm going to die here, I better do something with my life.' And I did. I started to go to school, take some time, and I moved down it to Talaquah, and I've been there off and on for the last twenty years." And Lee, speaking through his role as a tribal administrator, said:

I'm pro-education and it doesn't have anything to do with "Lee went to college," that doesn't mean nothing. I went to college and got a bachelor's degree, but in the business world today, that's about like graduating from high school. People say, "Well, I don't have a master's, I didn't specialize in this or say I got a BSE in education." They say, "Well you are not in your field," and they are right. Didn't really specialize on anything, and "Get a masters or go on from there." People don't realize in the business that you might have a bachelor's in this, but what did you specialize in, you can specialize in a lot of things. I see that daily that kids should be specializing in something.

But later he added:

Being public school or Indian school today, there is that focus on college, and Indian kids get into the Anglo world, the dominant society and just don't mesh. I'd be the smartest man in the world today if I could put my finger on why they don't. . . . They get timid, they get their feelings hurt, they walk with their head down, and then they go home. It's done, it's over. I wish I could put my finger on it. I see it all the time. I go and give talks to high school kids, I volunteer for the prison, go in and talk to the Indian prisoners and say, "Hey, we can rebound from this."

So Lee believes in the utility of education, and he has backed up the belief with a degree from one of the Oklahoma public universities and community action to urge Indian people to stay in or return to school. On the other hand, it is clear to him that the schools are failing many of their Indian students. Indian people know, even while they recognize school's usefulness, that the schools have not become Indian institutions; they remain organs of white society. So within this construction of school as useful is a discourse of reform. In this discourse, Indian people point out from their own experience the deficiencies of school—how it makes factual mistakes about Indian culture and history, or is blind to Indian perspectives—and they work to provide a more Indian school environment for Indian students.

One day when Julian and I were having lunch at a diner near his home, he talked about his experiences in both public and Christian schools where his Indian identity was not an issue but the education was blind to Indian perspectives. He voiced an impression of being left incomplete by the experience: "The things I learned growing up in school, the history books and so forth, I would always read things about basic wars and things, this was Custer et cetera, you might get just a little bit of information, like what specific tribe was involved, but never provided the kind of information I was looking for. Especially not anything in depth when it came to the Cherokee people, that was a part of me."

He recognized that the history and social studies classes he had taken were presented entirely from a white perspective. That perspective ignored his Cherokee heritage, even though all his schools were in Oklahoma, where it is likely that a large portion of any class will be Indian students. Julian believes that school should have done more about Indian people in Oklahoma, so he took it upon himself to learn what school left out. Many Indian students come to school knowing a great deal more about their heritage than Julian did, and school often contradicts that knowledge. Chris told me the story of her fifth-grade experience in a small-town Oklahoma public school:

> I can remember in fifth grade, my teacher vividly, I remember this vividly, I guess I always knew I was somehow different than children, non-Indian children, I guess even as a little (one) I guess I was a little bit militant and spoke my mind, I spoke out. . . . But in fifth grade our teacher kept

talking about Custer and teaching us about Custer and what a brave guy he was and how good he was. I went home and talked to my father and telling him this because this is not what I knew about Custer. My father told me, this, this, and this occurred and reminding me of history and teaching me some other real history about Custer. I went to school the next day and took my teacher aside and I said, "I want to talk to you." I'm in fifth grade now, so we went out in the hallway and I said, "You're teaching this classroom about Custer and how brave he was and what a good man he was and I'll tell you right now he was a coward. He murdered thousands of my people, he's a coward and he disobeyed orders so it isn't right for you to teach this wrong information to this class." This teacher was so caught by this, he just stood back and said, "Thank you very much for your input." We went back to the classroom, and we didn't hear about Custer anymore.

Chris the fifth-grader was confronted with a situation where her knowledge contradicted the teacher's, and she dealt with it as a political event. She confronted the teacher with her knowledge and did not allow her teacher to contradict what she knew to be true. Chris had many Indian classmates, but a government program moved Pat's family away from rural Oklahoma to a large Midwestern city, so there were few Indians in his high school class. Nonetheless, the story he told me, one morning in his home while he watched his infant son, was much the same as Chris's:

I remember the high school I went to my junior year, there were only two Indians in the entire school. I remember getting kicked out of a Western history class. When he got onto the part of the class when he was talking of Plains Indians, at that time we were still at war with the United States for one hundred years, within that one hundred year span. I knew my great-grandparents and all of the stories and things that they would tell us, and just being who I was, I knew this just wasn't factual. You would think someone would say, "Hey, we have a Cheyenne boy in here and we are discussing things and maybe we can talk or bring one of my family members like my grandmothers living at the time." But no, they threw me out of the classroom. They said, "No, no, that's not what we did. I know how to put a teepee together." I just couldn't take it anymore, so they kicked me out of the class.

Pat expected the school to get it wrong; after all, it was a white school in a white environment, and it had little or no experience with Indian people. It angered him, however, that the school was blind to him and his perspective. He felt that he brought an authentic knowledge to the subject that came through his family, and he was angry that his perspective had no standing with the school. To him the school was not merely blind to him and the truth he brought; it was also arrogant to believe that only the school had the truth, and probably racist, because it more than likely ignored him on the grounds that he was Indian.

It has been common for Indian students to feel that school is blind to their issues and perspectives. They have also felt that in many of the instances where a school does recognize Indian students, it is only for the purpose of exploiting them. To them, the school is getting money for teaching Indian students, but that money is added to the school's general funds without acknowledging Indian students in any other way. This combination of recognizing the utility of school, while at the same time understanding that school is a white institution that will not see Indian points of view without help, often results in an ideology that values making the schools more Indian. Some, like Sam Hair, expressed this value by working with academic professionals to make teaching materials for Indian students.

> Then in 1964 if I'm not mistaken, there's a fellow came around—he was a well educated doctor. His name was Willard Walker. He came around. So we made the books. A primer book in which you learn how to read and to speak Cherokee. The easiest way to learn, we thought that we made books. So the people could learn the Cherokee language, how to speak and how to read and how to write. So we worked on them primer books and sort of something else—some other things—Cherokee magazines that we made. (Hair 1972: 3)

The primer books and magazines that Sam Hair and Willard Walker wrote let the schools that used them affirm the value of the Cherokee language. They made the language something worthwhile to be learned, gave it parity with English and French and all the other languages of the school. Schools are being made more Indian not only with teaching materials but also through special Indian programs at all levels. Cory and Carol at one point worked together to start Indian studies programs in community colleges and universities in their area, and Chris has experienced programs for Indian students from the point of view of a student as well as an advocate. She describes a program for Indian students from her grade school years as a good thing:

> You know, we had Native American people involved with us, which is important, and it provided special presentations and special times for us, for what I believe in many respects . . . was good. Urban Indians is a new phenomenon that you are seeing now, especially here in Oklahoma. It kept those kids in touch with some things that maybe they wouldn't be in touch with. I'll tell you that . . . I applaud the [program], I think it is a good one.

This program was for Indian students, and it brought Indian people to the school to be a part of it. Chris formed continuing relationships with some of the community members who participated, and today is involved with other programs for local tribes. She makes the point about the value of these programs by first describing how one community conducts feasts, such as those for a funeral, and then she goes on to say:

> In Head Start they teach . . . them about that. How to sit down at a table and how to ask politely, "May I have, will you pass," and that sort of thing, because that's the way we have to conduct ourselves. Just as you sit down with your own children at the supper table. Other tribes have language-immersion programs, the Comanche Nation has a wonderful language-immersion program where they take little toddlers who are just beginning to speak and immersing them where nothing but Comanche is spoken.

These cases of Indian people working to make school more Indian may be isolated, and are, no doubt, too isolated, but they remain a good example of Indian people using the resources they have to strengthen Indian identity. They have taken the school systems that were originally intended to erase Indian culture, to turn Indians into whites, and made these systems, to a small extent, tools for cultural survival. They, of course, recognize that Indian children cannot learn to be Indian in school. Lee put it this way to me after I had said something about school being a white institution:

> The only time an Indian gets Indian culture or Indian way of thinking they got to come to this, I'm not saying Powwow, I'm saying Indian gathering part, it could be the gathering of a Stomp Dance, it could be a Powwow, it could be Native American Church meeting or Native Christian Church. Any kind of gathering that they have the Indians get around and tell stories of how it was and how we look at stuff.

## Conclusion

Ed told the story that her mother told her about how her name was taken away so that the school could get a nickel. While the story rests on the twin themes of white institutions and racial discrimination, it goes much deeper than that. The story goes back to Ed's grandmother and boarding schools:

> Grandma had two sisters . . . and a brother. . . . In their young lives the boarding school process separated them all, and Grandma . . . was sent to Haskell, one aunt was sent to Riverside in California, the other was

sent to Carlisle in Pennsylvania, and my great-uncle was sent to Chilocco. The idea of separating family certainly took place there. Grandma
absolutely hated the boarding school process, found a way to come home
and apparently sort of vowed that, by golly, she was not going to be an
Indian.

It looks like at this point Ed's grandmother represented a victory for
the assimilationists. She was going to act white, she would not speak the
language, she would not attend the ceremonies and dances, she would
not go to tribal meetings, and she would raise her children to be white.
Ed said there in her office that her mother

> remembers that very clearly. She remembers that Grandma didn't want
> them learning language or conducting themselves as Indians, so they
> didn't go to Powwows, they didn't associate on the local level with differ-
> ent related community activities. I have six siblings, three brothers and
> three sisters, and it wasn't until I was eight years old that Mom decided
> that it was okay to be Indian. We started participating at a local Pow-
> wow, we set up our camp there for the first time when I was nine years
> old in 1970–71, and we started participating, the whole family started
> dancing and learning and participating, and to this day everyone is still
> very much involved.

So after all, even though it took three generations, assimilation lost.
One of the reasons that assimilation has sometimes failed is in the nature
of Indian education itself. The structure of the white power center making
education for Indians creates with it a border between white and Indian,
and thus reinforces Indian identity. It is ironic that school became a force
for maintaining Indian identity rather than erasing it, as the assimilationists had planned. School is constructed in Indian identity in many
ways, not the least of which is a shared history of school as an agent of
cultural destruction. It was within this context that Indian people began
to appropriate school and both use it to survive in the white world and
change it to be more Indian, each of which maintained the white/Indian
divide. This is, however, a reactionary situation. Indian people reacted to
white schools and forced assimilation, but other aspects of Indian identity emerge more from within the community. Often these constructions
revolve around questions of authenticity, and community, often expressed
in terms of blood, but with a deep history in Indian discourse.

# PART III

# Survival and Change

# 5 *Blood Brothers*

Mr Beamer is not a full blood Cherokee, being probably
of three-quarters Indian blood, to one-quarter of white
blood. His surname indicates English ancestry on his
father's side, but he is usually considered a full Indian.

—Elisabeth Ross, description of Lewis Beamer
(Indian Pioneer Papers)

On its face, blood would seem to be a straightforward idea,
although that apparent simplicity does not survive very much thought. It
is clear, for instance, right from the first that the concept cannot actually
refer to blood. When people talk about three-quarters (or any other quantum) Indian blood, they cannot be referring to the red stuff that pulses
through our arteries and veins. We describe that substance in terms of
A, B, and O blood groups and rhesus factors (and, no doubt, many other
biomedical concepts of which I am not aware) that refer to all blood for
all humans. We cannot distinguish the blood in the veins of Indians from
white blood, or African blood, or Asian blood. So "blood" in the sense that
the Indian Pioneer fieldworker used the term to describe Lewis Beamer
as "three-quarters Indian blood" is a metaphor for the proportion of a
person's parents or grandparents in one racial category or another. But
Elisabeth Ross makes it clear that blood has this meaning and more when
she goes on to say that Mr. Beamer is considered a "full Indian." Blood
often refers to political factions, or to stands on issues. Blood may also
make reference to racial characteristics that are attributed to people on
the basis of certain proportions of Indian blood that they are supposed to
carry. And, in many cases, blood refers to Indian communities and the
values that keep them together.

Churchill (1999) makes a good point when he argues that blood as an identifier of Indianness is an imposition of a European idea on indigenous North American cultures. Be that as it may, blood is now, and has been for a long time, part of how Indian people talk about themselves and who they are as Indians. In this chapter I want to explore some of the major themes that Indian people express in their talk about blood. All the themes I will explore span the entire twentieth century. They emerge in the Indian Pioneer and Doris Duke interviews and from the talks I have had with people over the past ten years. Two of these threads of discourse refer to divisions within Indian communities. Perhaps because the idea came from Euro-American thinking, blood has had race at its core of meaning. In the late nineteenth and early twentieth centuries, the idea of race was defined by scientific racism, which held that the various races were hierarchically arranged—that some races (white) were naturally better than others (black, Indian). Many Indian people talk about blood in this way, using blood quantum as a measure of Indianness. Almost as a derivative of this measure, Indian people also sometimes understand political divisions along lines of blood, with the "less Indian" favoring progress and the "more Indian" opposed to white success. It is clear to Indian people that these expressions of the idea of blood are divisive, so blood also contributes to a dialogue on community that negotiates the values and beliefs that bring Indian people together.

## Race

The CDIB (Certificate of Degree of Indian Blood) is one of the oddest manifestations of "race" that I can imagine. Under this rubric, the United States government certifies that a certain person belongs in a specified

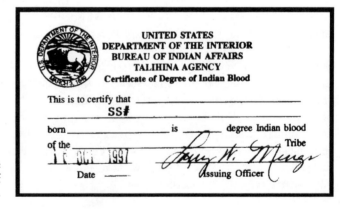

Certificate of Degree of Indian Blood.

proportion to a particular race, which is a direct outgrowth of the scientific racism that characterized thinking a century ago. It is odd now in the early twenty-first century, because it represents support of these racist ideas by the government of the United States. (As my mother would say, "You'd think they'd have more pride than that.") For some tribes, this certification is presented in terms of a degree of blood, or blood quantum, one-half, one-quarter, one-thirty-second, one one thousand twenty-fourth (and even more complex fractions), and so on. Even though the term *Certified Degree of Indian Blood* promises a degree, the certificates issued for some tribes do not list blood quantum. From the non-Indian perspective, it would seem that this racialization of Indian/ non-Indian differences could only serve to make the general policy of assimilation more difficult to achieve, yet it remains current today. On the other hand, many Indian people in Oklahoma who see the CDIB as a racist imposition of the U. S. government, at the same time, require it for any legitimate claim of Indian identity. Even though complex, however, these meanings are significant for Indian people in the construction of Indian ethnicity. One chilly early April morning when I was talking to Carol, the issue came up. She said:

> Some people have said that Indians are the only ones who have to have a pedigree, like animals. Most people will say well, they have some Scottish or Irish blood, but they don't have to prove it, and of course blacks don't have to prove their blood and Asians don't have to prove their blood, and it's curious that for historical reasons Indians have to. You can be black and be all shades of light to dark and you can have blond hair and be black, and of course the same thing is true for Indians as well, but the quantum issue remains.

Carol knows about CDIBs. She sees them regularly and is aware that the top line of the document reads "United States" and the next line reads "Department of the Interior." She knows, therefore, that when she says things like "the only ones who have to have a pedigree, like animals," she is clearly pointing to the division that the Unites States officially puts up between Indians and non-Indians through the CDIB. A little later she reexpressed this anger at the inherent racism of the document with a story that is commonly heard in Oklahoma:

> One of the interesting things, I know there are full-blood Cherokees who are not on the rolls who still speak Cherokee, not English, and they cannot vote with any tribe. I don't know to what extent that's true of some of the other larger tribes, I would guess it is, so again the ongoing question is, "Who is Indian?" When I was going through the Dawes

Rolls years ago, I was interested that lots of people were 1/320th at the beginning of the Rolls; what does that make them now?

Carol's concern about the legitimacy of the rolls is not a new story by any means. In 1938, Mrs. Kate Rackleff asked Nannie Lee Burns, the fieldworker interviewing her: "I should like to ask one question—My brothers are enrolled as fullbloods, my sisters as half-breeds and I am on the Rolls as three-quarters, Indian. Why?" (Rackleff 1938: 84)

Mrs. Rackleff, however, seems to see simple incompetence; Carol sees the CDIB as an example of Euro-American racism. Carol's statement also connects the CDIB to tribal membership, a feature that all tribes in the state share. While tribes have the right to establish their own membership rules, the U.S. government requires that all members have the document. Some tribes have membership rules, like the Cherokees', based on descent from an ancestor on the tribe's base rolls taken for allotment in the early twentieth century. The situation Carol describes here results when a Cherokee, for example, did not enroll for allotment, often as a political protest over the allotment program itself. Other tribes establish a minimum blood quantum for membership, but that quantum is also calculated from the tribe's base allotment roll, and is published on the CDIB. This often produces a situation where a man or woman's children cannot be members of their parent's tribe. This is true for Pat. He said: "Personally I think if you have a CDIB card you shouldn't list blood quantum on it. It's almost degrading. To me it's just been a degrading thing. I also have children who are right at one-half Indian. Various tribes. Not a single one of them can be enrolled. I have nephews and nieces and some of them can't be enrolled for those very reasons." A little later he returned to the subject of blood quantum and the CDIB, saying: "If the tribe will come along and say, 'Let's reverse this. Let's say you got blood if you can trace your ancestry. You're full blood, period.' That would change everything. It could actually make that tribe stronger. It would be extremely difficult to enforce quantums and it would be even more difficult to eliminate them."

Of course, the CDIB and the blood quantum it points to would not be an issue if there were no illegitimate claims to Indian identity—that is, if there were no hobbyists, non-Indians who dress in dance regalia and try to participate in Powwows, or wannabes, people who claim but cannot document (i.e., produce a CDIB) Indian ancestry. I heard many stories from Indian people around the state about confronting these hobbyists and wannabes by asking for a CDIB. So blood and blood quantum is at the symbolic core of Indian identity in Oklahoma. Furthermore, it

has been a central issue for at least the past century. The people I talked
to in the 1990s, the people in the Doris Duke interviews of the 1960s,
and people who participated in the Indian Pioneer project in the 1930s
all talk about blood and blood quantum.

On the surface, blood quantum refers to a rough count of the number of Indian ancestors a person has. Full-blood means both parents are
Indian; half that one parent is Indian; and so on. This count, however,
cannot account for the significance of blood in Indian identity, so it must
carry other meanings that add symbolic weight. Through these meanings,
blood points to the idea that Indianness is racial. Thus certain traits, like
speaking a tribal language, adhere to people, especially to full-bloods.
This racial context sometimes places individuals along a line from savage to civilized, roughly measured by blood quantum, that is used to
justify societal inequalities and to account for antisocial behavior. It
is commonly used to place people on one side or the other of political
issues, and to support political opinions. Blood is sometimes contrasted
with community as a central value of Indian ethnicity. Through all this,
however, the meanings of blood are negotiable, and are used in social
interactions to create Indian identities.

## THE NATURAL INDIAN

When Jess Rowlodge talked to Julia Jordan in April 1968, he talked a
little about Arapaho clothing and how Arapaho men wore breechcloths
in the late nineteenth century. And almost as an aside he said to Julia:

> You know in that connection I want to say this. Full blood Indians
>     don't have no body odor. Did you know that?
> Julia Jordan: I've sort of suspected it-
> Jess Rowlodge: They don't have no body odor. So the men of course,
>     they sweat—they can sweat all right. (Rowlodge 1972a: 15)

A little bit earlier, in the mid-1950s, my elder brother wanted to
participate in local Powwows. He was in high school, and two of his
classmates and close friends were members of a local Powwow club. My
brother wanted to make his regalia and Fancy Dance with them in the
club. He was not allowed to dance because he was less than one-quarter
blood. There was no dispute that our grandmother was Choctaw. She was
born in the Choctaw Nation in 1877, and her mother came to Choctaw
Nation on the trail of tears. She was in her twenties and married when
she put her name on the Dawes Commission Rolls of the Choctaw Tribe
and took her allotment. Our grandmother would talk about her life as
a Choctaw whenever we saw her. These facts made no difference, how-

ever, because our grandmother was on the Dawes Rolls as one-eighth blood quantum, making my brothers, sisters, and me one thirty-second, far below the one-quarter required for the federal government's lower limit. Thus my brother had no claim to being Indian, and the Powwow club would not admit him.

These two stories are interesting mainly because they point to a context—a place in time, space, and cultural values—where race was an important organizing concept. I, my brother, my entire family, my brother's high school friends, Jess Rowlodge, the Choctaw Tribe, the Powwow club, the United States government, and almost everybody else participated in organizing people by race. It was one of the traditional ways to think about people in Euro-American society, so nobody thought it was in any way misguided to conceive of being Indian, or any other race, on a biological basis. Maybe it would be better to say "natural" here rather than "biological," because many of the traits that became associated with the various races were not strictly biological. Being a full-blood Indian, for example, was often associated with speaking the tribal language. Whether natural or biological, however, this way of thinking associated these traits with races and the people in them, as a result not of their social life but of their essential being.

The fact that the concept of blood was used to racialize Indian ethnicity in the mid-1950s was nothing new; it had been a part of Indian identity for the entire century until then, and it continues to be part of the ethnic discourse today. Over that period, however, the concept has evolved. One interesting example of this is the quarter-blood rule that prevented my brother from dancing in the circle of the Powwow arena. This rule, like the CDIB, came from the federal government, which refused, at the time, to recognize anybody of less than one-quarter degree of Indian blood as an Indian eligible for treaty rights. Some prominent Indian people in Oklahoma supported this rule at the time of the Doris Duke project. As part of that project, the proceedings of an intertribal meeting sponsored by a group called Indian Citizens for Action were transcribed and included in the Doris Duke Collection. The meeting was held in the summer of 1969, and Senator Henry Bellmon (Republican of Oklahoma) was the guest speaker. Before Senator Bellmon delivered his remarks, several tribal leaders were recognized to address their concerns to the senator. One of those leaders was Charles Lohah, an officer of the Osage Nation Organization, who said: "We ask not only for our sakes but also for all tribes . . . that treatment be limited to those with not less than one-fourth degree of Indian blood, and their spouses and children."

No matter what support the quarter-blood rule had among Indian people and leaders, however, it was also causing some problems for many Indian people. Willis McNaughton, for example, who was at one time chief of the Peoria Tribe, mentioned some of the effort he went through as a result of the quarter-blood rule. Peggy Dycus interviewed Chief McNaughton, then in his midfifties, for the Doris Duke project in May 1969. At one point in the interview, he calculated his blood quantum and referred to why it was important:

> But, you see, my great grandfather, or my grandfather, D. L. Perry, mar-
> ried the daughter of Baptiste Peoria, who was our chief, and I, that's how
> I come in connected up. I am quarter. My mother was a half-breed. And
> I'm quarter. That's been regulated to quite a bit, in ways, and it showed
> some places that I was a sixteenth, and my brother was an eighth. (laugh-
> ter) That don't sound good, but it's the truth. But I've got my records
> straighten up. In fact, it shows up now and proves that I am a quarter.
> (McNaughton 1972: 5–6)

Clearly no one could deny Chief McNaughton's Peoria heritage; he was a direct descendant of a prominent Peoria chief and had been a part of the Indian community in Ottawa County, Oklahoma, throughout his life. The quarter-blood rule was the only way his Indian identity could be questioned, and Chief McNaughton took that threat seriously enough to go through the tedious process of amending government records. The quarter-blood rule is no longer in effect, and by the end of the twentieth century the meaning of blood quantum as it related to Indian identity had also changed. It had gone from the general acceptance of a minimum blood quantum for Indian identity to an emphasis on descent as a crite- rion for Indian identity. One day when I was talking to Lee in his office the topic came up. He framed the issue, as he often did, in terms of wis- dom from the elders.

> They were fighting that quarter-blood issue and . . . that man that came
> from Washington, D.C., and that big group and he asked, "Well you guys
> are Indian, you are a quarter-blood or more," he said."What's the issue
> here, what makes you think you have an issue?" This old man stood up
> and said, "Because no matter how much Indian you are, even if like that
> one little drop they say, you bleed or you get a nose bleed, it's gone. You
> are a direct descendant of that full-blood that you [i.e., the U.S. govern-
> ment] made that promise to—a direct descendant."

Lee makes reference here to what some in Oklahoma call a "nose- bleed" Indian, that is, one who will lose all his or her Indian blood if he or she gets a nose bleed. Lee cites his elder as saying the treaty commitments

the United States government made to full-bloods in the past applies even
to today's nose-bleed Indians. This statement stands in stark contrast to
Charles Lohah's remarks to Senator Bellmon. Under current thinking,
things have changed; my brother can be a member of the Choctaw Tribe,
and most, if not all, Indian organizations that sponsor Powwows would
be happy to have him participate. These changes in membership rules
and the etiquette of participation are a natural outcome of a broader shift
in how people think about the relationship of blood quantum to Indian
identity. A good example of how blood quantum related to Indianness
earlier in the twentieth century shows in the 1938 interview that Nannie Lee Burns conducted with Sarah Longbone, a Shawnee woman. Sarah
was about fifty years old at the time, and she talked a little bit about how
the Shawnee dressed when she was growing up. She said:

> The Eastern Shawnees are very particular about their clothes. They never
> wore each other's clothes and were also careful to take baths. They would
> buy yards of cloth. It was not cut and sewn into a dress in those days.
> They wrapped and draped it around themselves. When wash day came,
> they would go to the creek, and seat themselves in the water, and take
> off and wash the suit they had on. Wash it clean on their hands, and if
> they had only the one suit, would wear it until it was dry. They usu-
> ally had an extra suit and both suits would be washed. Grandmother
> used to say to me "you won't do that way, you'll learn to do the white
> man's way."
> Grandmother often used to tell me "Some day, the Indian language will
> fade away, be no more Indians. We have full bloods and half bloods now,
> some day they be one eighth, one-thirty second, one sixty-fourth, black
> eyes and black hair be gone, all be white." (Longbone 1938: 196–97)

In telling this story about clothing, Sarah Longbone identifies the important features of the Indian race: black eyes, black hair, and language define
the race, and blood quantum measures it. Thirty years later in 1968, Reverend James Martin, an Osage, echoed many of the same themes when
he was interviewed by Katherine Red Corn.

> It's funny to think that one day, that our particular tribe, the way that
> we're branching out into the different races . . . that even now it's hard
> to find a full-blood Indian, Osage. But it seems, though, that we're going
> out fast. Our old people are dying off, our young people are marrying into
> different races, establishing themselves. Just in the real near future, it
> will be hard for us to find a real genuine Osage. (Martin 1972: 4–5)

James Martin was an ordained Baptist minister who had led many
Indian congregations during his career. He participated in many tribal

organizations, and among these, his participation on the tribal War Dance committee deserves note. The conventional wisdom of the area has it that Christian Indians and Powwow Indians stay apart, but Reverend Martin breaks that mold. Even at that, however, he believes the "real genuine Osage" are "full-bloods." Today there is a growing emphasis not only on the quantity of blood but also on its quality, and many people talk in terms of "pure" (ancestors in only one tribe) and "mixed" (ancestors in many tribes) blood, with secondary reference to blood quantum. Leslie explained it to me like this:

> As for myself, I consider myself a mixed blood. My son is mixed blood, even though he is half Irish. My mother would really be mixed blood . . . and I always say there aren't any pure bloods. After this long a time, I don't care whether some tribes are really, "I'm better than you are because our people have a high quantity (of blood)." I say, "Okay, even in an area like Navaho, there could be, but it's an awful long way from Athabaska to here, and there's a lot of stops along the way before they met the Spaniards or before they met the Pueblos, and before they met the Apaches, before they met the Utes." Any time you get people together, you're going to come out with . . . as my uncle says, "a volunteer here or there," whether it is official or not.

Leslie's inclusive stance—everybody is a mixed blood—notwithstanding, concepts of blood quantity and blood quality remain important issues in Indian communities. One Saturday afternoon when I was talking to Lee during a break in the arena activities at a Powwow, he described some of the ways that blood enters into the public decisions that Indian people make:

> Politically, it's always going to be that pure-bloods or full-bloods or I'm more Indian than you. If you got control of something, let's say you are running a simple program, "Why you, you're only half Indian or you're only a sixteenth. You are telling the Indians what to do." It shouldn't be like that. The Indian people would do that to ourselves, I point fingers at us. We shouldn't do that, but we are doing that. We are making us way out on that little island with no way to get off. We should be back on the mainland, come back on the real deal, if that person, I don't care if it's Mickey Mouse, could run that program better than any pure-blood, full-blood Indian, that's who I want!

The comments that Leslie and Lee make are alike in that they both acknowledge that the significance of blood quantum and purity of tribal ancestry in discourse about Indian identity, but they challenge its effectiveness in maintaining Indian communities. Carol expressed this theme explicitly in her discussion of the Oklahoma Indian Chamber of Commerce:

> Somebody stands up in an Indian Chamber meeting and you are supposed to tell your tribe, well, when I even tell my tribe, what does that mean? I can identify with two tribes. . . . People do not only tell their tribes but they will say, "I'm full-blood," it's a mark somehow that makes them superior to other people, so what I would call an accident of birth makes you superior. That anyone can claim that what happened to them is a result of colonization and what happened to the dilution of their genes accordingly is somehow something that they can claim makes them superior is kind of curious. But it's also the reverse of what happened once upon a time where people were trying to pass desperately to survive. So if you can claim you are full-blood, it makes every bit of sense that you somehow did survive as a full-blood. So there is that to some extent, in spite of the problems of you couldn't pass and you survived, so there is that element to it.

Over the twentieth century, the meaning of blood was transformed from the immutable naturalness of race to the negotiated significance of ethnic identity. For Sarah Longbone and James Martin, the real Indians were the black-haired, black-eyed full-bloods who spoke their tribal languages. Today that exclusive claim is being questioned and contested by fair-skinned people with some non-Indian ancestors. The same period also saw significant shifts in how people in Euro-American society think about the issues of race and ethnic identity. Earlier in the twentieth century, people often thought about race in terms of a line stretching between the poles of savage and civilized, with the white race and ways at the civilized pole and other societies somewhere behind them on the continuum. In this model, the inferior people and cultures were sometimes considered dangerously violent and incurably ignorant. It is also true that this way of thinking is less prevalent in Euro-American thinking than before, and is being replaced by ideas that view race and ethnicity more in social and cultural terms and less in natural and biological terms. The extent to which Indian people earlier in the century adopted the earlier model, and the ways Indian people today take a more interactive view of the meaning of blood quantum, may be examples of how the meanings of social identities, whether ethnic or cultural, are negotiated by all parties in the system, in this case both Indian and white people. No matter why, however, much of the Indian Pioneer and Doris Duke material seems to reflect the earlier attitude, and many Indian people today challenge the idea that quantity of Indian ancestry is the most significant definer of Indian identity.

## Culture

The hierarchy of one society being superior to other inferior societies, inherent in earlier racial thinking, necessarily arranges the defining racial traits in a similar hierarchy. This was evident in some of the material on education discussed earlier. The cultural hierarchy is evident when Agnes Burnett criticizes Barkley Delano for going back to the Indian ways even after his Haskell education (Burnett 1972: 9), and both Lottie Choate (1938: 25) and Eastman Ward (1938: 129) put language and the ability to benefit from school as critical on the savage-to-civilized scale. This association between speaking the tribal language and blood quantum is common in the earlier interviews, especially the Indian Pioneer Papers. For example, in his 1937 Indian Pioneer interview, Sol C. Ketchum, in his midseventies at the time, describes his three-quarter-blood father's difficulty with English to the Works Progress Administration fieldworker J. R. Carselowey: "My father, a three-quarter blood Delaware Indian, could talk very little English in his younger days, and talked brokenly up to the time of his death" (Ketchum 1938: 450). Sol C. Ketchum does not describe his father's first-language fluency here, and so expresses the hierarchy that places English above Delaware (or Cherokee) or whatever language was his father's mother tongue.

Elliston Labor associates language with ancestry almost paradigmatically when he describes his father's language fluency in an Indian Pioneer interview: "My father was a part Choctaw Indian, and also had some white blood in him but most of his blood was Spanish. He could speak English, Choctaw and Spanish. He was just like one of those full-blood Indians in his ways and actions. He was considered a leader among the Choctaws where he lived, they came to him for advice on anything they wanted to know" (Labor 1938: 19).

These two form an interesting pair of interviews, because both are talking about the interviewee's father's language, and they both put language and blood together. Within this context, however, they are distinct, in that Sol C. Ketchum describes the situation from the point of view of white society, whereas Elliston Labor takes a more Indian perspective. He invites you to believe that his father was prominent in his Indian community because of his language skills and in spite of his blood quantum.

In another Indian Pioneer interview, the fieldworker, Billie Byrd, talked to Jessie McDermott, a Creek of Tulwa Town. Jessie McDermott talked about some of the place names in Oklahoma and told this about how Stroud, Oklahoma came to be called "Trout Town" in Creek:

The non-English speaking full-bloods and some of those that could speak English never could fully pronounce some English words but they took what little pronunciation they understood within a word and broke it into what meaning they could into an Indian word.

In the proper word Stroud, the name of a town in Lincoln County and in the Sac and Fox country, the Muskogee-Creeks couldn't say the full word Stroud but they did recognize the latter part of the town name as nearly meaning to them as being "Trout" so that the name of the town was called and is still often so named by the older Indians as "Cha-lo Ta-lo-fa" which means "Trout Town." (McDermott 1938: 54)

He goes on to give his understanding about the origins of several more place names around Oklahoma, including Keokuk Falls in Potawatomi County, Wewoka in Hughes County, Okmulgee, and Tulsa (McDermott 1938: 54–56). At the end of this interview (and of many others) is a little disclaimer by an unidentified editor. The disclaimer reads: "NOTE: No change is made in manuscripts of Billie Byrd for they are typically Indian and their value lies not only in the text but also in the diction. ED" (McDermott 1938: 56).

Nobody I know would disagree with this editor that it is as important to know how people say things as it is to know what they say. It seems to me, however, that the presence of this disclaimer points to the hierarchy that puts English over others. The interview is reported in English, but the editor feels compelled to explain why that English does not meet some unstated standard.

Indian people were aware of the language/culture hierarchy, and in some cases even played with it. A good example of this is the story Elizabeth Ballard Sanders told of her girlhood experiences. She was a Cherokee born in 1868, so she was about seventy years old when Ella Robinson interviewed her in 1938. The incident she relates involves language, culture, and religion: "We often had full blood Indian preachers who came to the school house and preached. One day I had a girl friend who was white visiting me and asked her to go with me to hear the Indian preacher. She went but got dreadfully frightened as she did not understand anything the preacher said, fearing that he might be planning to massacre the whites" (Sanders 1938: 109).

Elizabeth Ballard Sanders teases her friend a little bit by exposing her to a familiar situation (church) in an unfamiliar context (Cherokee language), and plays on the white girl's fears of savage Indians. This story associates full-bloods with the Cherokee language and massacres, but it is not alone in expressing the theme that full-bloods are dangerous. For example, Sallie (Johnson) Butler, in her midseventies when

James R. Carselowey interviewed her in 1937, related how her cousin, Frank Brown, was killed: "To make matters worse, a fullblood boy by the name of Sampson Sixkiller came to our place one day and begged some apples. While eating them on the porch in company with my Aunt Peggy's son, Frank Brown, the Indian stuck a knife in Frank Brown's back and killed him. Frank lived long enough to tell us that the Indian had said, 'You damn mean boy,' and then stabbed him" (Butler 1938: 165).

The full-blood boy Sampson Sixkiller takes the family's charity and eats their food but then kills a member of the family in cold blood. It is hard to get more savage than that. These passages often express the theme of full-blood savagery by putting the helpless—the elderly, women, or children—in the path of cruel, violent, and unpredictable outbursts. In November 1937, Lula Austin interviewed Meta B. Hatchett, a Choctaw, in Durant. Mrs. Hatchett related how her family had lived near the border with Texas, so alcohol was easy to obtain: "My grandmother would often be obliged to open her door at night to a drunken Full Blood and she would be very much frightened" (Hatchett 1938: 154).

About two weeks before this interview, Lula Austin talked to Joe Underwood, a full-blood Chickasaw, who first expressed the general theme of full-blood savagery, and then gave a specific instance from his own life.

> All I know is Indian used to kill Indian when he get mad at him—that is why we are all about killed out. I don't know why I didn't get killed.
>     One day my wife's sister, Beekie Riley, and her little boy were riding horseback to church at Rock Creek when Tom Billy and Malbert Nelson, both fullbloods, called for Beekie to dismount; they wanted her horse. She wouldn't get off and they began to shoot around her until she jumped off. She ran to George Yarborough's house and told him and he took the horse away from these two fullbloods. (Underwood 1938: 15)

Surely these threats traumatized Beekie Riley (they certainly would have traumatized me), but for the purposes of understanding Indian ethnic identity, the significance of this and other reports in the Indian Pioneer and Doris Duke interviews is more that they are framed in terms of blood. Joe Underwood did not portray Tom Billy and Malbert Nelson as local toughs, or outlaws, or anything else; rather they were characterized as full-bloods. This theme does not merely describe the people involved in the incident; it also creates and maintains the group they are considered part of. This particular grouping—full-blood means more Indian, mixed-blood means more white—permeated all areas of life, especially politics. Throughout the earlier interviews, people commonly understood political issues in terms of blood quantum, so commonly that the Lewis Beamer interview cited at the beginning of this chapter mentions that Mr. Beamer, "unlike many of the full bloods . . . took rather small interest in politics" (Beamer 1938: 132).

Lewis Beamer embodies some of the contradictions within this savage/civilized model that conflates the natural with the cultural. According to the interview, he is not a full-blood ("probably of three-quarters Indian blood, to one-quarter of white blood"), but he is a full-blood ("usually considered a full Indian") (Beamer 1938: 131); and as a full-blood, he should be interested in politics, but he is not. These contradictions about Lewis Beamer imply that meanings of particular blood quanta are negotiable, but only according to the dimensions established in the community. In this case, positions on political issues, and the makeup of political parties, are understood in full-blood/mixed-blood terms. This is sometimes even expressed in the names of political parties.

One small example of this in Cherokee politics relates to divisions between supporters of John Ross and Major Ridge, which are often cited in discussion of the complexity of blood politics. Ross, who was one-eighth Cherokee, had his backing in the mixed-blood faction but joined with the full-bloods in opposition to the Treaty of New Echota and removal. Ridge, seven-eighths Cherokee, was a leader of the full-blood faction but signed the treaty. After the removal, the Ross Party and Ridge Party remained the major forces in Cherokee Nation politics and were understood along the mixed-blood/full-blood axis. Thus Ridge symbolized the full-blood faction, even though he was considered a traitor to Cherokee interests. This contradiction was resolved later, as Charles Scott explained in a 1937 Indian Pioneer interview. "The Downing Party was started by Louis Downing, who was elected Principal Chief. Since he received so many votes of the fullbloods, and the fullbloods hated the name Ridge; which was the name of the party to which he, belonged, he changed the name to Downing" (Scott 1938: 27).

Conceptualizing this political division as between full-bloods and mixed-bloods is not only deep in time, stretching back to pre-removal times; its rhetoric is emotionally deep, often playing on provocative themes. One good example that exposes both of these is the story that Clarence Starr gave to the Indian Pioneer project of some of the violence the removal process precipitated. One of the interesting things about this interview is that these are not Clarence Starr's words but those of J. C. Starr, Clarence's father. J. C. Starr was a newspaper reporter, educated at the Cherokee Male Seminary, and in that capacity had written an account of what he called the "Tom Starr War," which took place in Cherokee Nation in the years following removal. J. C. Starr sets up the Tom Starr War by first recounting the well-known story of the reprisals taken against the signers of the Treaty of New Echota.

> As soon as the Anti-Treaty people landed in the Cherokee Nation they stirred up dissension and strife, out of which grew the Tom Starr War. The Anti-Treaty people were very much dissatisfied with the new country and with the Ridge Party for making the treaty, and very soon began to emphasize their displeasure by an organized attempt to kill all the leaders who had been instrumental in making it.
>
> The Full Bloods armed themselves and went in bands all over the country to murder any leader of the Ridge Party whom they could find. They deposed Chief John Jolly and elected John Ross Chief of the Cherokees, and then followed the declaration of war between these two powerful parties. The Anti-Treaty people went so far as to declare that they would kill every man who had signed the treaty with the United States Government, and started blood to flowing by killing the leaders of the opposite party.
>
> Early one morning a party of Full-Bloods rode up to the home of Elias C. Boudinot and Major Ridge and shot them down in cold blood. They afterward tied John West to a tree, stripped him of his clothing and gave him one hundred lashes on his bare back. The man who executed this command of the Anti-Treaty people tied West to a tree. He then cut ten young hickory sprouts, one year old, and would give him ten licks with one switch, throw it down and give him some water and then take another switch and give him ten more licks and so on until a hundred stripes were applied. (Starr 1938: 72–73)

J. C. Starr's story goes on from here to describe a failed attempt by the pro-treaty faction to establish a second Cherokee Nation for the treaty signers in Colorado. This attempt ended when J. C. Starr's grandfather, Ezekiel, died in 1846 while negotiating with the U.S. government in Washington, D.C. J. C. Starr reported that during the period when Ezekiel was on his mission, the war started with a raid on the home of James Starr (Ezekiel's brother and Tom Starr's father):

> Full-Bloods rode up to his house and shot him down on his porch. His son, Buck Starr, ran away, was pursued and shot several times and died a month later.
>
> From the Starr home the Full-Bloods went to the home of Polly Rider and killed Sewell Rider in his own yard. When Rider fell to the ground, mortally wounded, a Full-Blood named Stan jumped over into the yard and plunged a big knife into the wounded man's heart. A few minutes later the Full-Bloods met Wash Starr in the road and opened fire on him.

He fled to the brush desperately wounded but made good his escape and afterwards recovered. Wash Starr was a brother of Tom Starr. (Starr 1938: 76–77)

Tom, fearing for his life, did not go to the funerals, but a few days later visited the gravesides and "made a solemn vow that he would avenge his death, and that he would kill every Full-Blood who had had anything to do with the death of his father, James Starr. He at once organized a band of followers, composed of his brothers and cousins and a white man named Mack Gerring, and started out on his career of vengeance" (Starr 1938: 77). The story goes on from here to recount lots of bloodshed and several narrow escapes, until finally: "Tom Starr's war with the Anti-Treaty Cherokees over the murder of his father lasted about five years. The Full-Bloods finally concluded that they could not capture him and his band and realizing that they would finally all be killed, if the struggle went on made the overtures of peace which were accepted" (Starr 1938: 85–86)

But that is not the end of the story. J. C. Starr reported that the treachery and bloodshed continued even after the peace agreement, but new players became involved. Up to this point in the interview, the principals in the war were Tom Starr and his band versus the anti-treaty full-bloods, but in the final episode, "half-bloods" come in and perpetrate the continued violence.

> Early one morning soon after the treaty of peace was concluded a number of Half-Blood Cherokees went to the home of Mat Gerring who had been with Tom Starr through his war and killed him. The next day they went to the place where Ellis Starr was staying and called him out in the yard and killed him. From this place they went to Sallisaw, took Washington Starr out of his sick bed and returned to the very spot where they had killed Ellis Starr, and there killed Washington Starr.
>
> They went to the Choctaw Nation to capture Creek Starr and Ike Gerring. When they captured these men Ike Gerring was killed and Creek Starr made a prisoner.
>
> They started back to Goingsnake District with Creek Starr to kill him, and while enroute stopped to feed their horses. Watching his opportunity, Creek Starr mounted a fine horse, made a dash for liberty and escaped unharmed amid a shower of bullets. He was afterwards killed in a duel with a Creek Indian. . . .
>
> Repeated attempts to kill Tom Starr failed and also failed to provoke him to hostilities, if he could avoid them. On the other hand the Half-Bloods tired of the struggle and finally gave it up. In order to avoid further trouble with these people, who so flagrantly violated these terms of the treaty of peace, Starr moved to Canadian District where he spent

the remainder of his days in peace and became very wealthy. (Starr 1938: 87–88)

Tom Starr is clearly the hero of the story. His friends and family are unjustly and brutally killed, and his actions are either in self-defense or to extract justice where the civil authorities will not. His enemies, on the other hand, are portrayed as treacherous cowards. They sue for peace because they fear for their lives, not for any more noble reason, and they quickly break their word with more killings. Tom Starr's enemies are always described in terms of their blood quantum, either full-blood or half-blood; his blood quantum is never specified. He and his family are associated with the pro-treaty party, so we are invited to conclude that they were Cherokee, but even that is never stated. The opposition that this narrative sets up therefore pits Indians, full-bloods and half-bloods, against treaty supporters. The Indians, furthermore, are clearly depicted on the savage side of the line, whereas Tom Starr and his supporters are champions of justice and (white) civilization.

This process of understanding political debate in terms of blood quantum extended even to Euro-American politics. Mrs. Ella Coody Robinson was the daughter of a wealthy (slave-owning) and influential Cherokee family. She was born in 1847, which put her in her late teens during the American Civil War. In 1938 she gave a long interview to Miss Ella Robinson for the Indian Pioneer project. (The interview does not specify how or if Miss Ella Robinson is related to Mrs. Ella Coody Robinson.) In the interview, Mrs. Robinson describes the hardships she and her family suffered as a result of the Civil War, and in one passage she states: "Another source of annoyance with which we had to contend was the 'Pin Indians,' a band of full-bloods who were not slave owners, nor did they belong to either Army, although they were Union sympathizers" (Robinson 1938: 111).

The Cherokee Nation sided with the South in the Civil War (Wright 1986: 70), and, given her family's prominence and wealth, I presume that Ella Coody Robinson also supported the Confederate states. The interesting thing here is the easy application of blood politics to this Euro-American issue. Furthermore, in almost all cases in these interviews, political positions are constructed in terms of full-blood, Indian, and conservative versus mixed-blood, white, and progressive groups. A particularly brutal example of this race politics can be seen in the description of what an Indian Pioneer interviewee calls the Wilson War, which, according to the interviewee, was fought over the issue of fencing range land. This interview was conducted by Hazel B. Greene, who talked to

Wilson Locke in May 1938. The fieldworker starts the process by showing Mr. Locke a newspaper article:

> In the Sunday Oklahoman, under date of March 28, 1937 appeared an
> article, and pictures of the old water mill near Valliant. I was showing
> it to Wilson Locke, 60 year old quarter breed Indian. He told the follow-
> ing story:
> My grandfather, John Wilson, built that mill, from the ground up.
> Cleared the land, cut the first tree, built the dam and everything. The
> mill, his home and store were all there.
> He was a half breed Choctaw Indian, as was also my grandmother.
> Where they met and married I do not know, neither do I know when he
> was born or when he came to the Indian Territory. (Locke 1938: 62)

After this introduction, Mr. Locke goes on to describe his family tree in
some detail. This genealogical thread ends when Mr. Locke describes
his grandfather, John Wilson, and lays out the issues and events that led
to the war.

> Grandfather was County Judge of Towson County, and was altogether a
> prominent and useful man among his people as well as the white peo-
> ple, but the full blood Indians hated to see the white and mixed breeds
> prosper. Hated to see civilization come to this country. So a sort of feud
> was started. The full bloods would catch his stock out on the prairie or
> in the woods and kill them. Not for food, but just to torment the mixed
> breeds and white men. Things just kept getting worse and worse, until my
> father saw that he could not live there, so he just abandoned our home,
> where I was born, where Oak Hill Negro Academy is now located, one
> half mile west of Valliant, and father and mother moved to Goodland,
> New Goodland, we called it. (Locke 1938: 63–64)

This clearly puts mixed-bloods in league with whites and stands
them in opposition to full-bloods, but it also characterized the two sides
in moral terms. The full-bloods are against prosperity and civilization,
and, by extension, the mixed-bloods and whites stand for these social
goods. The full-bloods, furthermore, play dirty. They wantonly kill live-
stock to terrorize the whites and mixed-bloods. This tactic works to some
extent and drives Mr. Locke's family from their home. At the new home,
Grandfather builds a mill and conducts business, but political disputes
continue:

> Among our friends, white and mixed breeds, I mean those who helped
> Grandfather against the full blood Indians were, of course, his sons, Julius
> Victor, who had married his son's widow, V. M. Locke, Sr., my father,
> B. Frank Locke (M.B.), Jimmy and Jerry Gardener (Jefferson Gardener,
> who was once Chief of the Choctaws, did not help). Also, Dick Kelly.

We had other friends whose names I don't recall now. There was an old negro, they called him 'Grundy'; I don't know if that was his first or last name; but anyway he posed as Grandfather's friend, and he found out all he could and then told it to the full bloods.

Grandfather and his friends found out that this old negro was betraying them. They caught him out someplace, he was horse hunting, and had a boy with him and they killed him and threw his body on a pile of brush and burned it. People for a long time referred to that killing as "The barbecued nigger." Some of the men wanted to kill the boy. Grandfather was opposed to killing a boy, said he didn't mind killing a man who deserved it, but not a boy. While they were discussing it, someone shot the boy. There was a crowd of them together, and Grandfather never knew for certain who did it.

Another traitor to our cause was a full blood named Grayson Jacobs, full-blood sheriff of Towson County. He was shot by a firing squad of whites and mixed breeds. Grandfather said he never saw a braver man. In the face of death, he never flinched, stood as steady as a wall. You see, the full-bloods were trying to run the Wilsons and friends out of the country. One morning, pretty early, they surrounded the mill and store and began shooting. The shots were returned by the Wilsons. When the firing ceased, three Indians were dead on the ground, and John Wilson was wounded. (He carried that bullet in his knee till he died about 1910 or 1912, somewhere along about that time). The full-bloods were routed, but left with the promise that they would soon return with reinforcements. The wounded lad and Grandmother were put in a buggy; other members of the family, with provisions, bedding etc, were loaded into wagons. Others rode horseback and they "lit a shuck" for Hook's ferry. (Lit a shuck, Mr Locke explained, meant they hurried). Hook's ferry was on Red river about five miles away. Grandfather had a big yellow horse called old Isaac. He rode him and would not hurry, tho' the balance of the family did and urged him to do so. Old Isaac would never go out of a fast walk with Grandfather upon him. So he "walked" him to the river, with Uncle Edward begging, "Hurry Daddy, they will catch us." Grandfather said, "No, I'll never run from my home. I toiled too hard to make it, to run from it." The family were waiting at the ferry for him and they had just gotten ferried across when a band of Indians ran up on the side they had just left, firing at them as they got out of range.

Remember now, that the store and mill was left wide open, for anybody to ransack who wanted to do so. Dick Kelly wanted to slip back over there and put strychnine in the flour and other eatables, but Grandfather would not permit that. That was just too bad because that would kill innocent men, women and children. Those goods were precious, had cost lots of money, but there was nothing to do but just leave them. Taking a few for consumption. The Indians didn't want to steal anything, they just wanted to destroy the property of the white and near white men. Oh! They might have taken a few groceries for immediate consumption, but not much. When they killed the cattle and hogs, they did it for spite and left them lying wherever killed. They were opposed to this country being fenced up. They wanted it to remain in a virgin state and these white men and half breeds had brought barbed wire over here and fenced good grass that God had made to be free for all and the Indians cut every barbed wire fence they found all the time. And in their council they passed a law prohibiting fencing with barbed wire. So these Indians were defending what they believed to be their God-given rights. Later, this law was amended, allowing each individual to fence a certain number of acres, and so many acres for each child. That law was never repealed.

Grandfather had hauled those precious goods from Paris Texas, by wagon pulled by oxen. They had cost him lots of snake root, hides, furs, etc. Nobody much had any money. Some of the goods were brought up the river by boat and hauled from Hooks' ferry to the store.

It was in the Spring of the year when my people were driven over into Texas. They stayed about three months, when through the wise counsel of Principal Chief Jack McCurtain, who called his tribe together and advised them that development was best for the country and that it was wrong to do things by force and bloodshed. They were allowed to return and rebuild all that had been torn down and partially destroyed. He gathered up the remnants of his stock and by careful management got a good start again and died quite wealthy. (Locke 1938: 66–70)

Peace is made and John Wilson, like Tom Starr, dies wealthy, but that is not the only similarity between the two stories. John Wilson, also like Tom Starr, is clearly the hero of the story and represents goodness and truth. He opposes, but cannot prevent, killing the boy; he will not poison the food he leaves behind in his store because it may kill innocent looters; and he refuses to run away from his home. Not only is he portrayed as a man who acts on principles but also he stands on the side of progress and civilization in this particular dispute. His enemies, on the other hand, are treacherous spies and terrorists who stand in the way of progress and civilization, and have no respect for others. The stories differ, however, in the degree to which they are explicitly racialized. J. C. Starr never specifies Tom Starr's blood quantum, and depicts the violence as between pro-treaty Cherokees and anti-treaty full-bloods. Wilson Locke specifies John Wilson's blood quantum from the very start, and portrays the opposing sides in racial terms. On one side are full-bloods and African-Choctaws, and on the other side "white and near white men."

Jackson F. McCurtain was principal chief of the Choctaw Nation from 1880 to 1884 (Wright 1986: 115), so the events that Wilson Locke described took place before the passage of the Dawes, or General Allotment, Act in 1887 (3). Of course, allotment was a matter of intense political debate throughout Indian Territory, so it is no surprise that people thought of pro- and anti-allotment stands along blood lines. Tom Devine, who was in his forties when the Cherokee Nation was allotted in the early twentieth century, and his family were "in favor of the allotment. There were many acres of land claimed by full bloods who would not use it to their advantage, and many Cherokees that would make a showing did not have any at all" (Devine 1938: 197–98).

Mr. Devine expresses the political division over the issue in terms of blood and makes reference to the savage/civilized continuum in his justification of his position. On the other side of the issue, Columbus Wm. Ervin was in his teens when the Choctaw Nation was allotted, and his family opposed allotment. He said about his father: "My father was William Ervin, known all over the western part of the Choctaw Nation as 'Bill.' He was more Indian than I, practically a full blood. He was one of the old type Choctaws; a man who believed in the old ways and customs and who felt that the Territory should be for the Indians alone" (Ervin 1938: 173).

Mr. Ervin explicitly expresses the idea that the higher the blood quantum, the more Indian a person is, and he invites the conclusion that anti-allotment positions were an attribute of being full-blood. He also introduces the idea that blood quantum and Indianness are contestable and negotiable features of individuals in Indian communities. The blood quantum on a CDIB is a mathematical calculation assigned by the United States government. The blood quantum that Columbus Wm. Ervin refers to, in contrast, is a judgment made in Indian communities and is much more complex than a simple accounting of a person's Indian ancestors.

## Community

The language of blood is commonly cast in numbers. The "degree of Indian blood" in the CDIB, the phrases "full-blood" and "half-breed," and the entire notion of "blood quantum" all express a numeric approach to their meanings. If the discourse on blood had only mathematical significance, however, it would be worthy of only minimal time and effort. So it is not surprising that blood indexes, or refers to, the racial divisions between Indians and non-Indians and the political factions within Indian groups. But blood is a complex idea, and in addition to these numeric and divisive meanings, it also signifies and participates in an extended discourse on community.

Philemon Berry was a Plains Apache man in his sixties when Bill Savage interviewed him for the Doris Duke project. The Plains Apache have lived with and near their neighbors the Comanche and Kiowa since before contact with Europeans (Wright 1986). In the interview he talked about the issue of a separate versus a combined constitution for the Apache, Kiowa, and Comanche tribes. He said:

> And another things [I] want to pass this on why I am also against separate constitution. We have in our tribes all three a lot of mixed blood and we have some that are Kiowa and Apache some that are Kiowa and Comanche and also Apache and Comanche. And some that are all three. That's who you gonna hurt. If you support anybody that is wanting a separate constitution. You gonna hurt those people and they may be your own. (Berry 1972: 7)

Here Mr. Berry acknowledges that Indianness is real and argues that it should be expressed even in the formal, legal reality of tribal constitutions. The significance of blood here is not to divide communities, as it is in race and politics, but to merge peoples into one community. The tribes, to Philemon Berry's way of thinking, should not have separate constitutions because those who would be hurt are necessarily of one's own blood, one's own community. This is a theme of blood as community, of Indian people as the people of blood, and the focus of this theme is the community rather than the quantification of the CDIB. James Carnes made this idea explicit when he talked to fieldworker Johnson H. Hampton for the Indian Pioneer project. James Carnes was a Choctaw man in his midsixties when the interview was conducted. "I am an Indian, not a full blood, about three quarters I guess; but I sure can speak the Choctaw language fluently. I have lived here always, and have attended the Indian meetings and also the cries. We used to have some good meetings at that time for there were lots of Indians in the country then, but now all but a few of them are gone—very few full-blood Indians here now" (Carnes 1938: 65).

James Carnes starts with an assertion of his Indian identity and then qualifies that with the quantification. Once all the blood quantum stuff is done, he tells us why he is an Indian: because he speaks the language, lives in the community, and attends the ceremonies. The last phrase in this passage about "full-blood Indians" is interesting because it seems to negate the significance of his three-quarter blood quantum. He first attaches himself to "Indian" because he does the Indian things and then attaches that notion of Indian to "full-blood." In other words, James Carnes is a full-blood despite the fact that one of his grandparents may have been non-Indian. This interplay between the mathematics of blood quantum and the significance of community for Indian identity continues today. During my stay in Oklahoma, Indian people often brought up the divisiveness of blood quantum. For example, Cory once said to me: "Blood is just a way to keep Indian people apart." One day in early spring Leslie came around to the subject and related it to the tribal automobile licenses that tribal members have the right to display instead of the Oklahoma license tags:

> We have others who were enrolled with one tribe and then years later wanted to get off that roll and onto ours or off of our roll and onto another, one that was getting land payment or something and now want[s] to come back. We have some who are, of course, more than one tribe, which most of the people are now, and it's strange, because in one particular case the gentleman works for one tribe and has a tribal tag of another and blames everything on his father who is another tribe.

A little later she returned to the theme of car tags and identity: "My aunt's children came in from out of state and got tags. I said, 'How can you do that?' Well, I guess they are using her address, that type of thing. It's nice to be out somewhere else and see a tag like 'Oh! There's one of our people' and you go in and look around and—" "You don't recognize anybody," I interjected, and Leslie went on:

> In that way they are kind of playing with the blood and using it again like a credit card or something to get services. It just depends on how you feel. Even though I consider myself a traditional person, I still don't take as much part as I would really like to or should. Again, because we are way up here and have family obligations and things, so we really don't get down thirty miles away to attend a lot of things that I want to or take part in the politics because of everything else that personally goes on, just maintaining my little group.

Leslie juxtaposes official blood quantum with community here. On the quantum side, the official tribe provides services (car tags, land payments, etc.), while participation marks the community side. The car tags are ambiguous, because while they are a tribal service, there is usually little or no economic advantage to having them. The tribes usually charge about as much as the state for the tags, so tribal members purchase them, at least partly, to express their identity. But to Leslie, participation in the community defines her identity, so she is taken aback when she sees a license plate that claims membership but does not recognize the driver of the car. To Leslie, quantum is associated with politics and the official tribe, whereas community and participation are associated with cultural identity. At another point in the interview she said:

> Tribe to tribe they decide what they will take, like in the Cherokee Nation whether it's an open-end thing as long as you can prove you are,

then you are. Other tribes say you have to be at least a fourth, some say a half, but as the generations go on, it becomes less and less. There's a question of, for myself for instance, I am four-fourths, I'm a full-blood, but my father is Seminole, so that brings me down to half, but then that was a very strange thing, when I went back east, one of the elders there said, "Your politics down there get really strange." I said "Yes," and they said, "Well, do they buy votes?" I said, "Yes," and they said, "How do you do that?" I said, "In a way they do it with blood." They said, "What do you mean?" I said, "Well, my sister ended up almost full-blood," and I said, "We are full siblings and I ended up twenty-seven/thirty-two on the roll. I don't know if it is because I am eight years younger than she is or because when the candidate came around to me and asked, 'Would you vote for me?' I said, 'No,' right out, and my sister said, 'Maybe,' so on the roll she ended up more blood quantum than myself."

The old formula that blood quantum is a measure of Indianness is under attack here. Leslie knows she is a full-blood, and she knows that her CDIB does not reflect that. She also knows that she could not be more Indian than she is, because she is committed to her tribe and her Indian identity. Chris is like Leslie in this respect. She also knows that she could not be more Indian than she is because she speaks at least some of her tribal language, is committed to the local Indian community, and attends the ceremonies. And when the topic of blood came up in our conversation, her reaction was much like Leslie's.

I think that the identity as far as a Native American, and I think I was easily intimidated because there are many people in the Native American community, Osage and otherwise, that talk about "Well, I'm a full-blood" that makes this blood quantum nonsense, and I think my age and maturity and coming to realizations about things, I think now I have a different attitude. Now I'm like, I know who I am and I know who I come from and I know who I descend from and I know more, I don't need to prove anything to you. That attitude, and you have people from other tribes who want to . . . I don't know if it's territorial or what it is, but there is this prevailing attitude sometimes especially around the Powwow circuit like, "I know everything because I'm full-blood," and you have to say, "You're not my elder and you're not in my tribe." There's certain times, I'm not saying you should be disrespectful, what I'm saying is there are certain times I have learned it can be appropriate for me to say, "You know what? I don't need to prove anything to you, I know who I am and where I come from, I speak a little bit of my language," both my tribes' language. I take care of my family, this other thing out here, this blood quantum stuff, is a bunch of nonsense anyway, that was a white thing, the Feds came up with that business, and they did that for a reason, they did that to see that we diminished and disappeared. They're still trying that, and unfortunately a lot of tribes have bought into that nonsense, I think times are changing. That's kinda of where I've been or what I've come to as a member of the community.

At this point I interjected the idea that in some cases it is difficult to tell who is and who is not an Indian just by looking at them, and Chris went on:

> You know it is, and I'll tell you, it's something that has developed post-Cavalry, post-removal, because Comanches for instance raided villages a lot, they took prisoners, it was not uncommon for them to take people with them, and they often became Comanches, and they were Comanches as much as the next warrior. This blood quantum thing, a lot of people want to take that to say, "I'm half, my husband is nearly half." They think because they are full-blood or because they are half, that somehow gives them the privilege, and this is a very few people I'm talking about, a very small portion of the Native Americans community, because as a whole I think the Native American people are probably whether—Osages, Comanche, or Cheyenne or whatever—are very welcoming and open. Very inclusive.

Chris recognizes in this passage the divisive constructions of blood, which, she argues, emanate from contact with Euro-American culture. She uses her knowledge of tribal culture in the pre-reservation past to support a more inclusive meaning of blood on grounds of Indian tradition. Pat said almost exactly the same thing.

> I find it odd that of all these people in the world that we have to have some kind of pedigree card. I found that just kind of strange that a lot of the tribes . . . let me put it this way: a lot of tribes in the past, in past history had taken in other peoples, other tribes, Native Americans, whether it was by an act of war against another tribe and they took some of them in and used them, or if they adopted somebody from another tribe and took them in. Even with some of the Plains tribes, I'm not so sure there is such a thing as a full-blood. I'm not so sure there is such a thing as a full-blood one hundred years ago. Even today, some of the full-bloods who adamantly say we are this and everything, it may be so, somewhat, but the way it comes about is usually when they have these people and they are there so long they just take them into the tribe. They become a part of that tribe and a part of the people. My tribe, a lot of times they ended up with women or children from another tribe because of some battle or some other reason, they would train them. They would usually set them with an older woman and they would train them, teach them the language and stuff like that, but when they reached a certain age they would give them a choice, "Do you want to go home?" If they did, they took them home; if they didn't and they wanted, they became part of the tribe.

Pat, like Chris, refers to Euro-American society and to the divisions inherent to blood quantum, but Pat uses the CDIB (pedigree card) rather than the Cavalry. After that, the two positions are essentially the same. Both take the stand that Indian tradition decided questions of membership in the group on social rather than biological criteria. Pat expresses his criteria as knowledge, saying:

> I've seen people who have come into a group of Indians, maybe full-blood—maybe, and you say, "I'm full-blood," and they come in and know absolutely nothing about their ways, their people's ways. But will come in and be so adamant about, "Oh, we've got to keep this whole, we have to keep this certain amount of blood." We have patience with them because they are going to be learning here.

As does Chris:

> I think that's why probably a lot of people have picked back up some things that maybe their own families left behind a few generations ago, picking it back up and trying to pass it on to their children. I think there is a new generation of us who are mixed-bloods, and I respect our elders; I respect those who know far more than I will ever know, but it's up to us now.

Whereas Leslie thinks of Indianness more in terms of participation:

> I have a full-blood sister who just sits and doesn't do anything. That irritates me of course, we go to Green Corn and sometimes she goes, she just sits at the camp, she hardly ever goes to the longhouse. I say, "Why do you bother to come? What are you?" She doesn't like the idea, but, "Are you a Christian like your father?" That's your attitude, you got here somehow, and you sure look like him. On the other hand, why do you come here if you don't take part? Maybe it's here to just absorb, but you're fifty feet from what's going on, why don't you get from here and go out there and at least sit on the bench?

While they may approach it in different ways, all three speak to the same point: that Indians are people of blood, but not of blood quantum. They recognize blood quantum as a white imposition on Indian communities, and they agree that blood quantum can only serve to divide those communities. They also diminish blood quantum as an important measure of Indian identity in favor of considerably more emphasis on living as an Indian. It is important that Indian people respect the tribal languages, and even those who do not speak the language should learn as much about it as they can. It is important for Indian people to be active in their communities, and to participate in the community's rituals.

These factors, these measures of commitment to Indian people and to being an Indian, along with others, have emerged as the moral focus of Indian ethnicity.

There has probably never been a time in Indian Territory/Oklahoma when blood has not been a central theme in talk among and about Indian people. It has always been a complex idea and has always played a part in symbolic exchanges that carried an internal tension between division and unity. From the late nineteenth century until today, it has indexed political factions within tribes, even though many full-bloods supported mixed-blood parties and causes and many mixed-bloods supported full-blood factions. Because those meanings are still alive in Oklahoma today, it is not uncommon to hear people talk about political factions in those same mixed-blood/full-blood terms. Earlier in the twentieth century, blood was a central symbol in a highly racialized environment that placed Indian people at the lower end of a continuum from savage to civilized. As a result of this way of thinking, Indian people were considered backward and indolent, and they were thought to stand in the way of progress. Today those racialized meanings are less prominent. Indian people are thinking of Indianness not in terms of blood quantum but in terms of participation in Indian communities. While these communitarian meanings of blood have always been part of blood's symbolic inventory, today they seem to be gaining in strength as the concept of race has shifted away from the biological toward the social in American society in general. These communities of blood, however, require more than ancestry to maintain themselves. Communities are communities because the people in them interact with one another on a regular basis. Religion is one of the most important institutions that facilitate these interactions across the world, and that is also true in the particular case of Indian people in Oklahoma. There are two sources of religion for Indian people in Oklahoma: Christianity brought by Euro-Americans, and indigenous religious traditions that have evolved from tribal belief systems.

# 6  The Jesus Way

I was raised Christian like most white Americans or essentially white Americans. That's what I embraced even at the age of five and on up. For my own decision, I kept that, and I had a relationship with God, the Creator, but before that time.

I want to learn, but it's to learn to give words for what you feel, hopefully, rather than taking of descriptive of things and trying to make up for that with something inside. As humans we constantly search.

After I became dissatisfied with a lot of the things in the Christian realm, I decided to go, and because I still had a relationship with God, I still pray, I still felt this connection, I had questions that couldn't really be answered with the information that was available to me as far as the Christian belief system, et cetera. If I found an answer over here it conflicted with this group over here, and I was like, okay. I said forget all of this for awhile and maintain the connection that I have and just set it aside, not run from it, just set it aside.

There were certain scriptures that always stood out to me—paraphrasing—the signature, the fingerprint, of the Creator is in his creation, and it seemed logical, and it felt [like] something I knew, this God, this Creator, this force, et cetera, if there is benevolence there, and if there is a power, an authority, this connection to his creation (or her), if it is really there, [if] this truth like this exist[s], I should be able to—if I'm confused and can't find my way, if I am honestly seeking, it should become apparent to me.

So I felt I had enough faith in that original connection that I could kind of abandon some of these things and keep walking and searching like that and try to listen to the voice inside of me. I hate this kind of talk, it's so cliché, I do, I really do.

—Julian

The old Fountain Church. Drawing. Indian Pioneer Papers, Western History Collections, University of Oklahoma, Norman, Oklahoma, 72:119.

    I met Julian in church. It is an Indian Baptist church in a poor urban neighborhood, and on the Sunday I first met him, there was a guest preacher who identified himself as a Cheyenne. His homily to the mostly Indian congregation concerned how the scriptures applied to Indian people even though Jesus preached in the Holy Land. The hymns were sung in Cheyenne, Cherokee, Kiowa, and Creek, and testimonials during the service asked God to bless the Indian way and ease the suffering of the Indian people. Julian and I talked after the service, and he agreed to talk to me for my work.

    I was at the church because an old teacher of mine at the University of Tulsa had told me something to the effect that there are two major institutions, church and Powwow, around which Indian communities form in the state. That was, but should not have been, a surprise to me. I certainly knew about Powwows. I had attended them as a spectator since my teens, and more recently I had been attending large and small Powwows around the state in my attempts to understand Indian ethnic identity. I also knew, as an anthropologist, that religion was an important unifying institution in communities around the world. Since I was raised in Oklahoma around Indian people, I should have been aware of Indian Christianity, but I was not. As I talked to others who were familiar with Indian people in Oklahoma, a model emerged in my mind that these two institutions represented exclusive communities. I began to look at them as communities in opposition; the Powwow Indian people somehow viewed the Christians as sellouts, and the Christians looked upon the Powwow people as heathens and sinners.

The Indian Pioneer and Doris Duke interviews, along with what I learned from others like Julian, describe a more complex reality. People in these interviews talk about a wide variety of religious experiences that sometimes express this ideology of separation but often do not. People commonly belittle the ideology as un-Christian, and often attend both church services and Powwows. Furthermore, these experiences are articulated in multiple ways to a wide variety of religions traditions. Baptists, Presbyterians, Catholics, and the other Christian denominations are in the mix, as are people from the many tribal traditions. To many, Christianity structures the core of their lives every day, while others have encountered Christianity only at school and have avoided it in other contexts. Some have been converts to Christianity from indigenous religions and have attended services conducted by Euro-American missionaries, and others have attended community churches where the Indian ministers and members of the congregation were lifelong Christians. These are examples of Indian Christianity, but many, like Julian, draw a distinction between them and white Christianity with ministries that are not concerned with Indian people as Indians.

In the next two chapters I want to explore this religious complexity, especially as it relates to Indian ethnic identity in Oklahoma. Chapter 7 will focus on indigenous religions and how they relate to Indian ethnic identity, but here the emphasis is on Christianity, and on the Indian Christian traditions that span the twentieth century. The picture that emerges from what people said in their interviews about their experiences with Christianity is one of strong Indian Christian communities supported by both ritual and organization. These statements also acknowledge the diversity of religions within the whole of the Indian communities, and recognize that Indian churches and congregations are distinct from their white-world counterparts. These distinctions form an important part of the symbolic boundaries between white and Indian ethnicity.

## Church Community

Powwow and church are different in some important ways. Powwows are clearly Indian events, for example, where church events are not. When people make an effort and go to a Powwow, they expect to find Indian people doing Indian things. People who participate in the Powwow are expected to present themselves as Indian people, through their dress and through their activities, such as dancing or joining the drum. Churches, on the other hand, are not necessarily Indian, in fact most are not Indian at all. If a non-Indian Baptist went to services at the church where I met Julian, she or he might be surprised at the congregation made up of mostly Indian people, the hymns in North American Indian languages, and a sermon that focused on Indian issues, but she or he would be very comfortable with the service itself. Because Indian churches are not as visible, the communities of Indian people that coalesce around churches are more hidden, harder to see, than those that form around Powwow. There were times and places in Indian Territory, however, where Indian Christianity was as public and Indian as Powwow is today.

## CHURCHES

Church and Powwow are similar, in that both are associated with specific spaces where communities come together periodically. Where the Powwow spaces are usually open-air grounds, often surrounded by sites where families camp during the weekend event, churches are usually buildings. Sometimes these buildings have been grand structures like the medieval cathedrals of Europe, but for Indian people in Indian Territory they have usually been more humble. Nancy Miashintubbee described the churches she attended in Choctaw Nation to the Indian Pioneer project fieldworker Johnson H. Hampton.

> We attended Indian churches. The church house was built out of pine logs hewed on two sides, and floored it with split logs; and the benches were made out of split logs. They had camp houses built of logs and boards made out of red or white oak trees. They would feed and take care of the people who came to attend the meeting, which would last about four or five days. They had these camp meetings about every three months. (Miashintubbee 1938: 14)

These church buildings were, of course, expressions in wood and stone of their congregations' faith and needs. They were, in this, integral parts of social life and bespeak interactions between people in their daily lives. It is not surprising, therefore, that people talk about these churches when they are interviewed about their experiences. Jefferson Berryhill, who was a Creek and a fieldworker for the Indian Pioneer project, compiled a report on some of the churches and congregations around

Okmulgee. He starts his report by expressing the common assumption of his day that Indians were vanishing and would soon be gone:

> There are many churches of different denominations. It is important that I should make a report on them because the Indian churches are being abandoned or deserted not just because of losing faith but because of the vanishing of the older Indians who had been the backbone of the church. There are some that have ceased to be the meeting place of the Indians because these fullbloods are dead. Little Cussetah, a Baptist Church two and a half miles west and a mile south of Preston, Oklahoma, is now deserted because the people who lived there are all dead. Tallahassee Church, a Methodist Church, has also been deserted for the same reason. Rock Creek Church, a Methodist Church located one mile and a half mile south of Sapulpa, Oklahoma has only a few members. Creek Chapel, a Methodist Church one and a half miles west of Clearview, has many members. Concharty Church, a Methodist Church about twenty miles northeast of Okmulgee, has many members. Spring Town, about nine miles east of Coweta, has a few members; it is also a Methodist Church. New Town Church is a Methodist Church located one mile north, one mile west, and a half a mile north of Okmulgee. Big Cussetah is a Methodist Church located three miles east and five miles south of Okmulgee. Honey Creek, a Methodist church, is located eight and a half miles southwest of Okmulgee, on Route 3. Montezuma is located west of Tusklekee, Pickett Chapel is located seven miles south of Sapulpa. Tulsa Canadian, which was located south of Hitchita, was destroyed by fire. Here are some of the Indians churches that I have not been able to locate: Arbeka Church, Hickory Ground Church, Hopehocco Church, Green Leaf Church, Haikey Chapel, Eufaula Church, Little Coweta is located about three miles north of Sapulpa. (Berryhill 1938: 67–68)

The churches that Jefferson Berryhill lists here are being abandoned not because Christianity is being replaced but because the Indian communities that support them are dissolving. That notwithstanding, however, the number of churches this report lists in a relatively limited area indicates something of the significance Christianity had for Indian people, and the fact that churches are founded, fluoresce, and disappear indicates something of a life cycle for these rural congregations. Furthermore, the report is not about churches in general; rather it concerns Indian churches and thus exposes the existence of Indian Christian communities long before Julian and I met at church. Jacob Rolland described one way that life cycle went for a Yuchi church near Bixby, Oklahoma:

> Snake Creek was Buck Chapel. John Buck, old time Indian, started this church in 1900. He was an old Indian fiddler, aged about 85 years, when

he started this church. He talked the Euchee language, and the Creek language.

A storm blowed his house over and that scared him so bad that he began to preach and started this church. He had lots of members belonging to this church. This church is out of existence now, and all of the members are dead, except John Cooper and Sam Cooper. (Rolland 1938b: 20)

A common man, John Buck, began preaching late in his life and attracted followers. The church died as the congregation died. It is easy to presume that this was not an unusual sequence of events, and that churches often formed around charismatic leaders. This was not the only way churches went out of existence, however. Sometimes churches died because of actions a congregation took. Arten White related one such case when he gave his account of the birth of the Tulli Bok church in a Indian Pioneer interview.

I live near Ludlow, Oklahoma, am a full blood Choctaw Indian, member and minister of the Gospel of my church and am fifty-nine years of age.

Rock Creek (*Tulli Bok*) Church, a Choctaw dialect [name, (?)] is an organized Choctaw Indian Church of several members, though most of them have died. A few in number still live near the old church of their belief. This church is on a ten acre tract bought by members for their church ground surrounded with about five or six camps built of hewn log structure, chimney of rock and wood daubed with red clay and straw mixture as built in the olden days. It was first organized in the year 1896, a short distance south from the present location across Rock Creek, named after this creek which the name fits well.

There was another church, *"Tulli Holita,"* located a few miles east, where all the people in the community attended until one day, a disagreement over religious element came up when some of the members withdrew from the congregation and organized the Tulli Bok Church under a Cumberland Presbyterian doctrine. Such men as Jesse Wallace, Payson Ludlow, Willis Ludlow, Elias Ward and Arnis Whale and their families played an important role in withdrawing their membership from this church to the new organization which they had planned, although all of these members have since died. Jesse Wallace was the only man out of this list who was an ordained minister, the rest were all members, elders and church campers. *Tullli Holita* Church was forever discontinued. (White 1938: 102–3)

In this case, congregational politics brought an end to the Tulli Holita Church while it was in the process of instituting a new church at Tulli Bok, but the ties that held individuals to their congregations were not so

strong as to always require this drastic a move. Individuals could independently change congregations for any of a number of reasons. Thomas
Gilroy's first church, for example, did not satisfy his needs in religion.

> When I was a small boy I was sprinkled in the Church and later I was
> admitted into the church but when I got old enough to do my own think-
> ing, I wasn't satisfied with the sprinkling and joined the Arbeca Baptist
> Church one mile west of Bryant, by immersion. Then I was ordained
> later, as Deacon of that church.
>
> When the church decided to ordain me as Deacon, it called these men
> to do the ordination: Ministers; Irans Grayson, Rolla Sands of Okemah,
> Hampsy Roberts of Cromwell, Mose Walla of Dustin and the Pastor of
> Arbeca, G. B. Looney; Deacons: John Chupko of Weleetka, Jimmie Ash-
> berry of Weleetka, Mose Birdcreek of Weleetka, Oscar Harjo of Hickory
> Ground, Danna Watson of Dustin, William Fisher of Weleetka and Henry
> Day of Dustin.
>
> When a man is ordained Deacon, he dies a deacon unless he is ordained
> a Minister; but a Class leader is disqualified if he does anything that is
> unfit for a Class leader to do, and then he is just a plain church member.
> (Gilroy 1938: 143)

Living institutions require more than spaces to exist. They also need
organization and people to fill necessary positions so that they can perform the rituals that help create their communities. Nancy Miashintubbee mentioned one of those important community rituals when she
referred to camp meetings, and John Buck and Arten White were ministers of their churches, which could also have deacons, class leaders, and
church members.

When people are organized, they occupy positions that are often
named and carry with them specific duties and sometimes more vague
expectations of proper behavior. These organizations not only divide
the labor to get things done but also structure the communities by dif-
ferentiating people and social roles. This is as true of Indian Christian
communities as it is of any other, and positions like minister, deacon,
camper, or church member all point to people within these church groups
and to a social life that included these people as more than individuals,
as representatives of the positions they filled. Some of these positions,
like member, minister, and deacon, came from Christianity as it was
expressed in the specific denomination of the church, but others emerged
from the community, and Tucker W. Morton said: "When I came here in
1883, services in the churches of the Creek Nation were well attended
and quietly conducted. The men and women sat on opposite sides of
the church. A man, called a 'Dog-puncher,' kept the church free of such

animals during services and with a cane could inform people they were wanted outside, etc., without undue talking" (Morton 1938: 199).

I am sure that the dog-punchers were honored that their fellow church members chose them for the position, but this role facilitated the services that were the central focus of the community. It was the ministers' role to conduct these services for the community, and this central role in public prayer often translated to respect and prominence in the wider community. Meta B. Hatchett identified herself as a Baptist in her interview with Lula Austin, and went on to praise some Presbyterian ministers:

> It was not possible to attend church very often for there were few ministers. The ministers were called Circuit Riders and usually came no oftener than twice a month. The minister with whom we were the most closely associated in my youth was the Reverend Mr Reed. He was a Presbyterian and we were Baptists but we were all delighted to have him make our home his stopping place.
>
> There were other circuit riders who were just as worthy in every way but I shall mention only two others of whom it can safely be said that the country is better for their having lived in it; the Reverend Mr Frank Wright and the Reverend Mr Dixon Durant. Both were Choctaws by birth and Presbyterians by faith. The Reverend Mr Wright was a young man during Indian Territory days, a pleasant speaker and a well educated man, who later became an evangelist. The Reverend Mr Durant, the first resident of Durant and for whom the town was named, was a much older man than Reverend Wright. (Hatchett 1938: 163–64)

Meta B. Hatchett's respect for these clergymen is clear, but the passage also points to the integration of Christianity into the general Choctaw community of the day. The circuit rider was an institution in the community, and his visits were frequent enough to allow for the development of personal relationships within the community. Meta B. Hatchett singles out two of the many circuit riders for praise, pointing to a relatively large class of these ministers in Choctaw Nation. These preachers were not only a phenomenon of the Choctaw Nation. William Wolfe, who was born in 1850, recalled Cherokee circuit riders to the Indian Pioneer project fieldworker Gus Hummingbird:

> Churches were not established immediately after the coming of the Cherokees. Mr Wolfe did not have a church to go to before the Civil War, but *Coo-wee-scoo-wee*, an Indian preacher, would sometimes come through the country and held services at people's homes.
>
> After the Civil War a Sunday School and Church was organized in Mulberry Hollow. Among the early organizers of this church and Sun-

day School, was a Cherokee preacher named *Qu-The-Sce-Woad* and John Jones, a white man, who was sent to the Indian country as a missionary.

The Big Shed on the Peavine Creek was the first strong church that was organized in the Cherokee Nation. The Gritts, Coons, Smallwoods, and Hogners were the early converts. For a long time every church in the Cherokee Nation had to meet at Big Shed once a year. (Wolfe 1938: 465)

William Wolfe remembered Cherokee circuit riders from before the Civil War, and some of the people instrumental in founding the churches that were built after the war. These churches, indeed all churches, were made up of two physical components: congregations and the spaces they occupied. Christian churches have been common in Oklahoma Indian communities, and in the aggregate have represented essentially all the denominations of Christianity available in the larger society. These churches are not merely Christian, they are Indian, and in earlier eras they were tribal: Cherokee Baptist or Choctaw Presbyterian, for example. The churches provide organization to their communities by defining specific roles and expectations for their members that the wider communities knew and respected. William Wolf also recalled that when church buildings were built, they were related in a mother-daughter structure. This relationship was expressed in the requirement that congregations meet for services each year at the mother church. It is these services, these events that bring the community together for prayer and offering, that are, of course, the point of the whole thing.

## SERVICES

Communities perform some rituals, such as funerals and marriages, as needed, and others, like Sunday services, on a periodic basis. No matter what the scheduling mechanism, ritual remains a central element of religion, and does several things for communities. For example, it becomes a powerful symbolic expression of a community's values and the congregation's commitment to them. For Indian people in Oklahoma, this often translated into symbolic expressions that include both Euro-American Christian and traditional Indian elements. In other words, Christianity was a vehicle through which tribal and Indian identities were expressed. Ritual also brings people together, and in doing so serves to maintain a community's integrity. This was especially important in earlier eras, when travel was more difficult and access to professional religious specialists such as ministers and preachers was more rare. From the descriptions in the Indian Pioneer and Doris Duke interviews, camp meetings appear to be common, if not spectacular, examples of these community gatherings. Many of the passages that refer to camp meetings mention little more than attending the services, much as Henry Labor reported in his 1937 interview: they are brief and to the point, for example, "I used to attend the Indian Camp meetings at *Chishoktek*, this is the name of the place in Choctaw but in English it would be Postoak Prairie; it was a Presbyterian Indian Church. This church is still being used. This church was there when I was a boy and it is still there and being used, but the Choctaws are about all gone now who used to attend this church" (Labor 1938: 26).

Some of these interviews, however, contain much richer detail on these meetings and provide some insight into the strength of the communities that performed these services and the importance of them to those communities. David Jones was born in 1886 and was almost twenty-one years old when Oklahoma became a state in 1907. He told the Indian Pioneer project fieldworker Johnson H. Hampton something about the place camp meeting had throughout his life:

> We used to go to the camp meeting when they would have them. We used to camp with them, and help the others to feed the Indians or any other people that came to the meeting. We used to have good meetings while they lasted, they would run about three or four days. It sure did take lots to feed those Indians that came to the meeting, but we had most of the things that we raised at home, but we would have to buy flour, coffee and sugar. In order to buy this stuff, we would sell some cattle—enough to buy what we needed. After my father's death, my mother still used to camp for the meetings. After she died, we did not camp any more for a long time until I got grown and married, then I started to camping like my parents used to do, but after a while I left that part of the country, then I did not camp any more. (Jones 1938: 16–17)

David Jones camped most of his life. When he was a child his family not only camped but helped feed the other campers. This may have easily represented a significant drain on the family's resources, and to that degree points to the importance of camp meetings to David Jones and his family. The importance of camping to David Jones is reflected in his history of participation. Except for a period when he was an unmarried adult, Mr. Jones attended camp meetings until he moved out of his natal community. This is significant, I think, because it points to the power of these communities in people's lives. People attend camp meetings not only for the religious services but also for the community that forms around them. The resources that people put into institutions like camp meetings and the degree to which they participate in these institutions both measure the value of the institution. That value is also expressed symbolically in the details of the performance. Emeziah Bohanan was in his midfifties when he gave his Indian Pioneer project interview to Peter W. Cole. He describes camp meeting in some detail, from the construction of the camps to how ministers conducted the services:

> It has often been repeated that the Indians are great believers in the Great Spirit, and the Choctaw Indians are no exception. At a meeting of any Indian Church, the campers of old days would put up their sheds by placing two corner posts in front and two in the rear some six to ten inches lower than the front posts, nail cross pieces and boards across, and cover with boards. The different campers, depending on the number of camps to be erected, would arrange their sheds in uniform lines near and around the church, and would be ready for the occasion on time. Usually they would move to their camps on Thursday before the preaching. The groceries would be bought, the meat killed, the wood hauled, and everything planned for the meeting would be ready and carried out to the letter, and not a hitch would be made during the stay, such as killing meat on Saturday or Sunday or going to town for more groceries. It was the custom that everything must be arranged and ready to last for several days. If in winter, the campers would drag heavy logs and haul the wood with oxen, which were common in those days. This work must be finished by Friday 12 o'clock noon.
>
> At any time after Friday noon to six o'clock P.M. the minister would arrive. As soon as he arrived, the deacon or elder of the church would ring the bell for the church service, which would continue until the breaking up on Monday morning. Sunrise service was conducted before breakfast on Monday morning [with the] farewell handshaking of all persons at church, then breakfast, after which each family would start on their journey back home. Every body went away happy after enjoying the meeting, and love for their neighbor and respect for others was exchanged and acknowledged. Occasionally one could notice a string of wagons filing down the road, while riders on horseback would follow behind. Women riding horseback on side saddles were common in those days.
>
> Where there was just one horse in the family, the husband would ride, carrying the baby or bundles; if more than one child, the others would ride behind, and the woman would walk ahead on foot. If they had to go any distance the man would walk and the woman ride. This was the only way of traveling in those days.
>
> Each individual believed that a promise or idea planned ahead must be carried out when the time arrived. Therefore, knowing that it was time for a big meeting at any certain place, he went or took his family in a wagon or horseback and went regardless of weather.
>
> Very often where there was no church bell, the deacon usually had a ram, cow horn, or oyster shell which he blew for church service. At the

last blow of the horn, each person or crowd would leave for church. Each one would fall in line in the direction they came; the first line arrived will march in order, then the next line until the last line marched in before the minister would make any attempt to make announcements or to proceed with the service.

I knew of a minister who always expected to be at his appointment by Friday noon or before, and on his arrival, expected service to open immediately. Between services they would gather around the pulpit and practice singing out of an old songbook, "Christian Harmony," which contained only notes. Very often they would stay up all night.

The deacon usually had a place reserved in the church house for some peace officer, and at the beginning of the opening service he (the peace officer) would announce to the congregation with reference to law and order that there would be no drinking nor disturbance permitted around or near the church or premises, after which he would take his post near and around the church, where service was being held. After service he would stay some distance from the church to see if any drinking was gong on, or very often some horse thieves would take advantage of the meeting and steal some belongings or horses. It was the duty of the offi-cer to be on the watch and protect belongings and property.

Before leaving for church the mother of children would warn them to behave while in church or else the officer would take them to the jail. This was deeply impressed on them that they would not dare to leave church until the services was over.

The boys up to eighteen years would enter church with their father and remain by side of him until dismissed; and girls with their mother did likewise. This was in tradition with the "Puritans."

For lamps we burned mutton grease poured into a bored wood about four inches in diameter and three to four inches deep. A bundle of yarn or twine was saturated in grease until hardened. Another bored block to fit the first block was nailed to the wall and the candle block fit to it. When lighted it gave good light.

One cold winter I attended a meeting when there was not enough rooms to accommodate all visitors, and my father and I were obliged to make a pallet on the ground and went to sleep. Having my head covered up, it snowed during the night that I did not know anything about. Woke up the next morning, notice something heavy on top of blankets, to my surprise there was about four inches snow over us. I hated to get up the next morning as it was so nice and warm under the snow. (Bohanan 1938: 129–33)

I suspect that camp meetings were not confined to Indian Territory when Emeziah Bohanan was a teenager in the 1890s. Rural Christians all over America faced the same problems of limited traveling range and very few ministers. So the camp meeting of the 1890s may have a lot in common with the church where I met Julian; the church and very probably the camp meeting are common Christian rituals of their time, so, for both, their Indianness must be carried in the content of the services rather than their structure. Often, however, it was in the structure of the performance where the tribal or Indian was expressed. This was done in one of three ways. In some cases, where both traditional and Christian practices offered ways to accomplish the same end, such as marriage, the task was split, so that some of it was done traditionally and some on the Christian path, and sometimes both were performed in their entirety. Both of these would have a clear Christian part and a clear traditional part, so both maintained their integrity. In a third class of cases, Christian rituals changed to accommodate the traditional, so Christianity would become the vehicle by which traditional ways are performed.

The experience that Mrs. Eliza Cross related about her marriage may be a good example of the first. According to the Indian Pioneer project interview, Mrs. Cross was born in 1897, and her father was a full-blood Choctaw and a Methodist preacher. She described the way she was married to her first husband when she was sixteen years old, around 1913:

> While I attended Goodland school the last nine months an old full-blood Choctaw Indian Presbyterian preacher stayed at my daddy's house and labored for nothing. He would not charge my daddy anything, just laboring like in Bible days. So Daddy said that I must get married and settle down and I thought I just had to do what he said to do. And this preacher, Levi Harkins, was the one he selected for me. That was the Choctaw way, select husbands for the daughters. I had never gone with a boy anywhere. So we were married. He was a full-blood Choctaw Indian raised at Atoka. He died in 1927, and buried at little place called Bently. He was forty years old, I about sixteen. (Cross 1938: 80)

Mrs. Cross's Methodist father arranged for her to marry a Presbyterian, so most likely the marriage service itself was Christian, but the process of selecting the spouses was Native. Mrs. Cross herself identifies the process of fathers selecting husbands for their daughters as the Choctaw way, so the marriage is accomplished by a Choctaw betrothal followed by a Christian wedding. Mrs. Eliza Cross and the story she told about her marriage have a lot in common with Myrtle Morrell Unap, who told her story about thirty years later. Both were in their fifties when they were interviewed, both were married when they were about sixteen, and both their fathers arranged their first marriages. Mrs. Unap's story, however, is very different in its focus and a little different in its structure. Mrs. Unap's first words on the transcript outline some of those differences.: "I am Myrtle Morrell Unap, full-blood Osage, fifty years old. I want to relate the story, first about my life, and then my experience as a bride of

The Jesus Way     131

the Osage Indian traditional ceremony. I was raised in a Christian home with a loving mother and father" (Unap 1972: 1).

Mrs. Unap starts the interview with an announcement that she will talk about her experiences as a traditional Osage bride, which she follows with the disclaimer that she is a Christian. She then immediately launches into the detail of the traditional Osage wedding and her experience of it. The first order of business in this process is the betrothal:

> In 1934, my mother was still living. In the traditional Osage wedding, the first, you approach my family. That was in 1933 and, as I recollect, it was a usual day in the household—my mother was busy around the home and I believe my father was gone at that time and my younger sisters were there and there was the usual day, daily household, going about our ways. And the starting of the wedding, the first procedure in an Osage wedding, is the bridegroom, prospective bride groom's older members of his family approach the girl's family. They come and talk and ask for this girl, this family. It's between the families, not the boy and girl. (Unap 1972: 1)

Mrs. Unap then briefly described how the bride's family accepts the offer of marriage (the bride's family eats a meal at the groom's home), and she mentions that she was passive in the process—she watched the events unfold around her. The first of these events was the payment of the bride wealth:

> And, as we went about our daily task, I rode by through there on my way to town and back. And, down in the bottom, there was a creek and, there was a space there where they had horses. And they brought horses to this girl's family as gifts and in—in the English language, translated from the Osage language, they are buying the bride. Not in the actual sense of the word, but that's the way it is translated. And they bring horses, many horses, and, their prize horses, they brought as gifts. Well, that went on for several days, exchange. No we didn't exchange, the boy brought the gifts. (Unap 1972: 2)

When acceptable bride wealth was paid, the wedding day came, and Mrs. Unap described the advice her father gave her just before the ceremony began. First the participants dressed in elaborate clothing for the ceremony. The bride wore a coat of bright colors with an Osage sash on top of it and a wedding hat made from a silk top hat decorated with brightly colored plumes. Once dressed, the bridal company and the bride move to the groom's camp:

> I rode the first car and blankets on the car and a robe on my lap which were made of broadcloth, and yarn belts sewn across the broadcloth,

which are most elaborate. And as I recollect, my mother and my aunts spent many years collecting these blankets and these clothes that I am supposed to wear, which are all handmade. And from, and, as—as I rode the first vehicle or car, which was going to be given away and my matron of honor, she rode a car also, which was going to be given away, and the others rode horses and some of 'em just walked with their horse. And we were going down to the other camp, I remember, I believe the American Flag preceded the bride. And the Town Crier, is doing his duty at that time announcing that we are coming. And, at that time, it was—it's a public affair and there are many people there, many white people. And I believe, that I am the last, I am the last bride of the Osage traditional ceremony—wedding ceremony. A real, full, complete ceremony. So, as we were going to the other camp, the wedding procession, there was a race. They race for prizes. Who reaches the bride first, and so on down the line, they receive fabulous prizes. (Unap 1972: 3–4)

At the groom's camp a wedding feast is prepared for both parties, and gifts of wedding clothing are exchanged. It is at this point when the parallel Christian service is performed:

And from there, we were married in a civil ceremony by a Methodist Preacher, for everyone to witness. And we ate, and from there, the wedding was over for my part. And the next day, they return the bride back to her family with her bridegroom, which is another wedding procession. We rode back in a—in a buggy and a team of white horses. And the—his main—his main member of his wedding party, she rode a car, which is to be given to the bride's family. I believe, my matron of honor and his main person in his wedding procession, exchanged gifts which were the automobiles and—and we were in a procession on the way back to my family and, my home, which was led by the American Flag, and the Town Crier, announcing that we were coming back, which is a wedding procession—taking the bride home. And from there, I believe, there were other activities at that time of exchanging prize horses to my family, race horses were at that time, the finest horses they could get at that time, were given to my family, and my relatives, which were the boys of my family, the prize race horses at that time. My brother and my cousin, my uncle's oldest son, received the prize race horses, which were quite valuable and they had blankets on them and they received the blankets on the horses and saddles. And I believe there were maybe, forty head of horses given to my family at that time. After the wedding party reached my home, there was much feasting and, and just a good get-together of the two families. We ate together. And one day which is traditional in Osage people, in this sort of wedding, that they bring the elder members of the tribe, the chief and all prominent men at that time, to come and council the young couple on how to be and how to—what is going to be, and we were counciled in that manner. They sat around the room and they talked to us. (Unap 1972: 4–5)

Mrs. Unap was married with two wedding ceremonies; one, the Christian one, was brief and got only a few lines in her interview, whereas the other was long (because of the death of Mrs. Unap's mother, there was more than a year between betrothal and marriage, and the ceremony itself took at least two days), elaborate, and expensive. Mrs. Unap and her family clearly had a profound commitment to their traditional Osage ways as well as to their Christian beliefs. They used these parallel ceremonies to give proper and appropriate acknowledgment to each, but the Osage ceremony was the central focus. Like Mrs. Eliza Cross's Choctaw betrothal and Christian wedding, Myrtle Morrell Unap's two weddings keep the Christian distinct from the tribal traditions, but sometimes those tribal traditions are practiced through Christian forms. I believe that Choctaw Cry may be an example of this. Many people in the Indian Pioneer interviews mention these ceremonies, but none more completely than Mrs. Jancy Bell. She was in her early seventies at the time Johnson H. Hampton interviewed her for the Indian Pioneer project. She described her experience with Cries in this passage:

> We used to have those Indian Crys at the church most of the time but some times we would go to the grave and have the cry there. It used to be that when an Indian died they would not hold much ceremony over him at the grave but would wait about one year when they would set a date for the memorial, and we would all go over and spend the night there, and the next day at about eleven oclock the preacher would call the people together and preach the memorial. They would gather around the grave and cry and after the cry they would announce dinner when they would all gather around the table and eat, after which they would all go home. I think that the Indians have quit having those memorials because the white people would come and make fun or make a show of it until now the Indians don't have them any more. (Bell 1938: 22–23)

On the surface, almost everything about the Cry is Christian, even though the fact of the rite itself may seem a little odd. It is done at the church, or maybe at the graveside, and a preacher officiates at the ceremony. When it is considered in the light of traditional Choctaw funeral practices, however, the Christianity starts to look more like a veneer. In indigenous Choctaw burial customs, the body was first placed on a scaffold for a period of one to six months, after which a specialist cleaned the bones for internment. This specialist then presided over a feast in honor of the deceased (Debo 1972 [1934]: 4–5). The parallels between the indigenous custom and the Cry are unmistakable. In a change perhaps brought on by Christianity, the scaffold burial was replaced by internment, but the later ritual, presided over by a specialist, that brought the family together to remember the deceased remained in the form of the Cry.

This passage is interesting in another way because it speaks to symbolic divisions between white and Indian. Mrs. Jancy Bell speculates that Choctaw people stopped having these last rites to avoid white ridicule, which makes some sense in the context of the social Darwinist thinking of the day. If some peoples and ways of life are naturally superior to others, then the practice of the inferior has little to recommend it. It also divides the Indian from the white and therefore contributes to the boundaries that maintain Indian ethnicity. But this observation also indirectly points to another division that applies within Indian communities. From the Indian point of view, Christianity is inherently a European institution, and this is not eliminated when Christianity becomes the focus of Indian communities. It can, and often does, serve as a wedge within these communities.

## Division and Unity

Divisions, by their nature, have at least two sides, and one convenient way to look at the religious divisions within Indian communities is along Indian and Christian lines. In the early twentieth century, it may have been more appropriate to use a tribal/Christian split to approach this issue, but as ethnic Indian institutions have emerged, Indian has replaced tribal. This pie can also be cut, however, along ideal and real lines. I think people understand their world in idealized abstractions that they use to interpret what they experience. Of course, reality is always more complex than abstraction, so there is always a gap between the two, and this situation is no exception. The common abstraction many Indian people express pits Christianity against Indian institutions like Powwow and Stomp Dance, but many Indian people live both, easily crossing the borders between the two worlds that, it seems to me, are becoming more porous over time. This is not to say that the abstraction is false—some Indian ministers, no doubt, preach it from the pulpit, and some Indian people live it in their lives; but many others see no contradiction in participating in both worlds.

This standard theory that Christianity is inherently opposed to traditional expression comes up often in conversation. In one of the early interviews I recorded, for example, both Cory and Carol were participating, and the subject of religion came up. I was very happy about this, because the topic was on my agenda, and I had met Cory (like Julian) at church, so I hoped this would be the start of a discussion of Indian

Christianity. Cory started by saying: "The two things that have separated Indians from family culture was and still is education and religion. If you are going to be a Christian, then you have got to give up all your culture. You don't come over here to this church until you have given up all your religion." At this point Carol intervened with: "Culture is heathen. In many of the Indian churches you don't do your culture, that's bad, that's wrong, that's heathen. That's what we were saved from. And they can be full-blood saying this, it has nothing, in this case, to do with blood, it has to do with what they were taught by missionaries." And then Cory finished his point with the following:

> Recently here a particular church, I won't name the church or the denomination, was condemning people for participating in Powwow and such as that and really down on them, but even some things that we do here using cedar, cultural activities, they were condemning. That particular denomination that is doing all that condemning, I noticed on television, now, they are doing that cedar ceremony. Two dominant denominations here have done that. They have their own cedar ceremony before they begin their prayers or begin their whatever they are going to do, they have that in place now.

In this iteration of the ideal, the division is between the Christian and anything that may point to traditional Native American belief systems, whether it is ethnic Indian or tribal. Cory and Carol do not like the division, and they believe that Christianity is most at fault for making it. There is an element of power threaded through this discourse—Christianity represents the white dominating culture and has the power to enforce the split—as well as an element of hypocrisy. On the one hand, the white Christian church condemns native practice, while on the other it coopts them. In the early days of the twenty-first century, Carol and Cory expressed a division that reaches back at least into the nineteenth.

J. W. Barbee was a Shawnee man who came to Cherokee Nation at the age of four when his tribe was removed from its reservation in Kansas. He was born in 1867, so he was in his teens and early twenties in the 1880s. His Indian Pioneer project interview covered his genealogy, work history, and education, as well as this brief reference to religion: "I never tried to learn to speak the Cherokee language but when I was young, I could understand the Cherokees and could talk to them and can even yet understand what they are talking about. I have attended their churches and was raised among them but I have never attended a Stomp Dance. We had our picnics and singings, etc." (Barbee 1938: 169).

Here J. W. Barbee made only minimal ethnic distinction between Shawnee and Cherokee but emphasized religious distinctions. He attended Cherokee churches but not celebrations in the Ceremonial Ground religion of the traditional eastern Woodlands peoples, which he referred to as Stomp Dance. He reinforced the division when he said: "We had our own picnics and singings." He did not say why he did not attend the Stomp Dances. Winey Lewis was more direct on that point in the Indian Pioneer project interview she gave to Grace Kelley. The report mentions only that she was born before 1900 and gives no other indication of her age, so Winey Lewis may have been as young as her midthirties when she granted the interview.

> My father belonged to Nuyaka Town but I belong to Tuckabatcha Town. My husband is Kealigee. I belong to the wind clan. When a man marries he still belongs to his town but has to go to his wife's town too. He takes medicine at both towns but it doesn't hurt him for it is the same kind of medicine. He always belongs to his own town and is fined if he doesn't attend, but a real Christian never attends after his conversion for that is the same as a dance, to attend which is a sin. Some of the young boys go and then as they have backslid, they have to repent and rebuild. We belong to Arbeca Church. (Lewis 1938: 17)

Winey Lewis gives a very good outline of Creek social and political organization, and connects both to the Ceremonial Ground religion. Creek people were in her time expected to attend their town's celebrations or be fined, but Christians in the community did not attend because to do so would be a sin. This exposes a serious problem, and as Christianity becomes stronger in the community and more people exclude themselves from participation in the traditional religion, the traditional political system becomes weaker. She also makes it seem that the force behind the division came from the Christian side. The towns were not excluding the Christians, according to this account, but the Christians were excluding themselves. Some who report experiences from an earlier era indicate that the tribes sometimes took steps to suppress Christianity. Lilah D. Lindsey was probably in her seventies when she granted her Indian Pioneer project interview, in which she talked about the problems a white missionary had in setting up a mission in Creek Nation:

> Dr. Loughridge told me the story of his struggles to found a mission school; how he went to Coweta, a young missionary full of zeal to work for the good of the Indians. But the Creeks said: "No, No white man's religion." Loughridge said, "If I can't preach, may I teach?" Grudgingly they agreed. So he started a school in his one-room cabin. Realizing that by teaching he could preach, training the young generation, he decided to devote his life to that. (Lindsey 1938: 173–74)

It is not clear exactly when Dr. Loughridge had these experiences with the tribe, but Lilah D. Lindsey was teaching in the Coweta Mission school in the 1880s, so the school may have been founded as early as the pre–Civil War era. Sandy Fife was more explicit about the issue when he talked about Creek tribal suppression of Christianity in December 1937:

> It was against the Tribal Law for any of the Indians to go to meetings held by the Reverend Mr. Buckner, a traveling Baptist Missionary. I do not know the years when this took place but it was before the Civil War and I can only remember having known one of the persons punished. She was Sallie, the mother of Sam Logan. She and Sam are both dead now.
>
> Several were whipped at the same time that she was whipped and for a long time others were whipped. Sallie was kneeling down, praying while she was being whipped with some elm or hickory sprouts about the size of my finger.
>
> The committee of the Council met after this had been going on for quite a while and decided that their punishment was doing no good and that this new religion seemed to be doing no harm. These men had not been converted themselves though. They passed a rule to establish a religious meeting place and anyone who wanted to could meet, be converted, and carry on the work. They saw that these Indians were trying to do right and that it was a good thing. That was when The Big Arbor was established. (Fife 1938: 5–6)

Public flogging with hickory sticks seems like harsh suppression, but of more interest to me is the eventual official Creek Nation acceptance of Christianity. This construction of history allows Sandy Fife to be both Christian and Creek, but it cannot allow someone to be both Christian and Indian, because there is no official Indian hierarchy to sanction Christianity. In addition, neither official tribal hierarchies nor ethnic group expressions do very much directly to bring official Christianity along. As long as Christian ministers denounce expressions of tribal or Indian traditions as sin from the pulpit, the model of opposing Indian groups based on religion can be maintained. Today and in the past, both Indian and non-Indian ministers tell their congregations that participation in Powwow, Native American Church, and Stomp Dance is wrong and offends God. And probably just as long as that has been happening, Christian Indians have been ignoring this sermonizing and participating in their traditional communities. Sarah Longbone was born in 1887 and was nearing her fiftieth birthday when she was interviewed by Nannie Lee Burns for the Indian Pioneer project. She said of being both Christian and Indian:

> I joined the Baptist Church when in school at Lawrence, but I have always been glad to take part in the dances of my people, as all of them

have religious significance. The Stomp Dance is held any time that they want to have one. They would dance around a fire, one man leads them and four men follow him and when he talks, these men answer him. They dance a while and then the women join in the dance. They are glad to have lived and enjoyed life and to be there. (Longbone 1938: 200–201)

She barely acknowledges the tension between Christianity and Indian traditions, and emphasizes instead positive aspects of Indian religious expression in Stomp Dance. My impression is that Sarah Longbone was committed to her Christianity, but she was not going to let that stand in the way of participating in her traditional community, pronouncements from a preacher notwithstanding. Bertha Provost was a little more vocal about her opinion of Indian tradition as sin. She was in her sixties when William Bittle interviewed her for the Doris Duke project. She was Wichita and had been a Baptist since her midteens, and her nephew was a preacher at Rock Springs, a nearby Indian congregation. William Bittle asked her about missionaries among the Wichita. She had little to say about white missionaries but the following:

This ones that's there now, Rock Springs Church, Freemont Standing. He's my cousin's boy. And he tries to get very strict . . . .
    Any of his members go—like they have pow-wow somewhere, they go, he just thinks, they sin, and he don't like that. And he'll preach on that. Now he's just, I said—I called, him my nephew. In Wichita relationship, he's my nephew.
    I said, "Nephew, I want to tell you something. All these years, I been working in the church here." I said, "I was about fifteen years old I think when I—when I was converted." I said, "I have never seen an Indian like you go against things like that." I said, "I'm going to tell you something." I said, "You remember when Christ was going through a wheat field, and going around." I said, "The people were with him. Everywhere he went, Pharisees asked him for questions, 'Why is it you mingle and eat with the sinners?'" I said, "What was Christ's answer? He said He came into this world not for the righteous but for the wicked." And I said, "That's the one." I said, "You know good and well, when my husband was living yet, we used to always go where they have pow-wow gatherings. And what did the people do? If dinner hour comes the first thing, 'Reverend Provost, we want you to return thanks. You can say few words first.' He'd always get up and he's always willing."
    I said, "No wonder." I said, "There wasn't enough room in our church. People came every directions." I said, and he was a Sioux Indian. And he used to tell me, "My people are all Catholics." He said, "Don't ship my body home I want to be right here with your people because they're all good to me." (Provost 1972: 4–5)

Bertha Provost and Sarah Longbone belie the abstraction that Christian and traditional Indian people form two exclusive and antagonistic groups. Both were clearly Christian and both found important values in the traditions of Stomp Dance and Powwow. It is my impression that these two women represent the experiences of many, if not most, Indian people in Oklahoma today. I know of members of Native American Church who, after the end of Native American Church meetings on Sunday mornings, go straight to services with their local Baptist or Methodist congregations, and I know of many Indian ministers who dress out and dance in Powwows around the state. In short, although I have no statistics on the issue, I suspect that the majority of Indian people in Oklahoma are Christian, but they experience little or no personal conflict in participating in Indian spiritual life.

## Ethnic Boundaries

Christianity is a part of life for Indian people in Oklahoma and has been for the entire range of experiences represented by the Indian Pioneer and Doris Duke interviews. For many Indian people today and in the past, Christianity has offered a way for them to express their needs to participate in a spiritual life, but Christianity is by no means a monolith. While prior to statehood in the early twentieth century most congregations were predominantly Indian, today, with Indian people representing only about 10 percent of the total state population, almost all congregations are almost all non-Indian. Many of these churches recognize their local Indian heritage and try to include the sensibilities of Indian people in their ministries; far too many, however, are myopic in these issues and see only the dominating (white) culture's point of view. To many Indian people these churches represent the white world, and therefore, this mainstream Christianity can become one of the symbolic elements that help create Indian ethnic identity. This is expressed in several ways, in discourse that compares Indian to white, or constructs exclusive worlds so that one must choose Indian or white, or pits Indian in political opposition to white, or any number of other threads of discourse; but all fit into the same basic structure of meaning that attaches *Christianity* to *white*.

The general structure of comparative ethnic discourse in the interviews goes something like this: "White people say such-and-such about themselves (or Indians), but such-and-such is also true (or not true) about Indian people." Henry Armstrong followed this line when he gave this Indian Pioneer project interview in 1937:

The first man created was the red man, Adam, the name given to the first man, means "red."

When Noah built the ark and gathered all that were to be saved into it, before the great flood, there was no red man in the ark.

There is no water above the clouds and the red man had gone to the high peaks above the clouds and stayed there until after the flood.

The lost villages that have been uncovered in later years, are the Indian villages that were covered with mud from the flood.

The red man was here before the flood, the same as the white man. The white man wonders where the Indian came from and the Indian wonders the same about the white man. (Armstrong 1938b: 8)

In this passage Henry Armstrong relates an Indian perspective on two biblical creation stories. First he states that the biblical Adam was red, Indian, then he tells how red, Indian, people survived the biblical flood, thus equating Indian people with the descendants of Noah in moral standing. Mr. Armstrong attaches Christianity to white by referring to scripture, and he puts the Indian on a level with white by making the first man not white but red, and placing Indian people among the righteous who were allowed to live through the flood. Over sixty years later, Lee picked up the same line of discourse one early spring afternoon. We were talking about Stomp Dance, and the issue of traditional medicine associated with Stomp Dance came up. Lee said:

It's nothing like people think, mostly more like a sacrament. What they—people get confused to me, Indians had a way of religion long before they were considered Catholics or Christianity, the Indians always had a real strong belief and we always—like you might have been told Bible stories—we were always told little stories that referred to the Creations of man and why we do things and why things are considered sacred to the Indian people.

For instance, cedar, they said there was once a man, a real godly man, who was here and walked among the Indian people, lived with them and when he left he talked to God and said I want to stay here on this earth to help Indian people and that's where that cedar comes in. He left a part of him as that tree, and that tree never dies, and he said when you pray or come together or get bad feelings, good feelings, sad—whatever you pray about burn a little of that cedar and that smoke or that mist, I refer to it as the Bible. The Bible says that after the third day, Jesus Christ arose as a mist, a vapor. The way we use that cedar, that vapor or mist will take your prayers and lay it before God Almighty and do your representation for you. That's how they use it today—messenger.

Lee does not put Indian people in the biblical stories as Henry Armstrong does; rather he draws parallels between the biblical-white-Christian and the Indian. Just as white Christians have Bible stories, so Indian people also have stories to tell them about good. Comparisons require categories, so inherent in these comparisons are ethnicities that are sometimes constructed to be exclusive with regard to religion. In other words, for some Indian people to adopt Christianity is to abandon the traditional. When Pat talked about this phenomenon, he expressed an understanding of it in terms of suspicion and mistrust:

> That's how I look at: here's the Christian Indians today and their churches, and it helps them, it helps them to maintain that. Over here are the traditionalists who maintain their understanding and their love for that and have a mistrust [that] it's hard to keep it and let it out to others that are entrusted with it. If it would all of a sudden come out, now [it] would be considered a cult. The Peyote ceremony came out in the 1920s when it started moving up into the United States.

Pat is talking about groups here. He refers to Christian Indians and traditionalists in opposition to one another, because the traditionalists recognize the power the Christians wield and fear they would use it to eradicate their beliefs. Leslie experienced the same thing except on a more personal level. He was talking about how it was difficult to reintegrate himself into his family after returning from school and then recalled his father:

> People who were once very traditional decided they were going to set it aside, like my father. I asked him, "What did you do with all your Indian things?" Course he was a Baptist minister, but he has the Bibles and the hymnals in Muskogian. I said, "I would like to have them one day." He said, "All the Indian stuff I put away in the cedar chest, I just put it all aside and became a trucker for Allied Van Line," a moving service, and he said, "I'm not that anymore." To me, I find that horrendous. It's like unscrewing your ankle. And I said, "Okay, that's your problem. I'll come and see you and talk to you." He loves to talk World War Two and things like that which is great.

Leslie thinks her father tried to give up his essence, his nature, what he was, and to Leslie that was not only horrid but impossible. At the core of Leslie's father's decision is the idea that there is a white, Christian divide from the Indian so that it is impossible to be both. It is precisely this idea the Pat accounts for through mistrust. This discourse of exclusivity is sometimes realized politically through resistance. Chris talked about early experiences with various white institutions, like church and school, that in her eyes belittled her Indian heritage. One particular experience in church stood out for her: "I was at the head of Sunday School class, this is one of many faux pas they made, but this was the last straw, they said that Indians were heathens and that we didn't know any thing about God and all this crap. It was just wrong, and I spoke up about that as well. I said, 'I think I'll be leaving now,' and I left that classroom and never went back."

Christianity insulted Chris's people by calling them heathens, and she refused to put up with that. But of course, resistance is only one side of the political story; there is also pressure and grievance. Pat feels that because organized Christianity has lost most of its contact with the spiritual, it has poached on traditional practice.

> I don't consider this a good or a bad thing at this point, but if it helps the individuals in that way, then maybe it was a good thing. However, what I'm seeing today is some of these people became Christians or Protestants or all these other religions as they came in. After so many generations, they started looking for something else. It's like all of a sudden rural areas that chose spiritualism. How do I as a spirit relate to this religion? Of course many people, I think, question. So they go back now in order to find some of their roots and some of their spirituality. Many different things came out of that, one of them being the Native American Church came out of it. Much of that has been Christianized. The sweats were still going into [present] time, but they are starting to come to that too.

In this construction, Pat connects Indian with spiritual and white with Christian, while expressing concern that the white is taking over the Indian. To him, Native American Church has been Christianized, and even the sweats may be changing to accommodate white sensibilities. Whether these things are true or not (and I suspect they are), one of the symbolic consequences of this structure is to strengthen the ethnic boundary that separated white and Indian. It is clear, however, that behind this simple abstraction is a far more complex relationship between Indian people and Christianity. It has been part of the traditions of the forty or so tribes in the state for at least the past century and a half, and during that period Indian Christian churches have provided people with places to come together and pray and build their communities. While it has given structure to these communities, Christianity also carries with it inherent divisions between itself and traditional beliefs and practices. These divisions have led some traditional and Christian people to view the two Indian communities as exclusive from one another, but at the same time, many Indian people participate in both. For its entire history, Indian Christianity has coexisted with these traditional beliefs and practices that today represent some of the most important cultural institutions Indian people use to express their Indian ethnicity. Among these are Native American Church, Powwow, and Stomp Dance.

# 7  *The Red Road*

---

The only time an Indian gets Indian culture or Indian
way of thinking they got to come to this, I'm not saying
Powwow, I'm saying Indian gathering part, it could be
the gathering of a Stomp Dance, it could be a Powwow,
it could be Native American Church meeting or Native
Christian Church. Any kind of gathering that they have
the Indians get around and tell stories of how it was and
how we look at stuff.

—Lee

This is the final chapter in which the focus is on what people
said in the Indian Pioneer and Doris Duke collections and in my research
interviews, and it is unique among those chapters. Chapter 3, "Betray-
als of Tears," and chapter 4, "The Great Wisdom," concerned the ways
people talked about things that Euro-American culture did to Indian
people—forced removals and education. Chapter 5, "Blood Brothers," and
chapter 6, "The Jesus Way," do not talk so much about these things done
to Indian people; rather they are about ideas—blood quantum and Christianity—that Euro-American culture brought to Indian people. While all
of these represent important threads in the construction of Indian identity and ethnicity, they all come from European roots. This chapter is
about ideas that have Native American roots, and that have grown into
important Indian institutions in the early twenty-first century.

The previous chapters demonstrate the distinction between Indian
institutions and institutions with Indian roots. There are many Indian
institutions in Oklahoma that are grounded firmly on Euro-American
cultural values. Indian chambers of commerce and other professional
organizations are clear cases of this. It may be argued that the tribes them-

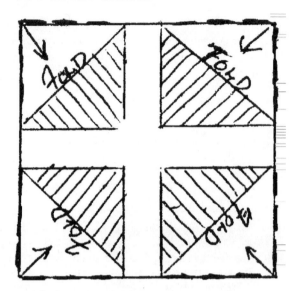

Crooked Foot's pad. Drawing by Julia Jordan, Doris
Duke Papers, Western History Collections, University of Oklahoma, Norman, Oklahoma, 5: 6

selves are in this category, because their major functions are to serve as
administrative units to deal with the United States government. On the
other hand, institutions with Indian roots emerge from indigenous values and patterns of thought. In Oklahoma these are often religions, but
even if they appear to be secular, they usually have religious overtones.
Powwow is one of these Indian expressions, and is very popular because,
of these institutions with Indian roots, it is one of the most accessible
for non-Indians.

## Common Ground

When I go to a Powwow, I often feel as if the physical process of just getting there takes me through a series of stages from the modernist Euro-
American world of white Oklahoma to a contemporary Indian world. To
me, the really good Powwows are off the beaten track, so the process starts
when I turn off the well-maintained U.S. or state highway onto local rural
roads. Even these lanes will often degenerate to dirt section lines before
the Powwow grounds come into sight. Sometimes there is a parking lot,
but it always overflows, so parking is usually in a field. Maybe there is a
sign on the way to the field saying, "No Alcohol, No Firearms, No 49s,"

but even if there is not, the white world is fading and the Indian emerging. For tourists and spectators like me, the footpath from the parking place to the Powwow events commonly passes by a series of vendors selling food and souvenirs who make the Indian world clear. At least one of the food stands may offer hamburgers and hotdogs, but fry bread and Indian tacos will be more common on the menu. All the souvenir sellers carry out the Indian theme. From T-shirts proclaiming "Indian country" to turquoise and silver jewelry and raw crafts materials such as beads and buckskins, the concessioners cater to an Indian clientele. By the time the arena comes into view, the transfer is almost complete. The arena itself is a roughly circular area defined by a border of backless benches often made of simple, sturdy two-by-twelve boards placed on concrete building blocks or some other such material. The Drum is set up in the center of the arena, and if the dancing has begun, it is surrounded by a group of men who are playing and singing the dance songs. Just outside the arena, a few yards behind the backless bench, people set up folding chairs, often in family groups behind a family member who has dressed out to dance and takes his or her place on the bench. In most larger Pow-wows, a series of bleachers are set up just outside the circle of folding chairs, where visitors can watch the goings-on inside the arena. I like to sit high in the stands so I can see more.

I like to get there early. I like to watch the empty arena fill with activity, and then ebb back. Sometimes I am lucky enough to arrive and see the Drum brought to the center and suspended above the ground on its collapsible frame, but usually the Gourd Dance has already started when I get there. On Friday of the Powwow, the Gourd Dancers often start in early evening, but on Saturday and Sunday they can begin in midafternoon. Sometimes the Gourd Dancers and their families have the arena pretty much to themselves, but by the time the emcee has asked the Drum to sing the last Gourd Dance song of the day, activity has picked up. After the last song, the Gourd Dancers put their eagle-feather fans and rattles away in the cedar boxes made for them, leave the arena, and prepare for the Grand Entry, which marks the beginning of the evening's events.

In some ways, the Grand Entry is a kind of index of personages. An appropriate song comes from the Drum, and participants in the Powwow dance in line into the arena through an opening left in the row of backless benches. State, national, and other flags head up the line followed by the head man dancer, head lady dancer, visiting tribal princesses, dancers dressed out in their competitive category regalia, members of the sponsoring Powwow committee, and others as they dance clockwise around the periphery of the arena. The emcee announces each important individual and each group as they come into the dance ground, until all are in the arena. Prayers, often in tribal languages, and a Flag Song from the Drum kick off the session's events, after which the Grand Entry participants dance out of the arena. By this time the rows of folding chairs and the bleachers are almost full, and the programmed events are about to begin.

Most spectators focus on the competitive dancing on the program, but that represents only one aspect of the Powwow. The dancers compete in categories divided by gender and age, and marked by the regalia dancers wear. For example, men's Fancy Dance regalia include two bustles, and women's Jingle Dancers wear a dress adorned with several hundred small metal cones that produce a soft clanking as the dancer moves. These competitions often take up less than half the program, which includes several other kinds of dances that are often called inter-tribals. During the evening there will be Honorings, Specials, Snake Dances, Two Steps, Round Dances, and a confusing myriad of other dances in the arena. Occasionally there will be a giveaway, in which someone being honored with, for example, an important position in the community, will publicly give special gifts to significant people in her or his life. Other times a young dancer may be "roached," in a ceremony that admits the dancer to the privilege of participating in the arena as an adult.

The Powwow activity extends beyond the arena. Volunteers circulate throughout the spectators, selling programs and chances on various raffles. Dancers and spectators alike mingle among the concessions, but late in the session the bleachers begin to clear out as spectators leave for home. After the last dance of the evening, the arena lights are turned off, and the Drum is taken down and put away. The journey from home to bleachers can leave the impression of traveling through a series of concentric circles to an Indian core, but that would be misleading. There is an Indian core at the Powwow, but it is not in the arena. It is in the camps next to the arena, where dancers, their families, and other participants spend the weekend. Often the individual camp sites will have been in the same family for generations, so many people in the camp have been visiting the same neighboring family at the Powwow for their entire lives. The events in the arena are one expression of the values and beliefs of the people in the camps, but the Indianness expressed in the arena activities resides in the camps, where Indian people talk with one another and create the "way they look at stuff."

After the lights have been turned out and the Drum has been put away, the arena often remains active, but there is a shift in the nature of the activity. Whereas the events on the Powwow program are carried out in a crowded bustle of activity, this new activity is carried out quietly and efficiently. In Stomp Dance, also called Busk Dance, a small fire is lit in the center of the arena once occupied by the Drum, and some women strap stout leather leggings to their lower legs. Attached to each of these leggings are twenty or more small cans (condensed milk are popular). Each can, emptied of its original contents, holds some small rocks, making a rattle. These women, called shell shakers, use these rattles to provide the musical accompaniment to the Stomp Dance. The only other activity is people milling around in small groups talking to one another. The beginning of the Stomp Dance activities also represents a shift in the symbolic universe. The eagle-feather fans, roaches, moccasins, buckskin, and gourd rattles give way to ten-gallon hats with finely beaded hatbands, fine cowboy boots, often made of exotic leather, ribbon shirts, and women's dresses that recall the nineteenth century.

The dance itself forms rapidly. Somewhere outside the ring of light cast by the fire, a silent signal triggers the dance. A line forms like a crystal near the fire behind a leader. Behind the leader is a shell shaker, behind her the next man, behind him another shell shaker, and so on, alternating woman-man to the end of the line. The leader makes a call and the line responds, the shell shakers dance the music into the night air, and the line snakes around the fire for several minutes. Then this dance is done, and the line disintegrates as rapidly as it had formed. Soon another line forms behind another leader, and the process repeats itself through the night and into the dawn.

The symbolic shift from moccasins to cowboy boots, and from Drum to fire, points to a difference in cultural origin. Most of the symbolic elements of Powwow point west to Plains peoples, and it may be that the structure of the event itself emerged from earlier tribal traditions from the plains. Stomp Dance, on the other hand, clearly points east to the Ceremonial Ground religions that characterized Native peoples in the East prior to removal. The Stomp Dance at the Powwow is, like the Powwow itself, a relatively secular event. It is a chance for people to socialize with one another as Indian people while expressing their Indian heritage. As a wider cultural phenomenon, however, it retains much if its religious character and is independent of Powwow.

Those Ceremonial Ground religions are active today, and have been active in Indian Territory/Oklahoma since the removals. Shawnee, Yuchi, Seneca, Cherokee, Creek, and Chickasaw people attend and participate in the Green Corn Dances and Bread Dances and Soup Dances and Strawberry Dances that define the various tribal cycles in Ceremonial Ground religions. Indian people not only participate in their own tribal ways but also attend the dances characteristic of their neighbors from other tribes. These major ritual cycles serve as a kind of cultural wellspring from which other realizations of Stomp Dance emerge. These range from tribally sponsored dances, such as the Miami Tribe's winter Stomp Dance, to the sometimes ad hoc dances after Powwow sessions, to small events that include only a few families. Stomp Dances are almost never advertised, so they are not nearly as well known, open, and public as Powwows, but they are nonetheless significant expressions of Indian identity.

Stomp Dance and Powwow come nowhere near making up the entirety of Indian socioreligious institutions that have roots in indigenous traditions. There are many others, but Sweat Lodge and Native American Church now draw many participants throughout the state. Both of these are as strictly religious as Ceremonial Ground practices and, as such, far less secular than the Powwow and the Stomp Dance that often follow. I drew a line earlier between the public and the private (mainly because we social scientists just like to draw these continua). On this particular continuum, the Stomp Dance is certainly not on the private extreme. Sweat Lodge may occupy a position on the line more private than even the family Stomp Dance known only to a few dozen people. Furthermore, just as Powwow and Stomp Dance use different symbolic elements, so the ceremonial Sweat Lodge introduces a third set of symbols. Here the things filled with meaning include the lodge itself, the structure, fire, stones heated in a fire, water, and nakedness. I doubt that ritual sweats can be localized in the same way as symbolic elements of Powwow and Stomp Dance, because I suspect that these ceremonies were practiced by most, if not all, of the peoples in North America prior to contact. Be that as it may, Indian people all over Oklahoma are sweating on a regular basis.

Usually Sweat Lodges are small, low structures that have a deceptively temporary look to them. They are roughly oval buildings that may be eight or ten feet wide, twelve to fifteen feet long, and no more than four feet tall. They are constructed by covering a flexible wooden frame—made of tree limbs two or three inches in diameter—with a cloth. The frame pieces are set into the ground at regular intervals (say, twelve to eighteen inches apart) and bent to the proper height on all four sides. The frame is then covered with a thick skin of heavy material like canvas or carpet. The long side of the structure is oriented along an east/west axis and an opening on the east end is covered with a flap of particularly heavy material, so that when the flap is closed, no light can enter. Inside the lodge, a pit about a foot deep and two feet in diameter is dug in the earth floor. Outside the structure, but near it, there is a hearth area where the fire is lit, and there is a cache of firewood and stones for heating in the fire.

The construction of the Sweat Lodge reminds me mostly of a tent (a flexible frame with a fabric cover), giving it a sort of impermanent quality, but that is misleading. These are not ad hoc buildings; rather they are necessarily small temples intended for long use. Some have been in regular use, often several times a week, for decades. Sweat Lodge ceremonies happen when people want them or feel they need them. They are not restricted to any particular time of day or day of the week, but the workaday world makes evenings and weekends popular times. Some traditionalists insist the Sweat Lodge is reserved for men, but this opinion does not represent the entire community. Sometimes the participants are only women, but often, maybe usually, both men and women pray together in the Sweat Lodge.

When people gather for the Sweat Lodge ceremony, a fire keeper lights the fire and begins heating the stones. Soon all who are likely to come have arrived, and the evening's participants strip to a bathing suit or less. On cold winter nights, many people at this point like to stand near the fire. Eventually the leader signals that it is time to start, and the participants enter the Lodge. Each participant stoops, almost crawling through the small opening, and says a short prayer acknowledging kinship with all, then files clockwise around the space until all the participants are seated around the perimeter of the lodge, with the leader to the west. The flap door may be closed for a first session of prayer at this point, or the leader may ask the fire keeper to bring the first round of heated rocks.

The ceremony itself proceeds inside the Lodge with rounds of prayer, testimonial, and song that the leader facilitates more than leads. When the fire keeper brings the stones to the lodge and closes the heavy flap door, the rocks glow red with heat. No matter what the outside temperature, the Lodge itself is warm from the rocks and the heat of the participants' bodies. The participants all sit cross-legged and crouched over, facing the pit in the center of the lodge, and soon they are all drenched with sweat. The leader will set the context of the sweat, pray, and encourage all to speak their hearts. Participants pray, often for help in a crisis; they give thanks for their lives; they testify to the role of the sweat in their lives. Sometimes people sing songs. They can be Christian hymns, or Peyote songs, or tribal songs, and so on. They can be sung in English, or a tribal language, or in vocables. At some points in the ceremony, the leader pours cool water on the glowing rocks. The water immediately vaporizes to steam, which quickly releases a throat-searing blast of heat as it condenses to water vapor. The fire keeper provides freshly heated stones to the pit when the leader asks, so the steam, heated stones, and participants' bodies keep the temperature high in the Lodge for the duration of the session. The ceremony can be brief—lasting only a half-hour or so—or long, going from sundown to the early hours of the morning. Sometimes the longer ceremonies are broken up into several short sessions, and sometimes they are conducted in one long session. At the end of the ceremony, the participants often stay together a little longer and share a potluck meal.

No matter what the diversity of how and when they are conducted, Sweat Lodge ceremonies are religious, and they are Indian. Unlike Powwow, which is essentially a secular event performed with religious overtones, or Stomp Dance, which is essentially a religious event that in some instances can be secular, Sweat Lodge is a religious ceremony. It has no secular component, but, curiously, it is not attached to any religion. While the use of "lodge" in the name does recall Plains traditions, and Sweat Lodges are part of larger ceremonial complexes, such as the Sun Dance, just as Stomp Dances are part of Ceremonial Ground religions, Sweat Lodge ceremonies are conducted completely independent of those traditions. Some Sweat Lodge practitioners do perform the ceremonies in a Shawnee, Cherokee, or Kiowa way, but not as part of a larger Plains or Ceremonial Ground religion, and many others make no reference to tribal origin at all. Rather than being a rite in a larger religion, or even a religion of its own, Sweat Lodge is one item on a relatively long menu of ways for Indian people to express their spirituality. Certain aspects of Powwow also fill this need, as do Stomp Dance and Native American Church, but among these, Sweat Lodge ranks high both in its intensity of spiritual experience and its accessibility.

I have been a spectator at Powwows since I was a teenager, and more recently have participated in Stomp Dances and Sweat Lodge ceremonies, but I have never attended a Native American Church meeting. While there are deep cultural traditions in North America for the sacramental use of peyote, Peyotism in the form of Native American Church emerged in southwest Oklahoma on the Comanche, Kiowa, and Apache Reservation in the late nineteenth and early twentieth centuries (Stewart 1987). Peyote itself, which members of Native American Church refer to as "medicine" or "the sacrament," grows on only a few places, and most comes from the peyote gardens of southern Texas (Swan 1999: 8). Of the two major types of Native American Church ceremonies, the most widespread is the "Little Moon" (referring to the ceremonial altar) or "Tepee

Way," and the other is the "Big Moon" or "Roundhouse" variety. The ceremonies are conducted by a "roadman," who conducts the ceremony, a "drum chief," a "cedar chief," one or two "firemen," and a "morning water woman." Little Moon rites take place in a tepee, whereas Big Moon meetings are held in permanent structures. Participants in the meeting pray with ritual tobacco, song, and sacramental peyote (23–25).

What strikes me in all of this, is that Powwow, Stomp Dance, Sweat Lodge, and Native American Church share the ground in common. A few Powwows, like Red Earth in Oklahoma City each summer, are held in large arenas or convention centers, but most are held deep in rural Oklahoma, where the dance arena is earth, not concrete. The same is true of Stomp Dance and the rites of the Ceremonial Ground religion from which it emerged. Native American Church meetings are held in tepees, and the participants sit on the ground. This may be a mere accident. It may be a consequence of the material conditions, that is, they are rural phenomena performed in rural conditions close to the earth. This would ignore the large portion of Oklahoma Indian people who live and work in the state's cities, and the expense and trouble these people go through to participate. Direct contact with earth is, of course, one of the central symbols of Sweat Lodge, and sometimes leaders talk about that in their prayers. The place where a Stomp Dance is held is called the Stomp Grounds, making earth a part of the name, and many participants view indoor Stomp Dances as less than valid.

They are also all performed in a circle. The dancers in a Powwow dance around the arena in a circle, and the Drum itself is the center of the circle of singers who sit around it on folding chairs. The Stomp Dancers dance around the fire, and participants sit around the perimeter of the Sweat Lodge and the tepee. It seems to me that the performance of these events on the ground and in a circle is in stark contrast to Christianity, where services are usually held in a church building (with a floor), and in a line, with the minister facing the congregation. The very performance serves the symbolic function of separating them from the white world, putting them into a class of Indian things. Chris articulated that clearly one day when we were talking about what being an Indian person meant to her, and she quickly got to the difference between how she and her parents approach being Indian. "My parents taught me some spiritual things, but as far as dancing, singing, any of those culturally identifiable things, I do that. My parents don't, they come occasionally but generally do not participate." I broke in at this point to ask if dancing referred to the Powwow circuit, and she replied: "Powwows, sweats, Native American Church meetings. My father has been in the meeting with me, but they generally don't . . . they are very supportive of me, but they don't do that stuff, I do that stuff." A few days later we were talking about the significance people put on their family's allotment, and she said:

> Some of those places still have, like for Osages some of them have origi-nal fireplaces for the Native American Church. I think culturally and personally those kinds of places can be very important. For some people that was an old home place that they have been coming to since they were a child or they were raised there and maybe raised their kids and their grandkids there. Just like with anyone who had an old home or house that has been in the family for generations, I think it's important in similar ways, but a lot of them establish a summer kitchen. Maybe they have Stomp Dances out there, maybe they have Native Ameri-can Church meetings or sweat, and for that reason those places may be important.

To Chris, at least part of being Indian is dancing in Powwows and participating in Native American Church meetings and Sweat Lodge cer-emonies. Along with that, Stomp Dances and Native American Church meetings on ancestral land provide that land with Indian significance. Chris is not alone in connecting Sweat Lodge, Powwow, Native Ameri-can Church, and Stomp Dance as culturally identifiable Indian things to do. That is the common understanding of these rites throughout the state, and that understanding is reinforced through the use of common symbolic elements. These elements include not only background simi-larities in performance but also a common history of emerging from local indigenous cultures rather than Euro-American ways. Two of this quartet, Stomp Dance and Native American Church, provide people with the opportunity to participate in an explicitly religious community, just as the various Indian congregations do for Christian Indians. And just as Indian communities form around these Christian congregations, they do so in these Indian religions.

## Ceremonial Ground

The social Stomp Dances at the end of an evening's Powwow events and the tribally sponsored winter indoor Stomp Dances are an easily accessible but relatively small aspect of Ceremonial Ground religions. These religions have their cultural origins among both northern and southeastern Woodlands peoples who were removed to Indian Territory. These religions are by no means monolithic, and tribal traditions con-tinue to be important aspects of their practice. These variants, however, are as related to one another as Baptists are to Methodists. The religions are characterized by an annual cycle of dances, sometimes referred to collectively as Green Corn Dance. These major festivals happen over several days and include communal meals, ritual games, and various dances, including those Stomp Dances in the wee hours of Powwow mornings. Communities participate in long traditions of ritual exchange where neighboring or otherwise related communities, often across tribal lines, attend one another's celebrations.

Fire occupies a central point in Stomp Dance symbolism that emanates from its Ceremonial Ground significance. The fire is the focal point of Stomp Dances, and leaders often seem to play with the fire with their bare hands. People use the fire as the focus of prayer, and they talk about the significance of particular fires. For example, it is not unusual to hear about the genealogies of different fires—for example, that such-and-such a fire was lit from another fire—or for people to mention that the fire at this Stomp Ground or that was carried by slow match over the trail of tears and kept lit since then. For example, Mose Wiley (Muskogee) talked about the "Sacred Fire of Okchiye Town" to Indian Pioneer project fieldworker Grace Kelley, and said:

> When they were getting ready to leave that country they selected two men to take care of the fire. Each of them took a burning piece of wood from the fire and each was to keep this piece of fire from going out on the journey. When they made a camp these men made a new fire from the burning wood they carried. When they broke camp they took two other pieces of burning wood and brought it on with them. When they got to this country they selected land for a new town or Stomp Ground. This was sandy land and these men dug a hole in the ground with their hands until the top of the ground came to their shoulders with the tips of their fingers on the bottom of the hole. Then they brought the fire and put it into the hole and added fuel to it. They kept a fire there a long time but it was finally put out and they have to rebuild a fire when they have a meeting there. (Wiley 1938: 18)

Sammie Narharkey picked up the same theme with an added twist about the genealogy of fires. He told the Indian Pioneer project fieldworker Reuben Partridge about a speech delivered by Eufaula Harjo, medicine man for the Lugaboga-Talasi, during the time that they held their Stomp Dances in Tulsa. In the speech, Eufaula Harjo is reported to have said that the Lugaboga-Talasi fire,

> which was brought from Alabama and never allowed to die out, was for their worship: That, 'the mountains and hills, that you see, are your backbone, and the gullies and the creeks, which are between the hills and mountains, are your heart veins. If your children do not obey their

parents, you must whip them with Pe-nos-lo-wa-ke (hickory limb).' The Lugaboga-Talasi fire in Tulsa is now gone, but fire was taken from it and moved to two other places, namely, Talasi Canadian Town and Little River Talasi town in Hughes and Seminole counties, respectively. (Narharkey 1938: 97)

Inside these stories, which can still be heard today, is an element of resistance that says, "Beginning with the removals, no matter what hardships were put in our way, we endured." The Ceremonial Ground symbolizes that endurance, and the fire becomes a metaphor for an Indian community that has persisted through time. This community can spread from Lugaboga-Talasi Town to Talasi Canadian Town and Little River Talasi Town, and even if the fire goes out, it can be rekindled. For Creek people, the Stomp, Busk, Grounds, and Town are the same thing and represent the focus of their social organizations, the seat of the political organization, and even regulated marriage. Like any human group, the Stomp Grounds/town adapts to the local social and physical environment. One mode of this adaptation is the fission described in Eufaula Harjo's speech. Another is the fusion that Nafa Butcher described in an Indian Pioneer project interview conducted by Billie Byrd:

> The members of the Okfuskee, Nuyaka, and Arbeka, northeastern part of present Okfuskee County, use[d] to be separate towns with their own separate chiefs (mekkos) with their own separate busk grounds. It has been some time since the Okfuskee and Arhbeka towns (tulwas) joined with the Nuyaka town (tulwas) which was a well organized and strong town with a lot of members. There were so few members in the Okfuskee and Arbeka towns.
> The Okfuskee town (tulwa) decided to reorganize and reestablish their own busk grounds and was started in 1936. Bunner Hicks has been selected as town chief (tulwa mekko) with Sparney Harjo as the town medicine man. (Butcher 1938: 71)

The depth to which religion is integrated into other aspects of culture, such as political and social organization, and the degree to which people adapt religious institutions to environmental changes both measure the significance of the religion in people's lives. Other good measures include the resources that people devote to the practice of the religion and the degree to which the material culture of the religion is considered sacred. If time is one of the resources that measure the significance of Ceremonial Ground religion to Indian people, the interview Ida Mae Hughes gave to the Indian Pioneer project indicates something of the importance of the Green Corn cycle to the Cherokee people in her community in the late nineteenth century:

When I was a girl I attended the dances at the old Stomp Ground between Lines and Bunch, in what is now Adair County, Oklahoma. It was called old Beaver Stomp Ground. The Indians would meet every year and sometimes three times a year, but mostly in August when corn was ripe. They had a Green Corn Dance, Stomp Dance, Stick Dances and several other kinds. They would stay sometimes ten days or more. (Hughes 1938: 220)

The investment of significant resources to the practice of Ceremonial Ground was not limited to Cherokee people. March Monday, a Creek man, was in his late fifties when he described the Green Corn Dance in an Indian Pioneer project interview. He is more specific about the "three times a year" that Ida Mae Hughes mentions, and he paints a picture of a complex ritual life that required significant investments of time and other resources.

July was usually the month for the Green Corn Dance. A Ribbon dance was held in the afternoon. They danced around in a 20 foot circle, to the accompanimentof four male singers. After the Ribbon dance, an Indian ball game was held between the men and women. The men used sticks and the women their hands. 20 points is the score limit. After supper, from 9:00 to 12:00 a midnight dance is held. The dancers then retire for the night. The women and children who are to take part in the Green corn dance take medicine prepared by an Indian Doctor.

The next morning, the men take their medicine. In the afternoon, the men have a feather dance. The feathers are obtained from cranes, called by the Indians "white birds."

They dance four sets with rests between. Then they dance four sets of real Indian Stomp Dance. This last dance is open to the public. At 5:00 P.M., they have the Buffalo dance. When this is over all get ready for supper.

At 9–10 P.M., they start in and dance until daylight. This dance is also open to the public. Before the meeting breaks up, arrangements are made for the next dances to be held.

The close of the season of Stomp Dances is marked by a squirrel hunt. A certain two days are designated for this event and [it] usually begins on Sunday. They have a rite known as "feeding the fireplace." Some of the squirrel soup is buried in a hole dug with a shovel or other instrument and which can't be touched with the hands. The men eat under an arbor and the women about 15 feet away on the ground. This squirrel hunt and feast is generally held in October. In May, they have a spring squirrel hunt to open the season for the Green Corn dance.

During the Stomp Dance, they have a Chief (Cussetah-Mecco) and have an Assistant Chief (Henneha). These are the directors of the dance.

The medicine for the Green Corn dance is made from the Red Root. The Chief appoints four men to obtain four large bundles of this root.

They are not allowed to wash, to drink or eat anything, until these roots are brought back and buried at the edge of the Stomp Grounds.

Formerly, they went on horseback, but in recent years they take care. It is not unusual for the men appointed to go 30 or 40 miles to get this root for the medicine.

They are allowed, however, the use of tobacco while on this mission.

The women usually aid the tom-tom by wearing tortoise shells, filled with pebbles, tied to their legs with leather thongs. The children's shells will consist of four for each leg while the women's will be maybe eight or ten. (Monday 1938: 80–82)

Here March Monday describes not only the Green Corn Dance itself but also a cycle of rituals into which it fits. These major events of the cycle mark important points during the year and take several days to complete. The participants in the Green Corn Dance share meals, dance, play ceremonial games, and take a sacramental medicine. He also mentions some of the ritual hierarchy of the community: the chief, assistant chief, and the four men who retrieve the red root for the medicine. Finally he talks a little about some of the ritual restrictions that apply in the religions, and a little of the sacred material culture in the cycle. I think there is also an interesting distribution of meaning in the passage. "Green Corn" refers not only to the dance in July but also to the entire cycle. And March Monday's identification of the chief and assistant chief as officials of the "Stomp Dance" attaches Stomp Dance to Green Corn with either widely overlapping meaning—that is, Stomp Dance and Green Corn mean much the same thing—or in a part-whole relationship—that is, Stomp Dance is part of Green Corn; or both. About thirty years later, Mandy Turkey Harjo Greenback, who had previously been married to a Seminole man, picked up some of the same meaning structures and themes. Velma Neiberding conducted the Doris Duke project interview and asked about doctoring the shells that shell shakers wear. Mandy Turkey Harjo Greenback replied:

Well, the way the Seminoles doctor their shells, they have their dance in the spring and they—the one that makes the shells, has to shake them before anyone else can shake 'em. They go to the Stomp Ground where they have four different arbors for the different clans that, are in these—stays in these arbors. And they have four leaders of men. And they scratch the womens legs with the—a piece of glass or a needle or something that makes 'em bleed. Then they have this medicine made of a different herbs that they use to wash their legs with and they also pour this medicine on to the shells. And they've got to shake 'em in this

Buffalo Dance first that they have that—the dance is a lot different from what we dance our Buffalo Dance around here. (Greenback 1972: 1)

Velma Neiberding asked if the turtle shells were real, and Mandy Turkey Harjo Greenback went on:

> Yes, that's the real shell—well, they doctor their cans too, but the real turtle shell they really are strict. And you are not supposed to loan them to anyone or no one is supposed to shake 'em at what we always say, you know, during the change of the moon—what we call. And they are not supposed to even handle 'em at that time. . . .
>
> The one that owns them doesn't handle them at that time. And they're supposed to put 'em out and sun 'em ever so often. And you are not supposed to play with them. Or you can't let anyone play with them, because if you do it will cause a storm or something. But they are not supposed to be played with anytime. (Greenback 1972: 1–2)

Mandy Turkey Harjo Greenback's description of how Seminole shell shakers introduce new shells to the dance reiterates March Monday's equation of Stomp Dance to the Ceremonial Ground. It also points to the sacred nature of Ceremonial Ground activities. To use these shells in the Stomp Ground, not only must the shell shaker participate in an arduous ceremony but also she must be sure to care for the shells in a ritually appropriate way. This points to a life commitment to the Ceremonial Grounds that extends from social dances after Powwow events to important annual celebrations. One time I asked Lee about that continuum, and he pointed to some of the moving Ceremonial Ground experiences he had had:

> In our area where we are, right here, after a Powwow it is a social gathering, a fun thing, it's easy for people to do, they don't require an elaborate costume, but the other part of it where you talk about the Creek, Seminoles. Yuchis, Cherokees, people that do it as a ceremonial, now that's a whole 'nother deal. The Cherokees they do it down at . . . where they brought that fire all the way from Cherokee, North Carolina, on the trail of tears, all the way back down here to Oklahoma. There's a fire they built in Cherokee, North Carolina, and brought here and it's never gone out.

To Lee even that fun social gathering Stomp Dance after the Powwow makes reference to the sacred fire in the Ceremonial Ground, and thus participates in its sacred nature. So at some level, all Stomp Dances are ritual expressions, and must be performed in accordance to ritual guidelines. For Stomp Dance those guidelines define not only the when and where of the Dance but also the proper attitude of the participants. Lee put it this way:

> In Stomp Dance there are certain rules. . . . People think about a leader and shell shaker then a follower, then a shell shaker, boy-girl-boy-girl. As far as those shell shakers go its boy, girl, boy, girl et cetera, and then after that it can be pretty much how they want to get in, they say that first seven should be boy-girl-boy-girl. If somebody from their own ground starts to lead after that seventh man, a visitor can get in, they go counterclockwise when they Stomp Dance.
>
> It's a common practice at night, but you don't Stomp Dance during the day. Them Shawnees believe you don't Stomp Dance indoors in the winter time or you are going to bring a bad winter upon you. There's a lot of little things each little tribe has that has a ceremonial part of it, but you kind of know where you're at, what's your doing.
>
> You go to any of these Ceremonial Grounds, they don't allow drinking. If I went and my wife went and we were arguing, we would be asked to leave. You don't bring that there, you don't start that stuff there. If you were drinking you would be asked to leave, if you cause a big fuss or get excited, you will be asked to leave. That's as plain and simple as it gets and everyone knows it.

The overall image of Stomp Dance that emerges from these passages is one of a ritual life that has carried deep significance for many Indian people in Indian Territory and Oklahoma up to today. People from the 1930s to the present talk about how the Ceremonial Ground's sacred fire coming from the East over the trails of tears symbolically connects the people of today with the founding ancestors. The Ceremonial Ground religions provide people with a community and help them organize themselves socially and politically. They provide meaningful social interaction in many formal and informal Indian contexts. Within these structural features, however, Stomp Dance never loses its connection to the sacred. As Lee said, after a long session of trying to get me to understand, "The question I use to ask as a young man was 'How come we Stomp Dance, how come we stay up all night?' The way it was told to me was, 'We didn't use to Stomp Dance, we use to stay up all night and talk about how we wanted things, we prayed, that made it hard, long . . . so the Stomp Dance made it fill in a little bit and let us pray in another way.'"

## Moon of Earth

To Lee, Indian people Stomp Dance as a way to pray, even when the dance is a social gathering after a day of Powwow. The social Stomp Dance at the Powwow is interesting because it establishes a place where the eastern symbolic complex of fire, shell shaker, and leader come into direct contact with Western traditions that emphasize the drum and the eagle feather. The symbolic overlap of the social Stomp Dance and Ceremonial Ground religions, along with that between Powwow and Native American Church, thus connects the Ceremonial Ground to Native American Church in the social Stomp Dance. As ways to pray, Ceremonial Ground religions also stand beside Native American Church in terms of their connections to tribal traditions and their use in expressions of Indian identity. This west-east symbolic distinction does not, however, refer to practice. Many members of Western tribes in the western part of Oklahoma Stomp Dance on a regular basis, and Native American Church meetings are common occurrences among descendants of those who were removed to Indian Territory in the nineteenth century. Jacob Rolland's 1938 description of Native American Church among the Creek speaks to both the wide distribution of its practice and the depth of its tradition in time.

> Indians here in the Creek Nation, and many other Indians in many other nations, have what is known as a Peyote religious worship. It is called the Union Native American Church. This religious worship was handed down to the Euchees here by the Caddo Indians. This Indian church is put up by the Indians. They worship God, our Creator, in a teepee. They put up 21 poles and put up a canvas tent over the poles and they have their church house built. When they have finished putting up the teepee, they build a moon out of dirt for an altar. They cut wood to burn in the dirt moon in order to keep light and warmth in the teepee.
>
> They worship and pray all night in the teepee. They have a man to conduct the Peyote religious meeting. The Peyote is an Indian herb that has been in use for many years.
>
> Apaches were the first ones to find this herb. Lots of people call this Peyote the bitter herb.
>
> The Indians use this herb for many kinds of sicknesses. It will also teach a person more about the good ways of God. (Rolland 1938b: 17–18)

This documents that in the first third of the twentieth century, Creek people were conducting Native American Church meetings in the heart of Ceremonial Ground territory. Jacob Rolland mentions many of the central symbolic elements on Native American Church, like the tepee, the fire, the altar, and the sacramental use of peyote. All the symbolic references aside, however, his main point is that Native American Church is an Indian church. He says that the Creek and "many other Indians in many other nations" have the religion. His history of the church mentions only Indian people—the Yuchi got the religion from the Caddo—and asserts that Indian people both define and build the church. That theme also comes clear in stories about how the religion came to Indian people. There are many versions of the story, but most include someone who is lost; experiencing hunger, thirst, and spiritual stress; and finds comfort through peyote personified (Swan 1999: 23), as does the version Jess Rowlodge told to Julia Jordan in a Doris Duke project interview. She asked him if he had heard how Indian people got the Peyote religion. He replied:

> Yes, through the Apaches I think that story has been concurred with by the Comanches. But the others might have different experience, but this one that concurred with the Arapaho and Apache way was that there were Apaches and Comanches and Arapahos and Cheyennes up around Texas country way back in the early days—southwest Texas. And down—raiding the, country, you know, in them days. And they said one man got lost. All right. He had to cross a lake or pond, and on each side was a dangerous spot to go through. So one night he stayed in the brush and then he swim across that night. He got across and he got safe and then he looked for his friends. Three or four days he looked on the hills and objects—course, they didn't have no telescopes—and early in the morning he'd get up on a high hill and look down and see where some Indians might be cooking breakfast—if he could see smoke. And sometimes he'd flare a looking glass—that's indication of signal, you know—for others to notice. Wouldn't be no answer coming. Well, one day he got probably somewhere south of San Antonio—somewhere in there. And he was alone. So he got pretty hungry. He had run out of food, and couldn't find no game to kill to eat. So one morning he went to bed. Went to sleep. He had his robe. And he slept that night and he dreamed that somebody came to him and says, "You been hungry. You haven't tried to find out what you can eat. Right ahead of you there's a green root—a green herb. When you wake up, you turn around and you're gonna see a bunch of it. Pull up one of those. It don't taste too good, but you're gonna eat that. Then forget your hungriness and your tiredness and your fear and your pain. It's got lot of juice in it, you could just sap it." So, sure enough, he woke up in the morning, looked around there and found some peyote growing right ahead of him, blooming. He said, "Maybe that's it." So he turned around and crawled over there and started—took his arrow spike and dug around there and pulled it out and started chewing on it. From that button. He kept chewing and pretty, soon a lot of saliva came to his mouth, and pretty soon that herb—the meat part of it—he said eat it. And he took that soft cotton fuzz off and all that and then he chew it and eat it. (Rowlodge 1972b: 19–20)

The miracle at the core of this story is a man's encounter with a spirit in a dream. Through that encounter, the spirit gives peyote and saves the man's life. The man is alone because he was separated from his three companions on a raiding party. The members of the raiding party represent four tribes—Apache, Kiowa, Arapaho, and Cheyenne—but Jess Rowlodge leaves the tribal identity of the man who encountered the spirit unspecified. This origin story, like the history Jacob Rolland told in the passage quoted earlier, is exclusively Indian. As a raiding party, it is a group, thus constructing a political boundary between the four tribes and the enemy. That group identity is reinforced when the peyote-bringer's tribe is not identified. Also like Jacob Rolland's history, this origin story is multitribal: Jacob mentions Creek, Yuchi, and Caddo, where Jess Rowlodge talks about the four tribes in the raiding party. Put another way, Euro-Americans have no part of this, but many tribes do. A lot of tribes are evident not only in talk about the origin and transmission of Native American Church but also in talk about the practice of the religion. Fred Bigman spoke to this issue in his Doris Duke project interview conducted by William Bittle. Bittle asked if he had ever been to one of the Native American Church meetings that they have in a building, and Fred Bigman replied:

> Round house, they call it. Yea, I went in there. One place . . . Osage, Osage man. Not a man, she's a woman. But her husband, he's a Omaha. His name is Fred Walker. They got a round house. I went up there one time, they got a double row (i.e. of participants). So many in the front, and so many in the back. I didn't like that. And they don't conduct the meeting like we do around here. They got it altogether different Nobody smoked in there, but he himself, the man who's conducting from the start. Only he makes smoke, cigarette, himself. The rest of us, we just sit there. And he goes to make that tobacco and prays. When he gets through we take that medicine and then the meetings starts, from right there. Close to that door, then when he goes the other way there's a man at gets up. One of the fireman [*sic*]. He goes drum for each man in the row, for all until he comes back to the door. When he gets back down there, and this next fireman, he gets up goes back. Same way, goes plumb around. . . .
> He drums for them, drums for them all around. And the third man, last man, he goes he does the same thing. He drums for each man, plumb around, It be about morning then. That's the way they conduct their meetings. I see that and after they get through in the morning well he say well alright, you boys go ahead and smoke now. Then we go ahead and smoke. Oh, you see them guys pull our their tailor mades (cigarettes). (Bigman 1972: 18–19)

Of course, the common theme that runs through Fred Bigman's narrative is the ever-present tension between structure and community. He critiques putting the participants in two rows (instead of one?), giving the roadman an exclusive role in tobacco offerings, and a similar monopoly held by the firemen. More interesting, to my mind anyway, is that these differences are constructed in tribal terms. Behind this passage is a phantom comparison between Osage (Omaha?) ways and the Apache ways that Fred Bigman grew up with. Similar distinctions among Christians, on the other hand, are normally constructed on theological grounds (i.e., Baptists versus Presbyterians). Fred Bigman went on to finish his description of Round House meetings with a few words about morning breakfast and adds that the Osage "claim they got this way from Moonhead, they call him. He might be a Caddo or something. He gave those ways to the Osage" (Bigman 1972: 19). A little later, he continues the theme of tribal variation when he brings Caddo ways into the conversation.

> We all smoke, but the Osage don't. The (Caddo) man that conduct it he take the tobacco and the rest smoke. The man that conducts that, he does the praying. Then when he gets through he puts his tobacco down and we put ours down too. Then we go ahead and use that medicine. But they always have water, setting inside all night . . . the Caddoes and the man that tends the fire he telling you how to go. He says well anytime you boys want water you ask the fireman. He give you a drink. So they had it there, all the time all night long, that water. In the morning those boys get fresh water. And they all go out in the morning they go out and wash, outside. Wash up. Everybody get through washing we march back into tipi. Then our breakfast comes in. For our breakfast we get a blessing from somebody . . . thanks for our breakfast So when we get there we go ahead and eat. Just like . . . we got ways like Osages about eating in the morning. Just like the water and things like that. From that meat, they got candy, just like Osages, and cookies and just like I tell you Hi-Hos. That what they do them Caddoes. But everybody smoke. They say anybody want a smoke during the night, maybe some of us got the habit smoking plenty tobacco here, or if somebody want to go ahead take this tobacco and pray it's alright that away. (Bigman 1972: 19)

Fred Bigman recognizes differences in the practice of Peyote religion and constructs those differences along tribal lines, much the way he and others construct the history of the religion and its spiritual origins. Some of the differences were, however, remarkably idiosyncratic, such as having women conduct meetings. Native American Church has a reputation around the state for adhering to a strict division of the ritual labor by gender, and assigning men the central roles in the meetings, so women who directly or indirectly take these men's roles are worthy of notice. Perhaps that is why Jess Rowlodge brought up such women in a Doris Duke project interview. He was talking about older forms of the Peyote meeting when he brought up an Arapaho woman named Crooked Foot: "We had one Arapaho woman that run her own meeting—her husband always run the meeting for her, but that was her form—Arapaho way. . . . And she was a jeweler, too—she was a silversmith. Long Hair's wife. Her name was Crooked Foot. She had her own way. She learned it her own self. She was Arapaho, yes. And she was a silversmith and was a good beader, too" (Rowlodge 1972b: 6).

The interviewer, Julia Jordan, picked up on this topic and asked where Crooked Foot had learned "her peyote way." Jess Rowlodge replied:

> The early Apaches and the Arapahoes. She start her own form. Made her own songs, and all that ritual inside was her own conduction, you know—conducted way. But she always let her man run it. She'd sit by him. She had a pad—when the water woman comes in—I saw that twice—when the water woman come in in the morning, she always carries her own pad, whether it's hers or some, other woman that carried water for the particular meeting. This pad was about that square. Black on one side and white on the other. And it had designs there—don't remember what those designs were—I think one of them was design of peyote. But anyhow, before she sat down, when she put her bucket down and she step back and throw that pad down and she'd turn every corner over—made a cross—white cross. You know what I mean? Like, if this is the white side and the other side—she'd turn this over like that and she'd turn this over like that and she'd turn this over like that and she'd turn this over and that made a cross. She set on it. See the form? (Jess is demonstrating with a piece of paper.) And then, of course she sat down and took care of the rest of it. She'd offer prayer and smoke herself and she'd hold out her cigarette like that and the fireman would get up and come by and get that cigarette and take it to the chief. And she, of course, would offer a prayer, and he give it to his drummer to offer a prayer and his cedarman would offer a prayer. And he give it back to the chief and he'd get up and put that smoke in front of—in ash part of the moon. I said I didn't notice that. Well, she knew all what she was doing, all the way through. (Rowlodge 1972b: 6–7)

It seems to me that while Crooked Foot may have been remarkably aggressive in Peyote meetings, the forms of meetings she directed her husband to conduct were not very much different from others. They still had all the main elements, like the prayer offerings of tobacco, and personnel like the cedar man, the firemen, and the water woman. So this particular variation in the practice of the religion came more from the fact that Crooked Foot was a woman, and not because she made the practice of Native American Church any less Indian. In fact, what emerges from all this is a kind of tribal Indianness, in which the connection to a tribe provides an Indian with legitimacy in Native American Church. The diffusion of the religion is always constructed along tribal terms, one tribe gets it from another tribe, and the chain never involves non-Indians. The same is true of stories that portray the religion's spiritual origins, even to the understanding of variation in the practice of the religion. Sometimes people make this Indianness of Native American Church explicit when they talk about it. In one such case, Fred Bigman was talking about his experience with a man who came to meetings after drinking alcohol.

> Yea, first time I seen that Shawnee guy come in like he did, he sit down, they give him smoke, he make tobacco and they light it for him, They had tea made, and he drink that tea, boy he drink a lot of it. He take medicine and he eat it. Next morning when we quit, he couldn't go over to dinner. It effect him you know, next day after we quit. . . .
> I brought it out next day to that Osage guy down there, southwest of Shawnee town. He married a Shawnee I said I seen that guy come drunk twice now, I said, I don't think it's right for him to come in like that. That belongs to the Indians, peyote Church, I said that's our church. For him to come in like that I said, for my part, I don't know what we can do if he's like that, but I don't use it and I don't go in like that I said. Cause I go in there to worship I said I don't go in there just to make a plaything out of it. That's my church. That Osage he say, you right, you right every bit. (Bigman 1972: 13)

To Fred Bigman, Native American Church "belongs to the Indians," so he believes that people should not attend meetings after drinking. And he makes it fairly explicit that he thinks being drunk at the meeting desecrates its Indianness. In another way, however, Fred Bigman is also trying to repair and strengthen the boundary between white and Indian here. The drunken Indian was in 1970 (as it was long before Fred Bigman's interview, and still is now) one of the negative stereotypes that Indian people were forced to suffer. Any drunk Indian only reinforced that stereotype, and a drunk Indian at a Peyote church meeting can only add sacrilege to the ethnic insult, so he resists that image. That boundary between white and Indian does not, of course, separate parallel ethnic groups. The relationship is, in fact, grossly out of balance, with white ethnicity dominating control of almost all formal and informal cultural institutions. It should come as no surprise, therefore, that the dominating society sometimes tries to restrict the practice of Native American Church through legislative and legal channels. In the late 1960s, the

Oklahoma legislature was considering such laws, and it is in this context that Pete Birdchief talked about his experience in the Peyote Way:

> Dad use peyote. I use it. And you can see what kind of a man—You can go down there to any bank—and I'm not bragging. I wish white man would leave us alone, treat us a little more decent about this peyote. It's used—I use it when I need it for medical purposes. That's the only time I use it. I don't use every day, no other time. No. Just when I need it. I use it when I am at home. I wish white man would give us a break and leave us alone. That's our church—Where we go. That's how we worship. We worship all night. Pray to Almighty. Like the war, we hope it would stop. We pray. (Birdchief 1972: 3)

The boundaries are clear to Pete Birdchief, as is the distribution of power between white and Indian ethnic groups. Native American Church serves as an important boundary symbol, partly because it has drawn so much attention in the white world. This attention from the white world notwithstanding, however, the religion would have little significance were it not for its deep traditions and widespread practice. While its symbolic sensibilities clearly emerged from Plains cultural traditions, it has appeal among Indian people who come from other, mostly eastern, cultural traditions in Oklahoma. It shares this feature with other roles it plays in Indian communities and in the lives of Indian people.

## Indian Religion

Native American Church, and its close relative, Powwow, as well as Ceremonial Ground religions and the social Stomp Dance that emanates from them, are as institutionally Indian as the Methodist Church is European. Everything about them, from their concepts of the spiritual world to the performance of their rituals, emerges from Indian constructions of reality. Even in those places, especially in Native American Church, where elements of Christianity have been brought into the belief structure or ritual, these Christian elements are expressions of Indianness, because those elements have been fully incorporated into the religions and in that process have been transformed into Indian. This contrast between the Indian and the non-Indian is necessary for Indian ethnicity, and it is evident in the way Indian people talk about these religions and religious expressions. Lee encapsulated these salient features late one evening in his home with his son sitting at his side:

> This reporter came down here one time and was asking this old Indian man and I was sitting close so I was listening. Said 'Why do you Stomp

Dance, why do you dance, why do you have Powwows, why do you do these things?' That old man didn't hesitate, he said, 'It's just like it was a hundred years ago when we come together as family, as friends, and eat and enjoy ourselves and dance and have a good time, we are not just honoring ourselves, but our creator.' I thought it made good sense, because we eat there, we visit, we talk about old things, how we would like to see new things come about, different changes from when the old folks were here and the way it is now, and how to keep this thing going, how to train our young kids, how to teach them.

I was really impressed by that, it made good sense to me. Stomp Dance, it happens all over Oklahoma. Again the Creeks, the Yuchis, the Cherokee, the Shawnee, all the different band of Shawnees and there are Stomp Grounds all over, everyone is aware of these.

Lee went on to talk about the pleasures of the social dances and the more serious Ceremonial Ground rituals, but he soon brought up some of the discomforts. He mentioned staying up all night for Stomp Dance and Native American Church meetings, and the hardships some of the rites require of their participants. He concluded with this comparison with Christianity:

I'm often asked why is the Indian way have to be so hard and tough like that? I wish a hundred times or more that I could go sit in church for an hour where it's clean and warm and cool and a nice suit of clothes and go home and feel like I'm done, I feel good, but it's not that way. That's the way these Indian people view their religion, you pay a price, you sacrifice a little bit of something. That's what that ceremony is all about, your paying that price, you sacrifice a little bit to be out there, to take part of it.

Lee is certainly not alone in his choice of religious expression. Many Indian people in Oklahoma elect to relate to the spiritual world through these, and other, totally Indian institutions. While Lee is not unique, other Indian people choose other alternatives. Many choose Indian Christian churches, others opt for regular mixed-race congregations and express their Indianness through Powwow or in other ways, and many do all, including Native American Church and Ceremonial Ground rites. These people are Indian not on the basis of the alternative they select but because they construct their lives on the basis of maintaining their Indian identities. They understand their histories from an Indian point of view, and they dispute white characterizations of the removals, the confinement to reservations, allotment, boarding schools, and blood quanta. They make extra efforts to participate in Indian communities, speak tribal languages, and symbolically display Indian identity in many ways, including how they style their hair, the clothing they wear, and the art that decorates their homes. Lee made clear that he understands this process of being Indian by living Indian in the quotation that begins this chapter, and he further understands that this process has not merely kept Indians alive, it has made Indianness flourish.

# 8  The End of the Trail

Now Jesus tells me, and I believe that it's true
The red man is in the sunset, too
We ripped off his land, and we won't give it back
And we sent Geronimo a Cadillac

—Michael Martin Murphy and Charles John Quarto,
  "Geronimo's Cadillac," as performed by the Lost
  Gonzo Band

It was early May, and it was clear to me that this experience in Oklahoma would soon be over. A strike of airline employees made getting back and forth between Oklahoma and Ohio difficult; consequently, I had not been able to spend time at home since winter, and I missed my family. Even if the attractions of home did not lure me out of the field, job obligations would soon force me back to my everyday life on faculty. These thoughts were on my mind as I drove from Norman to take four follow-up interviews in a big swing across the state. It was a beautiful day, with a clear blue sky, a mild temperature, and a light breeze. The leaves were fully out on the trees, and flowers were in bloom. Pat was first on my list, and I got to his house at about nine in the morning. Our conversation began with morning pleasantries, hot black coffee, a lot of fiddling with taping equipment (if that is what you want to call my thirty-nine-dollar cassette recorder), but soon Pat was talking about who he is by relating his significant experiences. These included life with kin on distant western and northern reservations, but quickly came to the path that brought him to a career as a health-care provider and the influence his grandmother had in defining the direction of that path. He said:

Getting into this medicine had kindled what she had been teaching us and I am incorporating a lot of what she taught. A lot of it was body work, hand work, manipulation of muscle and tissue, and then a lot of the herbal medicine. I started studying more and more into that. I also became more involved in my tribe's religion, and that's where she got her training, and consequently I ended up going deeper and deeper and deeper into it to the point that now I am a tribal priest. So that was part of our heritage and part of our life. Through this whole process of going back there and then looking forward I have come to a lot of conclusions, mostly my conclusions on my part. And so that's what guides me forward.

There's an old painting called "The End of the Trail." I used to look at that, and everywhere I go I'd see it, and people had it in their homes, and I would always think about it and couldn't figure out what it was about it that bothered me. It wasn't until a few years later that it hit me . . . end of what trail?

*The End of the Trail*, by James Earle Fraser. National Cowboy and Western Heritage Museum, Oklahoma City. Photo by the author.

I really thought about that, and I thought—there's no end of the trail here. My ancestors sacrificed just so we could still be here. They had rough times and times that they had to go through the same thing we're going through. They hunted and had to protect their families and go all through this. We are going through the same thing. We have to work to take care of our families and kids. There are things that we have to do and sacrifices we have to make in order to keep the lineage going. So that's why I dislike that "End of the Trail." I always tell people that, "I can't stand that thing." It's just not true, it's a big lie, and unfortunately around Indian country people still believe that. It's like they are in a perpetual state of mourning.

It was another of those moments when a nagging, ill-formed idea crystallizes. Like Leslie earlier with her story of how Oklahomas go either way, Pat's critique of the message in the popular painting synthesized an emerging understanding of my experiences in the field. The painting, and the 1894 James Earle Fraser sculpture it is taken from, expresses a popular view of Indians as vanishing race. My experience, on the other hand, with the people I was talking to, with community functions like Powwows I was attending, and the Indian Pioneer and Doris Duke interviews I was reading, pointed to growing, extensive, and strong Indian communities rooted in tradition but transcending tribal boundaries. In other words, the boundaries that contain these communities are not so much between Kiowas and Modocs as between Indians and whites, and are the symbolic expressions of historic, political, and cultural forces. All these sources clearly express this Indianness, whether in understandings of histories in terms of white and Indian, in the Indianization of Euro-American culture, or in direct Indian adaptations of Native cultural traditions.

## Indian People

Indian identity and Indianness are the results of complex interactions between Indians and non-Indians over the past centuries. Indian ethnicity comes about not because Indian people do what they do; rather it comes about because Indian people have to deal with white people and white people, for the most part, recognize them only as Indian and not as Choctaws or Kiowas. Furthermore, the white world in general is woefully ignorant of Indians not only as Indians but also as people with specific tribal origins. Indians and non-Indians alike, therefore, participated in the construction of Indian ethnic identity, and that construction is, at

least in part, made out of understandings of history that, for many Indian
people, are structured along a white/Indian divide.

For Indian people, that understanding of history points to the major
events that brought their ancestors to Indian Territory and Oklahoma
and produced the social landscape as it exists today. High on that list of
events are the removals that many of the tribes now in Oklahoma suffered, and the allotment of Indian land that paved the way for Oklahoma
statehood. Throughout the interviews reported here, Indian people talk
about the removals and their families' experiences with them. What they
say often focuses on themes of injustice and hardship, and so it is easy
to find places where people talk about their ancestors being driven from
their homes and treated like animals. People in the Indian Pioneer and
Doris Duke interviews commonly relate family stories of distant cousins,
uncles, and aunts who died on the trail and were buried unceremoniously
on the wayside. Sometimes this discourse of injustice and deprivation
is muted, especially among those peoples whose ancestors were first
removed from homelands, often in the upper Midwest, to small reservations in what is now Kansas, only to be moved again to even smaller
reservations in Indian Territory. They speak of removal in terms of their
own agency in the face of Euro-American duplicity, and they describe
the choice to come to Indian territory rather than assimilate into white
society in terms of their own family values. These threads of discourse
unite when people talk about their homes in Indian Territory. Here the
talk takes on a golden age theme, and life on the reservations and in the
Five Republics is described in glowing terms. People fondly relate stories
about the homes their ancestors built and the communities where they
lived.

The Five Republics of eastern Indian Territory—the small reservations that were shoehorned between their territories—and the large reservations in the west fostered communities in which day-to-day life was
largely defined and carried out in a tribal context. Tribal people were local
political leaders, they were often the merchants and schoolteachers, and
they were the religious leaders of the community. The allotment program
changed that fundamental fact of social life for Indian people in Indian
Territory. In the twenty years between the passage of the General Allotment Act in 1887 and Oklahoma statehood in 1907, Indian Territory was
transformed into a place where white Euro-Americans controlled every
aspect of daily life. Different Indian people around the state experienced
that transformation in very different ways. For some of the people on
the western reservations, the whole idea of private ownership of land

was alien and took energy and concentration to understand. On other reservations, Indian people had prior experience with private ownership. Many were offered allotments, taken from their tribes' Kansas reservations, in exchange for complete assimilation into white society. They had turned that down, often as a family decision to live in Indian communities rather than assimilate. Both groups seemed to take allotment as a given, and used whatever power they had in the process to select land that would keep their families together.

It is probably true that the tribes confined to reservations had few options to resist the allotment program. The five Indian republics in the eastern half of Indian Territory, however, saw it within their power to resist. As a result, the wisdom of the allotment program became a political issue in each of the Five Republics, and political parties took stands for and against the program. The divisions in the Five Republics over this issue were deep and often turned violent. Even these deep fissures in the Indian world, however, were couched in white/Indian terms. Indian political positions in favor of the allotment program were often articulated as a way to emerge from savagery and take advantage of the benefits of civilization. The savagery/civilization continuum was understood as the true (white) construction of the world. In other words, both sides accepted the idea of the savagery/civilization continuum, some choosing civilization while others desired to stay in savagery with the tribes.

The savagery/civilization model also appears in people's accounts of their experience with Indian education. In the years just before and after the turn of the twentieth century, Indian people in Indian Territory could take advantage of several educational alternatives. In many communities, subscription schools that recruited and paid their teachers on a per-student, per-month basis arose in response to local demand. The five Indian republics in eastern Indian Territory all had national school systems, Christian denominations opened mission schools, agency schools were available on reservations, and the United States government operated multitribal boarding schools throughout the country. All these schooling choices shared a common goal: forced assimilation of Indian students into white society by means of education.

This was not lost on the Indian students in the schools. Passages in the interviews commonly refer to the value of teachers trained in prestigious white institutions, and about the utility of Indian school training for success in the white world. The tools these schools used to force assimilation attacked the material, meaningful, and behavioral features of tribal life and sought to replace them with white ways. They were English-only institutions, and often the use of North American Indian languages was brutally punished. Often this meant that children experienced their first exposure to English in classrooms where they were expected to respond in English. Over and over again in the Indian Pioneer and Doris Duke interviews, English emerges as a central icon of white society and therefore represents a distinction, a boundary, between white and Indian. English was associated so closely with white society that the language came to stand for the society and became a major tool of those who used education to force assimilation. One result of this policy was a shift from native North American Indian languages to English, but that apparent victory for assimilation is mitigated by the fact that English has become the language of wider communication among Indian people in Oklahoma.

These schools also drew a symbolic connection between Euro-American culture and school when they replaced students' clothing with uniforms modeled after the United States military and imposed behavioral structures modeled on military lines. Indian people recall marching to every function in Indian school and being organized into military units, along with the scratchy uniforms they were forced to wear. If school draws an identification between white society and English, it also makes a strong distinction between white and tribal culture with the military regimentation of Indian students. When these students went to school, they took off their home clothing and put on uniforms modeled after their recent enemy's military, and at the same time they were taken out of their home's social organization and put into military-style organizations that emphasized hierarchy, command, and control. These schools were designed to draw powerful distinctions between white and Indian and, in doing so, constructed clear boundaries between the ethnic groups.

The schools were Christian institutions, whether private or government sponsored, and they suppressed the practice of Native religions. Many of the students experienced their first contact with Christianity in these schools, while others had never known any other religion. For all students, however, the school's commitment to Christianity was consistent and thorough. Every aspect of life was carried out with prayer, and church attendance was required several times each week. The capstone of this military Christian English curriculum was an emphasis on labor, which reflected white concepts of the proper economic roles Indian people could play in white society. Sometimes labor was included as a part of the formal curriculum, sometimes it was an important part of the school's economic base, and sometimes it was merely work for work's sake. The curricular and economic functions of student work for schools were often merged. Students worked because it was part of the training they received, but the fruits of that labor added, in one way or another, to the school's coffers. Work, however, clearly had value beyond its role in the production of wealth to the people who ran these schools. Whether this work was done for its own sake, or to contribute to the school's budget, or as part of a vocational curriculum, it was always viewed as one of the pillars of the assimilation policy. These schools were not there to develop academic skills; rather they were to train a low-paid working class. This imposed a distinction between white and Indian culture that helped form the foundation of Indian ethnicity.

The common theme that penetrates the experiences reported here is that the Indian schools were white institutions. Whether the school was operated by Christian missionaries, or an Indian national government, or the United States, its goal was to transform students from tribal peoples mired in the savage past into modern contributors to the white economy. The Indian schools share an important feature with the removals and the allotment program. All three of these emanate, in one way or another, from white cultural institutions. The United States government forced the removal of Indian peoples from the East, and it forced Indian peoples onto reservations. The United States government issued titles to small plots of land to all of the individual Indians in Indian territory. In these two cases, institutions of Euro-American culture carried out these policies. In the case of education, the school itself is implanted in Indian communities as a white cultural institution. Blood and blood quantum, too, are like these other cases, in that the idea of organizing people in this way also comes from white cultural roots. It is significantly different, however, from these previous examples because blood itself is not an institution but an idea. So the act of constructing an understanding of people based on blood quantum can be seen as an example of assimilation.

Be that as it may, blood and quantum are today, and have been for a long time, part of the construction of Indian ethnic identity. Of course, when people talk about blood in the context of Indian ethnicity, they are not talking about the biological organ that circulates gases through our bodies. Blood in the ethnic sense is a metaphor that carries multiple meanings in different times and places. The most obvious of these meanings incorporates the Euro-American idea of race in the understanding of Indian people. This approach produces odd results that, for many Indian people, do not match the reality they know. Indian people commonly tell stories about individuals they know whose children cannot be in their parent's tribe. These anomalies emerge in tribes that specify a minimum blood quantum for membership. Other tribes who, rather than specifying a minimum blood quantum, choose to require lineal descent from an ancestor on a base roll have their own anomalies. The stories about lineal descent tribes concern people with little or no connection with a tribe's cultural heritage acquiring some credentials and benefits of Indian identity. One way excludes people who should be included, but the other includes people with little understanding or loyalty to Indian values or traditions.

The racialization of Indian ethnic identity, of course, is often expressed in terms of the biological characteristics of Indians. In this stereotypic construction, Indians have copper-colored skin, straight black hair, and dark eyes and sometimes even lack body odor. The understanding of Indian people as a race is also a convenient entry into the discourse on Indians as vanishing peoples. In this way of thinking, as the blood quantum is reduced from generation to generation, Indianness is also reduced. The assumption behind this thinking is that Indian identity is biologically transmitted and is an essential quality of people with Indian blood to the degree that they have that blood. In this context, it is easy to understand how political issues in Indian communities were often characterized in terms of blood quantum. Usually this works out to progressives being labeled as mixed-blood, while traditionalists are considered full-blooded.

I think there is a deeper and more subtle meaning to blood in Indian communities that goes beyond thinking about Indian identity in terms of race. Often when Indian people bring blood into the conversation they recognize its racial meanings but reject them as decisive to Indian people. They do, on the other hand, associate blood with community, and blood in this sense is a metaphor for an individual's commitment to the community. The elements of this community commitment include respect for the tribal language and regular participation in community events. In this sense, Indians have transformed the idea of blood from the divisive accounting that emphasizes blood quantum numbers into a more inclusive approach that emphasizes people of blood and tradition.

Race, and its metaphoric extension in blood, are not the only European ideas that contribute to the makeup of Indian ethnicity in Oklahoma. Christianity also fills that function for many Indian people, both as a way to express their Indian identity and as a way to distinguish the Indian from the white. Christianity and blood, however, occupy very different realms as ideas. Blood and the understanding of human groups as races operate in the background of our understanding. They color all our interpretations, but they serve as the focus for relatively few of our social interactions. Christianity, on the other hand, structures the places and the times for much of social life. Church services are scheduled and structured events that take place in the church building, which also serves as the venue for other social functions. A church is both a place, a building, and a social group, a congregation. These two go hand in hand, and as the congregation dissipates, the building itself will no longer serve its function. This is as true for Indian people as it is for any other, and the role of Christianity in the lives of Indian people emerges clearly from the Indian Pioneer and Doris Duke interviews.

Those interviews show an Indian Christianity that is distinct from the non-Indian churches of various denominations, and that was central to the lives of many Indian people as Indians. From early times in Indian Territory, Indian congregations met in churches that they often built with their own hands. The services themselves represented great commitment to the church, because they were both difficult to attend and often lasted days. These churches were fully integrated into their communities, often emerging under the leadership of charismatic leaders, or dying by falling prey to internal political divisions. One of the important ways in which these churches were Indian churches was that the people involved were Indians. The congregations were Indian, although non-Indians were usually welcome, and the members of the local hierarchy were also Indian. The preacher was Indian, the deacons were Indians, all of the named officers of the church were Indians, and they preached and ministered to Indian people in their native languages.

Christian Indian people accommodated their cultural traditions in many ways. In some cases, they carried out traditional functions through Christian rites and institutions. Marriages were arranged using tribal values but were performed in Christian churches, for example. In some instances, the traditional and the Christian were performed in parallel, that is, with two weddings, one in tribal tradition and one in the church. And, rarely, traditional Indian ceremonies were Christianized, but in each of these, Christian Indians were part of the wider community and not only participated in the tribal religions but also encouraged traditionalists to join in with the Christians. While these churches served their Indian congregations at the local level, a wider ideology worked to divide Indian communities on the basis of religion. That ideology proclaimed that the only legitimate expression of religion was Christianity: that religious practices that emerged out of tribal ways were, at best, expressions of mere superstition, and at worst heathen, perhaps satanic, rites. When this ideology was preached from the pulpit, Indian people were belittled and berated for participating in traditional dances and religious expressions. This message is alive today, and many ministers and priests admonish the Indian people in their congregations to avoid Powwows and Stomp Dances. This vision of the world demands that Indian people abandon the "old" Indian ways and adopt the "new" white ways, and many Indians accept and articulate that ideology. Behind this public message, however, Indian people continue to find accommodation between the Christian and the traditional.

Fortunately, many Indian people in Oklahoma ignore these self-righteous pronouncements from the pulpit and participate in Powwows, sweats, Stomp Dances, and other expressions of Indian identity. These expressions distinguish themselves from each other on various dimensions. For example, Powwow and, often, Stomp Dances are public events that are both well advertised and sponsored by official Indian groups such as tribes, urban Indian clubs, and even student associations. Announcements for Powwow and Stomp Dances are easy to find tacked up on bulletin boards and kiosks around the state. On the other hand, Sweat Lodge ceremonies and Native American Church meetings are more private and open only to members of the local community and their guests. Powwows and some Stomp Dances are secular events, although they are performed with a consistently religious message. The eagle feathers and the dance arena itself are considered sacred to Powwow dancers and Stomp Dancers, who dance to celebrate their creator. The Native American Church meetings, Sweat Lodge ceremonies, and the Ceremonial Ground rites, on the other hand, are explicitly religious. While community renewal and social interaction is important to these gatherings, the people who attend them are there to pray.

More important than the differences that distinguish these institutions, however, are the similarities that they share. All of them, for example, are symbolic expressions of Indianness, and they share this feature with Indian Christianity, constructions of history, and understandings of their heritage. These religious and quasi-religious institutions also share a significant feature that distinguishes them from many other expressions of Indian ethnicity. Indian people in Oklahoma today understand the roots of Powwow, Stomp Dance, Sweat Lodge, and Native American Church in terms of tribal heritage and not as adoptions of Euro-American values or responses to the Euro-American atrocities. They are seen as Indian institutions with Indian origins that express Indian identity. Indian people articulate these understandings explicitly when they step through the Sweat Lodge door, or when they point with pride to the long histories of Stomp Ground fires that were brought over trails of tears and have been kept lit for nearly two centuries now. When the Powwow emcee asks the Drum for an Honor Song or retells the origin of the Grass

178 SURVIVAL AND CHANGE

Dance, he is making a statement that the celebration he and the audience are participating in is an Indian celebration that came from Indian cultural traditions.

## Oklahomas

These five things—the removal, reservation, and allotment histories; Indian education; meanings attached to blood and blood quantum; Indian Christian communities; and institutions that emerged from tribal rather than white traditions—fall into three relatively natural categories. The first of these involve Euro-American policies directed toward Indian people. All these are policies whose goals are the elimination of Indian people from white consciousness. The removals and reservations attempted this goal by physically getting rid of Native people, where education and allotment tried forced assimilation to achieve this end. It is no surprise that Indian people construct their understandings of these histories on adversarial white-versus-Indian terms, and that these histories are now significant symbolic boundaries in the construction of Indian ethnicity. The second group, blood and the meanings associated with blood quantum, is a Native reaction to white understanding of the nature of social groups. Nineteenth-century scientific racism attempted to justify its current social order in biological terms so that a person's place in the community emerged from his or her parentage. It was used to keep the Anglo-American ruling elite in power and in control of the society's wealth, and Euro-American society casts all discussion of cultural identity in its terms. It is perhaps understandable that Indian people adopted some of this, because white Americans dealing with Indian people insisted on understanding the world in this way. It is in this context that Indian people are contesting the association of blood quantum with ethnicity and requiring participation in community life along with ancestry for legitimate claims of Indian identity.

Where Indian people had the opportunity to define social life on their own terms, they created institutions structured on traditional values but adapted to current circumstances. Throughout the genesis of Indian ethnicity, Indian Christian churches have thrived. These congregations, sometimes tribal, often multitribal, are the focus of Indian communities in every part of Oklahoma. These churches are places where people meet to worship and to socialize with others in their communities. These communities define specific roles related to church membership and fill them from within, so prayer leaders, deacons, and ministers emerge from the community and lead the spiritual life of their fellow members. They sometimes participate in Indian ethnicity by accommodating its religious and quasi-religious institutions: I have shared Sweat Lodges with Indian Christian ministers and seen them dance in the Powwow arena. These churches also distinguish themselves from their non-Indian Christian counterparts in that they understand themselves as Indian institutions. They share this construction with Indian people who find their cultural and spiritual fulfillment in institutions that emerged from tribal cultures. Native American Church, Stomp Dance, and many other manifestations of Indian ethnicity can be traced to tribal traditions that adapted institutionally from tribal to Indian and symbolically as important boundary markers between the Indian and the white worlds.

Indian people around the state talk about Indian ethnicity in various terms. Indian people often refer to it as "intertribalism," or "pan-Indianism," or they may just toss it off as "that Powwow thing." The fact that this kind of vocabulary exists probably should alert any good social scientist that Indian ethnic identity and the symbolic structures that maintain it are not merely marks of ethnic division between whites and Indians but also point to political divisions within Native American groups. It does not matter very much whether or not I was alerted to this possibility; it is in fact true that Indian ethnicity is contested within Native American groups, and many people do not see it as a positive development. The argument is often couched in terms of competition between Indian and tribal identities, and many see Indian identity as a threat to tribal ways. They see many tribal members who are more devoted to Indian institutions like Powwow or Native American Church than they are to the tribal rituals, celebrations, and languages that keep them distinct as a people. They fear that these tribal brothers and sisters are nearing total assimilation into the white world. This is a life-and-death concern for many who see Indianness as bringing on the end of tribal culture.

On the other side, many people do not see the institutions of Indian ethnicity as a threat to tribal identity, and to many, those Indian institutions are the only way they have ever known to express their Native heritage. On the other hand, ethnically Indian people often point to those things they have in common with their kin who struggle to keep tribal cultures alive. They share a common understanding of history and point to many of the same historic events, like removals, confinement to reservations, and allotment, as being of central significance to them. One of the features that makes these events important for all sides is that they are constructed in terms of white versus "my people." I believe these approaches fail to see some of the complexities of the situation. I do not, for example, accept the sort of zero-sum game that many construct. I do not believe that Indian ethnicity is strengthened at the expense of tribal identity, so that as Indianness flourishes, tribal culture must wane. It is entirely possible that each can strengthen the other. At the same time, for ethnic Indians to deny there is a problem ignores an important voice within their communities, and doing that weakens all. While many people on all sides look at current tribal governments as a means to articulate with state and federal governments, rather than as protectors of ethnic heritage, they remain one of the few central tribal institutions. Many of them are much more, of course, and they often find ways to foster tribal traditions and languages as well as broader Indian expressions. Ultimately, of course, any ethnic identity is created only through participation, so both Indian and tribal identity require that people participate in the communities that the institutions, constructions of history, and understandings of nature symbolically demarcate.

# APPENDIX

## *The Indian Pioneer and Doris Duke Interviews*

In the mid-1990s, I spent six to ten weeks each summer in Oklahoma. During this time I began to explore Indian ethnicity, but I also took the chance to visit with my family. On visits with my sister in Norman, I would explore the resources at the University of Oklahoma, where I found the Western History Collections of the University's libraries. There I first learned about the Indian Pioneer and Doris Duke interviews. The interviews reported in the Indian Pioneer Papers were conducted in the late 1930s, and the Doris Duke Collection interviews in the late 1960s and early 1970s. In the two sets, fieldworkers interviewed Indian people, generally elders, about their memories, experiences, and thoughts as Indian people. These two sets of interviews provided information about Indian people—their thoughts and experiences from their own point of view—through the seventh decade of the twentieth century.

The fifty thousand or so pages of the Indian Pioneer Papers are divided into a little over one hundred volumes at the University of Oklahoma Western History Collections. They are the result of a Works Progress Administration program, and, for the most part, are reports of field interviews with either Indians or pioneers. The pioneers were non-Indians; the Indians were members of one of the forty or more tribes in the state. All the interviewees in the project were people who lived in the area before 1907, when Oklahoma became a state. Although the reports in the Indian Pioneer Papers are called interviews, this term must be taken with some caution. All the Indian Pioneer interviews used here were conducted in 1937 or 1938, long before tape recorders were available, so they are not transcripts of recorded conversations between people. They are more like newspaper stories that report the fieldworker's experiences. I could find no record of how fieldworkers were trained, but I get the sense, after reading several hundred of them, that a fieldworker would talk to an interviewee in his or her home, and then come back to a central office to type up a report. No doubt the interviewer took field notes, but the reports themselves do not mention field notes or the process the fieldworker went through to report the interview. Very rarely, perhaps once or twice in the twelve hundred pages I collected, a fieldworker would make reference to the procedures used in the project, but I have not been able to find any documentation of those procedures.

The reports vary widely along many dimensions. A few of them have hand-drawn illustrations or hand-written annotations in the margins of the typescript. Some of the reports are written in the third-person voice of the fieldworker, and some in the first-person voice of the interviewee. Some are very short, less than one page, while others are long, more than twenty pages. Within this diversity, however, there are some striking commonalities. The reports are never cast in the form of a question-and-answer dialogue between fieldworker and interviewee, but always expressed in clear, well-structured paragraphs. Blood and race are concepts expressed in almost every interview, and they are never contested; interviewer and consultant alike use these concepts to identify themselves and others. The reports often emphasize the same issues. They commonly refer to schooling, the Civil War, trading points, and the location of cemeteries. These topics are sometimes mentioned even when the interviewee has little or nothing to say about the subject. The reports are often organized into sections with headings reflecting these topics: "Education," "Trading Point," "Civil War," and so on. This indicated to me that the fieldworkers received some common training, and were all contributing to a common outline.

Other copies of the Indian Pioneer Papers are available elsewhere in the state, one of the most accessible being at the Oklahoma Historical Society in Oklahoma City. The two sets are, unfortunately, not catalogued the same way, so the volume and page numbers from the University collection do not correspond to the Historical Society catalogue. When I use this material here, I cite it according to interviewee (whom I consider the author) and by volume and page number. These refer to the University of Oklahoma's copy of the Indian Pioneer Papers, and anyone who wishes to look up the sources at the Oklahoma Historical Society should be aware of this and search the name of the person being interviewed.

The Doris Duke Collection is about half the size of the Indian Pioneer Papers and is organized into a little over fifty volumes. All the Doris Duke interviews that I collected for my data carry dates between 1968 and 1970, but the project was not completed until the following year. The typescripts were copied to microfiche in 1972. All the interviews were tape-recorded, and transcribed. This gives them a very different quality from the Indian Pioneer Papers. The Doris Duke Collection interviews are reported as dialogues, with technical problems with the tape recorders noted in the text. Each report is labeled with a tape number (included here in the bibliography), and the headings on each interview include the names of the fieldworker, the transcriber, and a proofreader, as well as the name of the interviewee. The Doris Duke data, therefore, are nearly verbatim accounts of what the interviewee actually said.

Where the Indian Pioneer Papers reported interviews from both Indians and non-Indians, Indian people are the focus of the Doris Duke Collection, and only a few reports include non-Indians. Like the Indian Pioneer Papers, most of the materials in the Doris Duke Collection are interviews, with a few other sorts of reports, such as transcripts of newspaper stories and political meetings. The subject matter of the interviews reflects the interest of the interviewers, who were often either graduate students or faculty at local universities. Religion, especially Native American Church, song, and kinship are common topics in these interviews.

To use any of the material for these two sets of interviews, I had to select it, copy it from the microfiche, and transcribe it to a word-processor file. I knew from the start that I could not collect all of the seventy-five thousand or so pages in the Indian Pioneer and Doris Duke collections. It was clear to me that I would have to take only a small portion of that, so I began with the goal of collecting about three thousand pages. As I learned more about the collections and about the process collecting the information, it became clear that even three thousand pages was too much. I did not have the time to do it all, so I lowered the total to two thousand pages. I wanted those two thousand pages, as much as possible, to cover the entire length of both collections. I therefore divided 159, the total number of volumes, into two thousand to estimate how many pages per volume I should collect. According to these calculations, I would need thirteen pages from each volume.

To ensure that I collected these data as evenhandedly as possible, I decided to take the first thirteen pages of interviews in each of the 159 volumes. I started with volume 1 of each collection and went through to the last volume. This simple process, however, produced a few complications. The first of these was that some of the interviews in the collections were with non-Indians. I recognized that non-Indians participated in the formation of Indian identity, but I felt that the most valuable contribution this work could make would be to document the issues, opinions, and feelings of Indian people in Oklahoma. For this reason, I decided to limit the scope of the research to Indian people and collect only interviews with Indians. This was pretty much irrelevant for the Doris Duke Collection, because virtually all the interviewees were Indian people. On the other hand, the Indian Pioneer Papers are heavily weighted to interviews of pioneers. I took no data on this issue, but I estimate that over two-thirds of the Indian Pioneer Papers consist of interviews with non-Indian people. I reviewed each interview to ensure that it was an interview with an Indian person.

I used several indicators to decide if a particular interview was with an Indian person. Many of the interviews began with a Works Progress Administration "biography form" or "legend and story form," and often these forms identified the interviewee as an Indian. Almost always, the interviewee identified himself or herself as an Indian, either directly, by saying, for example, "I am a full blood Choctaw," or indirectly, by referring to his or her family: "My father was half-blood Seminole."

Almost every interview in the Doris Duke Collection is longer than thirteen pages, and while the interviews in the Indian Pioneer Papers are usually shorter, collecting enough interviews in a volume to get to my thirteen-page minimum almost always produced more than thirteen pages. I decided immediately not to collect partial interviews, and when I reached the thirteen-page minimum in the middle of the interview, I went ahead and collected the entire interview. This produced a surplus that I adjusted as I went. When the surplus number of pages exceeded twenty-six pages, twice the target number of pages per volume, I skipped the next volume. Following these procedures, I collected a little over two thousand pages of interview data from the Indian Pioneer and Doris Duke collections. Included in those two thousand pages are 208 interviews (1,469 pages) from the Indian Pioneer Papers, and 37 interviews (657 pages) from the Doris Duke Collection. Ninety-six of the interviewees were women, and 149 were men. They came from twenty-seven of the thirty-nine Oklahoma tribes and ranged in age from their thirties to their nineties. Table 1 gives the distributions of these details.

The people who gave these interviews knew what they were doing. They had volunteered to participate in the process, and they were aware that the results of that participation would be made public to people like me who wanted to learn from what they said. I imagine, in fact, that the men and

*Table 1.* Doris Duke (DD) and Indian Pioneer (IP) Data by Tribe, Age, and Sex

| | Source | | Age | | | | | Sex | |
|---|---|---|---|---|---|---|---|---|---|
| Tribe | DD | IP | 20–40 | 41–60 | 61–80 | 81 & up | AU* | F | M |
| Total | 37 | 208 | 9 | 74 | 104 | 30 | 28 | 96 | 149 |
| Arapaho | 6 | 2 | — | 3 | | 5 | — | 2 | 6 |
| Caddo | 1 | 2 | — | 1 | 1 | — | 1 | 3 | — |
| Cherokee | 7 | 56 | 2 | 12 | 32 | 12 | 5 | 27 | 36 |
| Chickasaw | — | 7 | — | 5 | 2 | — | — | 5 | 2 |
| Choctaw | 2 | 54 | 2 | 22 | 23 | 4 | 5 | 20 | 36 |
| Cheyenne | 3 | 1 | — | — | 2 | 1 | 1 | 2 | 2 |
| Comanche | — | 6 | 2 | 1 | 1 | — | 2 | 1 | 5 |
| Creek | — | 37 | 1 | 9 | 19 | 2 | 6 | 13 | 24 |
| Delaware | 1 | 5 | — | — | 4 | — | 2 | 2 | 4 |
| Kaskaskia | — | 1 | — | — | 1 | — | — | 1 | — |
| Kiowa | 3 | 1 | — | — | 3 | — | 1 | 3 | 1 |
| Miami | — | 1 | — | — | 1 | — | — | 1 | — |
| Muskogee | — | 6 | — | 5 | 1 | — | — | 1 | 5 |
| Osage | 4 | — | — | 3 | — | — | 1 | 2 | 2 |
| Oto | — | 2 | 1 | 1 | — | — | — | 1 | 1 |
| Ottawa | — | 1 | 1 | 1 | — | — | — | 1 | 1 |
| Peoria | 2 | — | — | — | 1 | 1 | — | — | 2 |
| Plains Apache | 2 | — | — | — | 2 | — | — | — | 2 |
| Potawatomi | 1 | — | — | — | — | 1 | — | 1 | — |
| Quapaw | — | 2 | — | — | 1 | 1 | — | 1 | 1 |
| Sac and Fox | — | 7 | — | 4 | 3 | — | — | 2 | 5 |
| Seminole | — | 6 | 1 | — | 1 | 1 | 3 | 1 | 5 |
| Seneca | 2 | — | — | — | 1 | — | 1 | 2 | — |
| Shawnee | 2 | 3 | — | 1 | 3 | 1 | — | 2 | 3 |
| Wichita | 1 | — | — | — | 1 | — | — | 1 | — |
| Wyandotte | — | 1 | — | 1 | — | — | — | 1 | — |
| Yuchi | — | 7 | — | 5 | 1 | 1 | — | — | 7 |

*AU = Age Unknown

women who contributed to the Indian Pioneer Papers and the Doris Duke Collection wanted their thoughts and feelings to be read and used in the future. Given this, I believe their efforts and honesty should be acknowledged, so whenever I make reference to something one of them said I cite them by name. Not all the interviews I finally collected are used in this work, but each of them contributed to my understanding of Indianness and Indian identity in Oklahoma: all interviewees whose reports I collected are acknowledged in the list at the end of this appendix.

The efforts of these consultants would not be available now if it were not for the fieldworkers who conducted the interviews and saw that they were processed through to the final report or transcription. The names of those fieldworkers are also listed here.

The Indian Pioneer Papers and Doris Duke Collection provide firsthand information about the experiences Indian people had in Oklahoma (Indian Territory) in the 1930s and early 1970s, but they do not say anything about the last quarter of the twentieth century. To learn about those experiences, I had to talk to people across the state. In that fieldwork I attended student meetings at colleges, participated in classes on Indian culture, visited with Indian scholars, attended both Christian and Indian religious ceremonies, and visited tribal institutions—tribal headquarters, community program offices, and so on—around the state. In all these ways, I met and talked to many Indian people, and I did my best to hear and understand what they were saying to me about being Indian today. I also conducted over thirty hours of formal interviews with Indian people around Oklahoma. The interviews were recorded on audiotape, and later transcribed and added to the body of data I would use to understand Indian ethnicity in contemporary Oklahoma.

I wanted to learn about Indian identity from an Indian point of view, so the goal of the analysis of these data was to expose how people expressed their identities as Indians (or kinds of Indians such as Kiowa or Choctaw) in order to come to some understanding about being Indian in Oklahoma today. The general way to do that for people with my training and background is to take a funnel-shaped approach to the process of coming to understand. A good place to start is by asking very broad questions with little content of their own—"What is it like being Irish Catholic?"—and use the answers to those questions to explore issues further, in ever narrowing fields. This way of doing things requires time. The broad questions are asked early, and the more focused questions come later in follow-up interviews. This was the process I used in interviews with people I met in the field, but I had to adapt the process to the interviews I selected from the Doris Duke and Indian Pioneer data. These data allowed no opportunity to conduct follow-up interviews. I could not ask people to expand on a particular issue or how they felt about a particular incident they had related. While it is impossible to make up for the continuing refinement and clarification this approach provides, and while this problem cannot be truly solved, some of what is lost can be regained through volume. The different points of view expressed in a large number of instances can provide some of the depth achieved in follow-up conversations. This is why I collected as much as I could from the Indian Pioneer and Doris Duke collections.

The archival data has a second problem that requires adaptation of the live interview model. While these data are clearly intended to be used as data, they come from other eras and were generated by other minds. They reflect not only the technologies of their day—ink-ribbon manual typewriters versus tape recorders versus desk top computers—they also reflect the interests and sensibilities of their times. For example, there is much more discussion of the Civil War in the Indian Pioneer data than I would expect were the interviews to be given today. On the other hand, tribal sovereignty is prominent in many of the conversations I recorded, but almost absent in the earlier data. As a result, while the Indian Pioneer and Doris Duke interviews were probably coherent data in the context in which they were created, they have a fractured quality in terms of the needs of this project. It is not unusual for a few lines of interview in the Indian Pioneer Papers, for example, to mention blood quantum, education, religion, and tribal politics. I tried to compensate for this through the process of coding.

A code is a concept, idea, or value that describes some piece of text. Codes can come from anywhere; they can be theoretical concepts like "class" or "role," or they can emerge from the data. For example, this passage mentions Christianity, and could be (was) tagged with a code like "religion: Christianity": "'The teacher of this school was the Reverend John B. Jones, for a number of years engaged in missionary work among the Cherokees" (Beamer 1938: 131).

Researchers can decide before they look at the information they collect what codes they will use to understand the data, or they can create the codes as they go through the data, so the codes express the themes as they emerge. I chose to make codes that expressed the data, so I generated codes from the data as I went through it. When all the data are collected and all the text in the data is tagged with an appropriate code, then all of the similarly coded passages can be brought together to see what people said about the issues each code represents.

Because the researcher ultimately makes up the codes, coding is a significant source of researcher bias. It is a place where I can impose (and really cannot avoid imposing) my point of view on the data by the interpretations I place on them and the codes I elect to create. But imposing that view can easily warp the data to tell a story that is not there. To help avoid this problem, I read and took notes on about thirty Indian Pioneer interviews and about ten Doris Duke interviews before I began the process of creating codes and assigning codes to passages of text.

My initial set of about fifteen codes came from what I had read in the interviews. It included codes for text that mentions blood quantum, genealogy, education, removal, and allotment. As I continued coding, and learning more about, the data, I created more codes as they suggested themselves, until I ended up with fifty-nine. For each interview in the data set, I also noted its source (Indian Pioneer, Doris Duke, or my own interview) and the age, gender, and tribal affiliation of the consultant. While it is possible to do this work by hand, it is time-consuming and tedious, so I used a computer program named ATLAStiR designed for this purpose.

Almost all the codes I used were like those for mentions of blood quantum, food, house and home, or Powwow dances; that is, the passages tagged with the code usually contained the code word (passages codes for blood quantum contained the word "blood"). There are some, like the Lewis Beamer passage just quoted, where the code is derived more or less directly from the passage ("Christianity" is taken from the Reverend Jones being a missionary), but other codes, however, are more abstract. For example, consultants often talked about their economic life, and sometimes they emphasized things they provided for themselves—making their own clothing or growing their own food. Other times they emphasized their connections to others—working for wages, participating in reciprocal exchange networks, or bartering for goods at a trading post. I used one code for economic independence and another for economic integration for these passages, even though the words "economic," "independence," and "integration" never appear in the passages. The issues covered by these abstract codes include mentions of internal or external (to the tribe) politics; ethnic relations with other Indians, whites, or African Americans; and the gender roles of men and women.

I did occasionally give in to my fancy. For example, after I had coded a little over a hundred interviews, I came across a passage about dance regalia. I thought this was interesting, perhaps because regalia and the attention to it were so striking at the Powwows and Gourd Dances I had attended. Accordingly, I created a code for regalia. I reviewed the interviews I had already coded for mentions of regalia and kept it in my code list for the remainder of the analysis. In the entire corpus of data, perhaps four or five passages mentioned regalia (as opposed to more that two hundred that mentioned blood). The benefit of this code was not so much what it revealed about Indian identity in Oklahoma as the lesson it taught me about paying more attention to what interviewees were saying.

All the data—archival interviews, field notes, contemporary interviews—were analyzed using the codes I created. Once coded, all mentions of particular issues, codes, were brought together. While the text analysis software I used has many more capabilities, I did not want to go much further than this in the analysis of this material. I could, for example, have asked the software to generate all the instances where one code was mentioned with another, or defined various networks of related codes. It seemed to me, however, that these procedures took me away from my goal of staying as close to the data, the words of the people in the interviews, as I could. So I stayed at this low level of analysis and looked for the themes that expressed people's identity in what they said about the significant issues in their lives. To me, those issues sorted out into two major categories: mentions of the pressures toward assimilation to the white, Euro-American world—especially the removals, allotment, and education—and talk about Indian identity, especially in terms of blood quantum and religion.

*Indian Pioneer and Doris Duke Consultants*

George Abbot
Alex Alexander
Jesse Allen
Mary Alice Arendell (Gibson)
Henry Armstrong
Mrs. Lucy Bacon
Mrs. Pearl Baggette
Mattie Bailey
Butler Baker
Mrs. Jane Baptiste
J. W. Barbee
Angie Barnes
Isaac Batt
Mr. Ed Baxter
Lewis Beamer
Arthur J. Beames
Jennie Bell
Jasper Bell
Jancy Bell
Philemon Berry
Jefferson Berryhill
Mr. Big Nose
Fred Bigman
Mrs. Chas. A. Bilbo
Jeannette Billingslea
Pete Birdchief
Jay Black
Emeziah Bohanan
Mrs. Eliza Coker Breeding
Oliver Hazard Perry Brewer, Jr.
J. W. Brewer
Agnes Burnett
Nafa Butcher
Robert Butler
Sallie (Johnson) Butler
Mrs. C. B. Campbell
Jackson Carn
James Carnes
Bill Chisholm
Julius Choate
C. C. (Uncle Bud) Choate
Lottie Choate
Dr. Isabelle Cobb
Mrs. Jane Cole
Rosa Conner
Crawford Connor

Joe Creeping Bear
Mrs. Eliza Cross
Anna Anderson Davis
Tom Devine
Alvarado Taylor Dilbeck
Daniel Downing
George Duck
Mrs. John E. Duncan
Dickson Duncan (Na-ma-quo)
Ollie England
Columbus Wm. Ervin
Sandy Fife
Timmie Fife
Adam Folsom
Osmond Franklin
Mrs. Rachel Franklin
Lille Grayson Franks
Mrs. Mary Freeman
Ben Freeny
George French
Guy Froman
Thomas Gilroy
Milley Fish Gilroy
Winona Goodbear
Mrs. Mary Gordon (nee Scott)
Susan Riley Gott
Thomas Greece
Amos Green
Mary Jane Green
Mandy Turkey Harjo Greenback
Sam Hair
Walter O. Hale
Webster Halfbreed
Bessie Hall
Annie James Harkins
Mr. Silas G. Harkins
Meta B. Hatchett
Mrs. Mary Helms
Henry Henderson
Ed Hicks
Elmer Hill
Rev. Willie Honey
William Rex Howland
Alice Hudson
Ida Mae Hughes
Mr. Henry Hunter

Thomas W. Hunter
Charles Jefferson
David Jones
Mrs. Joanna Jones (nee McGhee)
Mrs. I. V. Jones
William Karty
Johnson Keener
Albert W. Keith
Ebenezer Cutnezer Kemp
Ellis Ketcher
Sol C. Ketchum
Mrs. V. I. Kikler
Henry Clay Kilgore
Julius Pinkey Killebrew
Elliston Labor
Henry Labor
Alexander Labors
Barney Leader
Mrs. Celeste Caby Leal
J. Norman Leard
Samuel Left Hand
Winey Lewis
Myrtle Lincoln
Lilah D. Lindsey
Wilson Locke
Charles W. Lofton
Mamie Turkey Long
Sarah Longbone
Alex Lowe
Mrs. Mahaley Lowe
Mary Ma-na-ka
Susie Ross Martin
James Martin, Jr.
Lindsey Mayes
W. B. McAlpin
Jessie McDermott
Mack McDonald
Lulah Elizabet McKinney
J. R. McLaughlin
Willis McNaughton
Robert Meigs
Jackson Miashintubbee
Nancy Miashintubbee
Mrs. D. H. Moffatt
March Monday
Mary Still Morris
Tucker W. Morton

Sammie Narharkey
Joel E. Oakes
John R. Osborne
Mrs. Elizabeth Lindsey Palmer
Eliza Palmer
Mrs. Mary Payne
Mary E. Payne
Andrew Perdasophy
John Perkins
Louie Perkins
Johnson Poahway
Mr. Walter Polecat
Charles W. Ponds
Thomas Poorboy
Charlotte Pressley (nee Greece)
Cora Pritchard
Louis Garnett Pritchard
Bertha Provost
Guy Quoetone
Mrs. Kate Rackleff
Joe Ralls
Leister Reed
Mrs. Jennie Campbell Reel
Mrs. Ella Coody Robinson
Clara Ward Robinson
Jacob Rolland
Peter Rolland
Mr. Cheape (Charlie) Ross
Jess Rowlodge
Elizabeth Ballard Sanders
Bose Scott
George Scott
Charles Scott
Cherokee Sells
Mrs. Irene Shafer
George Shakingbush
Garfield Shoals
Mrs. Annie Shorb
John Silk
Mrs. Molly Starr Sillers
Simmer
George W. Smith
George Smith
Clarence Starr
Ada Stratton
Eliza Strout
Mrs. Matilda Stultz

Ta-tek-ke Tiger
Tohnee Turtle
Myrtle Morrell Unap
Joe Underwood
John Wa-kah-quah
Jefferson Wade
David Wade
Mrs. Hugh Wakolee (Ma-ko-she)
Mrs. Arthur Walcott
Beatrice Wallingford
Mrs. John Walner
Jack Walton

Eastman Ward
Mrs. M. E. Whelchel
Nancy Whistler
Arten White
Bennie Whiteday
Mr. and Mrs. Charles Whitehorn
Mose Wiley (The-wah-lee)
Eunice Bluejacket Wilson
William Wolfe
Mary Frances Wood
Alice Apekaum Zanella

*Fieldworkers*

Oliver Abrams
Maurice R. Anderson
Lula Austin
Levina R. Beavers
Jesse S. Bell
Anna R. Berry
Jefferson Berryhill
W. J. B. Bigby
William Bittle
Robert H. Boatman
Susan Brandt
Jas. S. Buchanan
Nannie Lee Burns
Billie Byrd
Nettie Cain
James R. Carselowey
Jessie Chisholm
Peter W. Cole
Charline M. Culbertson
Augusta H. Custer
John F. Daugherty
Henry Day
Faye Delph
E. F. Dodson
Mary D. Dorward
Peggy Dycus
Ethel V. Elder
Jerome M. Emmons
Dawes Fife
James H. Fleming
Lillian Gassaway
Rufus George
Gomer Gower

James Russell Gray
Hazel B. Greene
Johnson H. Hampton
Ruth Hankowsky
Amelia F. Harris
Charles H. Holt
Otis Hume
Gus Hummingbird
Effie S. Jackson
David Jones
Julia A. Jordan
Grace Kelley
Kirk Kickingbird
Chester A. Lamb
Ida B. Lankford
George Littlejohn
Katherine Maker
Etta D. Mason
Loudolphus D. Maybee
Alene D. McDowell
Ida Merwin
Velma Neiberding
Warren D. Norse
Reuben Partridge
John M. Pearce
Dovey P. Read
Katherine Red Corn
Ella Robinson
Elizabeth Ross
Marvin G. Rowley
Lenna M. Rushing
Bill Savage
Carl R. Sherwood

Jr. Thad Smith
Joe Southern
Frank J. Still
Robert B. Thomas
Bessie L.Thomas
Wylie Thornton
B. D. Timmons

Joe Trimble
Hattie Turner
Jarvis W. Tyner
J. W. Tyner
Ophelia D. Vestal
L. W. Wilson
Ruby Wolfenbarger

# BIBLIOGRAPHY

Armstrong, Henry. 1938a. Interview by Alene D. McDowell. Indian Pioneer Papers, Western History Collections, University of Oklahoma, Norman, Oklahoma. 1:77–91.

———. 1938b. Interview by Alene D. McDowell. Indian Pioneer Papers, Western History Collections, University of Oklahoma, Norman, Oklahoma. 102:7–8.

Bacon, Lucy. 1938. Interview by Johnson H. Hampton. Indian Pioneer Papers, Western History Collections, University of Oklahoma, Norman, Oklahoma. 4:14–19.

Baptiste, Jane. 1938. Interview by Nannie Lee Burns. Indian Pioneer Papers, Western History Collections, University of Oklahoma, Norman, Oklahoma. 5:147–56.

Barbee, J. W. 1938. Interview by Nannie Lee Burns. Indian Pioneer Papers, Western History Collections, University of Oklahoma, Norman, Oklahoma. 5:162–70.

Barnes, Angie. 1972. Interview by Leonard Maker. Doris Duke Collection, Western History Collections, University of Oklahoma, Norman, Oklahoma. 46(T-367): 1–16.

Barth, Frederik. 1969. Introduction to *Ethnic Groups and Boundaries: The Social Organization of Cultural Difference,* edited by Frederik Barth, pp. 9–39. Boston: Little Brown.

Batt, Isaac. 1938. Interview by W. J. B. Bigby. Indian Pioneer Papers, Western History Collections, University of Oklahoma, Norman, Oklahoma. 6:48–52.

Beamer, Lewis. 1938. Interview by Elizabeth Ross. Indian Pioneer Papers, Western History Collections, University of Oklahoma, Norman, Oklahoma. 6:131–34.

Bell, Jennie. 1938. Interview by Jesse S. Bell. Indian Pioneer Papers, Western History Collections, University of Oklahoma, Norman, Oklahoma. 7:29–34.

Berry, Philemon. 1972. Interview by Bill Savage. Doris Duke Collection, Western History Collections, University of Oklahoma, Norman, Oklahoma. 39(T-): i–10.

Berryhill, Jefferson. 1938. "Location of Indian Churches." Indian Pioneer Papers, Western History Collections, University of Oklahoma, Norman, Oklahoma. 102:59–66.

Bigman, Fred. 1972. Interview by William Bittle. Doris Duke Collection, Western History Collections, University of Oklahoma, Norman, Oklahoma. 39(T-50):i–30.

Birchfield, Don L. 1998. "Intermediate Choctology," in *The Oklahoma Basic Intelligence Test: New and Collected Elementary, Epistolary, Autobiographical, and Oratorical Choctologies.* New York: Greenfield Review Press.

Birdchief, Pete. 1972. Interview by Joe Trimble. Doris Duke Collection, Western History Collections, University of Oklahoma, Norman, Oklahoma. 23(T-254):1–5.

Blochowiak, Mary Ann. 1993. "The Opening of the Cherokee Outlet." *Chronicles of Oklahoma* 71 (2): 116–17.

Blu, Karen I. 1980. *The Lumbee Problem: The Making of an American Indian People.* Cambridge: Cambridge University Press.

Bohanan, Emeziah. 1938. Interview by Pete W. Cole. Indian Pioneer Papers, Western History Collections, University of Oklahoma, Norman, Oklahoma. 9:125–46.

Brewer, J. W. 1938. Interview by W. J. B. Bigby. Indian Pioneer Papers, Western History Collections, University of Oklahoma, Norman, Oklahoma. 11:107–12.

Burnett, Agnes. 1972. Interview by Kirk Kickingbird. Doris Duke Collection, Western History Collections, University of Oklahoma, Norman, Oklahoma. 50(T-434):i–15.

Butcher, Nafa. 1938. Interview by Billie Byrd. Indian Pioneer Papers, Western History Collections, University of Oklahoma, Norman, Oklahoma. 14:70–71.

Butler, Sallie (Johnson). 1938. Interview with James R. Carselowey. Indian Pioneer Papers, Western History Collections, University of Oklahoma, Norman, Oklahoma. 14:162–172.

Carnes, James. 1938. Interview by Johnson H. Hampton. Indian Pioneer Papers, Western History Collections, University of Oklahoma, Norman, Oklahoma. 16:59–65.

Champagne, Duane. 1994. *Native America: Portrait of the Peoples.* Detroit: Visible Ink Press.

Choate, Lottie. 1938. Interview by Johnson H. Hampton. Indian Pioneer Papers, Western History Collections, University of Oklahoma, Norman, Oklahoma. 18:8–26.

Churchill, Ward. 1998. "The Tragedy and the Travesty: The Subversion of Indigenous Sovereignty in North America." *American Indian Culture and Research Journal* 22 (2): 1–70.

———. 1999. "The Crucible of American Indian Identity: Tradition versus Colonial Imposition in Post-Conquest North America." *American Indian Culture and Research Journal* 23 (1): 39–68.

Clark, Blue. 1999. *Lone Wolfe v. Hitchcock: Treaty Rights and Indian Law at the End of the Nineteenth Century.* Lincoln: University of Nebraska Press.

Cobb, Isabelle. 1938. "Cherokee Schools." Indian Pioneer Papers, Western History Collections, University of Oklahoma, Norman, Oklahoma. 104:2–36.

Cohen, Abner. 1996. "The Lesson of Ethnicity." In *Theories of Ethnicity: A Classical Reader,* edited by Werner Sollors, pp. 370–84. New York: New York University Press.

Creeping Bear, Joe. 1938. Interview by Ida B. Lankford. Indian Pioneer Papers, Western History Collections, University of Oklahoma, Norman, Oklahoma. 21:442–49.

Cross, Eliza. 1938. Interview by Hazel B. Greene. Indian Pioneer Papers, Western History Collections, University of Oklahoma, Norman, Oklahoma. 22:71–82.

Debo, Angie. 1972 [1934]. *The Rise and Fall of the Choctaw Republic*. Norman: University of Oklahoma Press.

———. 1987. *The Road to Disappearance*. Norman: University of Oklahoma Press.

Devine, Tom. 1938. Interview by Gus Hummingbird. Indian Pioneer Papers, Western History Collections, University of Oklahoma, Norman, Oklahoma. 24:191–98.

Duncan, Dickson. 1938. Interview by Lenna M. Rushing. Indian Pioneer Papers, Western History Collections, University of Oklahoma, Norman, Oklahoma. 26:185–88.

England, Ollie. 1938. Interview by W. J. B. Bigby. Indian Pioneer Papers, Western History Collections, University of Oklahoma, Norman, Oklahoma. 28:94–98.

Ervin, Columbus Wm. 1938. Interview by James Russell Gray. Indian Pioneer Papers, Western History Collections, University of Oklahoma, Norman, Oklahoma. 28:173–82.

Fife, Sandy. 1938. Interview by Billie Byrd. Indian Pioneer Papers, Western History Collections, University of Oklahoma, Norman, Oklahoma. 30:1–3.

Fogelson, Raymond D. 1998. "Perspectives on Native American Identity." In *Studying Native America: Problems and Perspectives*, edited by Russell Thornton, pp. 40–59. Madison: University of Wisconsin Press.

Folsom, Adam. 1938. Interview by Pete W. Cole. Indian Pioneer Papers, Western History Collections, University of Oklahoma, Norman, Oklahoma. 31:11–17.

Fowler, Loretta. 2002. *Tribal Sovereignty and the Historical Imagination: Cheyenne-Arapaho Politics*. Lincoln: University of Nebraska Press.

Franklin, Rachel. 1938. Interview by Lenna M. Rushing. Indian Pioneer Papers, Western History Collections, University of Oklahoma, Norman, Oklahoma. 32:32–34.

Freeman, Mary. 1938. Interview by Jerome M. Emmons. Indian Pioneer Papers, Western History Collections, University of Oklahoma, Norman, Oklahoma. 33:254–59.

French, George. 1938. Interview by Frank J. Still. Indian Pioneer Papers, Western History Collections, University of Oklahoma, Norman, Oklahoma. 33:79–80.

Gibson, Arrell Morgan. 1981. *Oklahoma: A History of Five Centuries*. 2nd ed. Norman: University of Oklahoma Press.

———. 1987. "The Centennial Legacy of the General Allotment Act." *Chronicles of Oklahoma* 65 (3): 228–51.

Gilroy, Thomas A. 1938. Interview by Grace Kelley. Indian Pioneer Papers, Western History Collections, University of Oklahoma, Norman, Oklahoma. 34:141–50.

Goddard, Ives. 1978. "Delaware." In *Handbook of North American Indians*, vol. 15, *Northeast*, edited by Bruce G. Trigger, pp. 213–39. Washington, D.C.: Smithsonian Institution.

Goodbear, Clara Winona. 1972. Interview by David Jones. Doris Duke Collection, Western History Collections, University of Oklahoma, Norman, Oklahoma. 25(T-63):i–27.

Green, Amos. 1937. Interview by Billie Byrd. Indian Pioneer Papers, Western History Collections, University of Oklahoma, Norman, Oklahoma. 36: 8–11.

Green, Donald. 1989. "The Oklahoma Land Run of 1889: A Centennial Re-Inter-pretation." *Chronicles of Oklahoma* 67 (2): 116–49.

Green, Michael D. 1982. *The Politics of Indian Removal.* Omaha: University of Nebraska Press.

Greenback, Mandy Turkey Harjo. 1972. Interview by Velma Neiberding. Doris Duke Collection, Western History Collections, University of Oklahoma, Nor-man, Oklahoma. 52(T-621):i–4.

Hair, Sam. 1972. Interview by Faye Delph. Doris Duke Collection, Western His-tory Collections, University of Oklahoma, Norman, Oklahoma. 15(T-412): i–8.

Harkins, Annie James. 1938. Interview by Mary D. Dorward. Indian Pioneer Papers, Western History Collections, University of Oklahoma, Norman, Okla-homa. 39:2–7.

Hatchett, Meta B. 1938. Interview by Lula Austin. Indian Pioneer Papers, Western History Collections, University of Oklahoma, Norman, Oklahoma. 40:153–67.

Howard, James H. 1990. *Oklahoma Seminoles.* Norman: University of Okla-homa Press.

Hughes, Ida Mae. 1938. Interview by Robert B. Thomas. Indian Pioneer Papers, Western History Collections, University of Oklahoma, Norman, Oklahoma. 45:217–22.

Irving, Washington. 1956 [1835]. *A Tour on the Prairies.* Norman: University of Oklahoma Press.

Jackson, Deborah Davis. 2002. *Our Elders Lived It: American Indian Identity in the City.* DeKalb: Northern Illinois University Press.

Jones, David. 1938. Interview by Johnson H. Hampton. Indian Pioneer Papers, Western History Collections, University of Oklahoma, Norman, Oklahoma. 49:13–18.

Jones, Joanna. 1938. Interview by Nannie Lee Burns. Indian Pioneer Papers, Western History Collections, University of Oklahoma, Norman, Oklahoma. 49:168–74.

Kappler, Charles J. 1904. *Indian Affairs: Laws and Treaties.* Vol 2. Wahington, D.C.: Government Printing Office.

Keith, Albert W. 1938. Interview by Anna R. Barry. Indian Pioneer Papers, West-ern History Collections, University of Oklahoma, Norman, Oklahoma. 50:93–104.

Ketchum, Sol C. 1938. Interview by J. R. Carselowey. Indian Pioneer Papers, Western History Collections, University of Oklahoma, Norman, Oklahoma. 50:449–60.

Killebrew, Julius Finkey. 1938. Interview by Nannie Lee Burns. Indian Pioneer Papers, Western History Collections, University of Oklahoma, Norman, Okla-homa. 51:35–44.

Labor, Elliston. 1938. Indian Pioneer Papers, Western History Collections, Uni-versity of Oklahoma, Norman, Oklahoma. 52:13–19.

Lewis, Winey. 1938. Interview by Grace Kelley. Indian Pioneer Papers, Western History Collections, University of Oklahoma, Norman, Oklahoma. 54:12–21.

Lindsey, Lilah D. 1938. Interview by Effie S. Jackson. Indian Pioneer Papers, Western History Collections, University of Oklahoma, Norman, Oklahoma. 54:171–77.

Locke, Wilson. 1938. Interview by Hazel B. Greene. Indian Pioneer Papers, Western History Collections, University of Oklahoma, Norman, Oklahoma. 55:61–71.

Loftin, Charles W. 1938. Interview by Gomer Gower. Indian Pioneer Papers, Western History Collections, University of Oklahoma, Norman, Oklahoma. 55:83–86.

Long, Mamie Turkey. 1972. Interview by Velma Neiberding. Doris Duke Collection, Western History Collections, University of Oklahoma, Norman, Oklahoma. 52(T-623):i–8.

Longbone, Sarah. 1938. Interview by Nannie Lee Burns. Indian Pioneer Papers, Western History Collections, University of Oklahoma, Norman, Oklahoma. 55:193–203.

Lowe, Mahaley. 1938. Interview by Jerome M. Emmons. Indian Pioneer Papers, Western History Collections, University of Oklahoma, Norman, Oklahoma. 54:37–41.

Martin, James. 1972. Interview by Katherine Red Corn. Doris Duke Collection, Western History Collections, University of Oklahoma, Norman, Oklahoma. 47(T-269): i–6.

Mayes, Lindsey. 1972. Interview by J. W. Tyner. Doris Duke Collection, Western History Collections, University of Oklahoma, Norman, Oklahoma. 17(T-305):i–11.

McDermott, Jessie. 1938. Interview by Billie Byrd. Indian Pioneer Papers, Western History Collections, University of Oklahoma, Norman, Oklahoma. 58:53–56.

McDonald, Mack. 1938. Interview by John F. Daugherty. Indian Pioneer Papers, Western History Collections, University of Oklahoma, Norman, Oklahoma. 58:63–66.

McElroy, Joseph Jefferson. 1938. Interview by Comer Gower. Indian Pioneer Papers, Western History Collections, University of Oklahoma, Norman, Oklahoma. 58:98–105.

McNaughton, Willis. 1972. Interview by Peggy Dycus. Doris Duke Collection, Western History Collections, University of Oklahoma, Norman, Oklahoma. 49(T-472-2):i–21.

Miashintubbee, Jackson. Interview by Johnson H. Hampton. Indian Pioneer Papers, Western History Collections, University of Oklahoma, Norman, Oklahoma. 63:2–8.

Miashintubbee, Nancy. 1938. Interview by Johnson H. Hampton. Indian Pioneer Papers, Western History Collections, University of Oklahoma, Norman, Oklahoma. 63:10–15.

Monday, March. 1938. Interview by Jerome M. Emmons. Indian Pioneer Papers, Western History Collections, University of Oklahoma, Norman, Oklahoma. 64:74–83.

Morris, John W., Charles R. Goins, and Edwin C. McReynolds. 1986. *Historical Atlas of Oklahoma*. Norman: University of Oklahoma Press.

Morton, Tucker W. 1938. Interview by Jerome M. Emmons. Indian Pioneer Papers, Western History Collections, University of Oklahoma, Norman, Oklahoma. 65:195–201.

Narharkey, Sammie. 1938. Interview by Reuben Pattridge. Indian Pioneer Papers, Western History Collections, University of Oklahoma, Norman, Oklahoma. 66:96–97.

Oakes, Joel E. 1938. Interview by Hazel B. Greene. Indian Pioneer Papers, Western History Collections, University of Oklahoma, Norman, Oklahoma. 68:15–25.

Palmer, Eliza. 1938. Interview by Grace Kelley. Indian Pioneer Papers, Western History Collections, University of Oklahoma, Norman, Oklahoma. 69:71–77.

Payne, Mary E. 1938. Interview by Elizabeth Ross. Indian Pioneer Papers, Western History Collections, University of Oklahoma, Norman, Oklahoma. 70:79–86.

Perdasophy, Andrew. 1938. Interview by Ophelia D. Vestal. Indian Pioneer Papers, Western History Collections, University of Oklahoma, Norman, Oklahoma. 71:5–8.

Provost, Bertha. 1972. Interview by William Bittle. Doris Duke Collection, Western History Collections, University of Oklahoma, Norman, Oklahoma. 54(T-686):i–12.

Rackleff, Mrs. Kate. 1938. Interview by Nannie Lee Burns. Indian Pioneer Papers, Western History Collections, University of Oklahoma, Norman, Oklahoma. 74:74–84.

Reed, Leister. 1938. Interview by Nettie Cain. Indian Pioneer Papers, Western History Collections, University of Oklahoma, Norman, Oklahoma. 75:65–67.

Risser, Paul G., and Jeannine Hale Risser. 1980. *A Concept Plan for the Unique Wildlife Ecosystems of Oklahoma.* Norman: University of Oklahoma Press.

Robinson, Ella Coody. 1938. Interview by Ella Robinson. Indian Pioneer Papers, Western History Collections, University of Oklahoma, Norman, Oklahoma. 77:94–127.

Rolland, Jacob. 1938a. Interview by Rufus George. Indian Pioneer Papers, Western History Collections, University of Oklahoma, Norman, Oklahoma. 78:17–18.

———. 1938b. Interview by Rufus George. Indian Pioneer Papers, Western History Collections, University of Oklahoma, Norman, Oklahoma. 78:20.

Rowlodge, Jess. 1972a. Interview by Julia A. Jordan. Doris Duke Collection, Western History Collections, University of Oklahoma, Norman, Oklahoma. 7(T-265):i–30.

———. 1972b. Interview by Julie A. Jordan. Doris Duke Collection, Western History Collections, University of Oklahoma, Norman, Oklahoma. 5(T-235): i–20.

———. 1972c. Interview by Julia A. Jordan. Doris Duke Collection, Western History Collections, University of Oklahoma, Norman, Oklahoma. 5(T-170): i–20.

Sanders, Elizabeth Ballard. 1938. Interview by Ella Robinson. Indian Pioneer Papers, Western History Collections, University of Oklahoma, Norman, Oklahoma. 80:105–10.

Sattler, Richard A. 1998. "Cowboys and Indians: Creek and Seminole Stock Raising, 1700–1900." *American Indian Culture and Research Journal* 22 (3):79–99.

Scott, Bose. 1938. Interview by Jas. S. Buchanan. Indian Pioneer Papers, Western History Collections, University of Oklahoma, Norman, Oklahoma. 81:14–18.

Shafer, Irene. 1938. Interview by Nannie Lee Burns. Indian Pioneer Papers, Western History Collections, University of Oklahoma, Norman, Oklahoma. 82:30–34.

Shoals, Garfield. 1972. Interview by Ruth Hankowsky. Doris Duke Collection, Western History Collections, University of Oklahoma, Norman, Oklahoma. 45(T-286):i–4.

Silver, Shirley, and Wick R. Miller. 1997. *American Indian Languages: Cultural and Social Contexts.* Tucson: University of Arizona Press.

Starr, Clarence. 1938. Interview by James R. Carselowey. Indian Pioneer Papers, Western History Collections, University of Oklahoma, Norman, Oklahoma. 87:70–88.

Stewart, Omer. 1987. *Peyote Religion: A History.* Norman: University of Oklahoma Press.

Strickland, Rennard. 1980. *The Indians in Oklahoma.* Norman: University of Oklahoma Press.

Swan, Daniel C. 1999. *Peyote Religious Art: Symbols of Faith and Belief.* Jackson: University Press of Mississippi.

Unap, Myrtle Morrell. 1972. Interview by Katherine Maker. Doris Duke Collection, Western History Collections, University of Oklahoma, Norman, Oklahoma. 48(T-340):i–15.

Underwood, Joe. 1938. Interview by Lula Austin. Indian Pioneer Papers, Western History Collections, University of Oklahoma, Norman, Oklahoma. 93:14–15.

Wade, David. 1938. Interview by Warren G. Rowley. Indian Pioneer Papers, Western History Collections, University of Oklahoma, Norman, Oklahoma. 94:39–41.

Ward, Eastmen. 1938. Interview by Johnson H. Hampton. Indian Pioneer Papers, Western History Collections, University of Oklahoma, Norman, Oklahoma. 95:126–30.

Whistler, Nancy. 1938. Interview by Gomer Gower. Indian Pioneer Papers, Western History Collections, University of Oklahoma, Norman, Oklahoma. 97:69–76.

White, Arten. 1938. Interview by Pete W. Cole. Indian Pioneer Papers, Western History Collections, University of Oklahoma, Norman, Oklahoma. 97:102–5.

Wiley, Mose. 1938. Interview by Billie Byrd. Indian Pioneer Papers, Western History Collections, University of Oklahoma, Norman, Oklahoma. 98:25–32.

Wilson, Eunice Bluejacket. 1972. Interview by J. W. Tyner. Doris Duke Collection, Western History Collections, University of Oklahoma, Norman, Oklahoma. 53(T-539):i–13.

Wilson, Frazer E. 1894. *The Treaty of Greenville.* Piqua, Ohio: Correspondent Press.

Wolfe, William. 1938. Interview by Gus Hummingbird. Indian Pioneer Papers, Western History Collections, University of Oklahoma, Norman, Oklahoma. 99:462–69.

Wright, J. Leitch. 1990. *Creeks and Seminoles.* Omaha: University of Nebraska Press.

Wright, Muriel H. 1930. "Early Navigation and Commerce along the Arkansas and Red Rivers in Oklahoma." *Chronicles of Oklahoma* 8 (1): 65–80.

———. 1986. *A Guide to the Indian Tribes of Oklahoma.* Norman: University of Oklahoma Press.

# INDEX

Abihkas (tribe), 21
abuse, 59, 61
academies, 64, 69; Christian, 66
Adair, Walter, 40–41
Adair County, Oklahoma, 155
African Americans, 22, 109, 110; children, 64, 67, 73
age, 6, 146. *See also* elders
agency, 38, 171
agents, Indian, 27, 28
agriculture, 22. *See also* farming
Alabama, 21, 22, 23, 153; removal from, 8, 21, 24
alcohol, restrictions on, 144, 158, 164
alliances, 22
allotments, 36, 47–61, 171; and family, 47, 51, 54, 152, 172; for Five Tribes members, 39, 44, 111; legislation on, 29–31, 47, 48–49, 53, 58; now, 59–61; opposition to, 47, 52–58, 59, 111, 172; and politics, 110–11; of republics, 53–58; of reservations, 48–53; rolls for, 48, 59, 94, 114; sale of, 50; selection of, 51–52; for Small Tribes members, 43, 44; support for, 53–58, 111; those without, 54, 57–58
altars, 159
ancestors, 9, 101, 158, 170, 175, 178; non-Indian, 100
Anglo-Europeans, 68, 82. *See also* Euro-Americans; Europeans; whites
Apache, Oklahoma, 17
Apaches, 3, 52, 99; and Native American Church, 150, 162; and Peyote, 159–61, 163; reservations for, 27, 150
Apaches, Plains: and blood quanta,

111–12; homeland of, 14, 16–17; language of, 72
Apuckshenubbee (chief), 20
Arapaho, 16, 81; and allotment, 51; chiefs of, 80; clothing of, 95; and education, 75; homeland of, 14; and land, 49; and Native American Church, 163; and peyote, 160–61; reservations for, 17, 27, 30, 48
Arbeca Baptist Church, 124, 136
Arbeka (tribe), 154
Arkansas, 17, 38, 41
Armstrong, Henry, 52–53, 64, 139–40
art, 167
Ashberry, Jimmie, 124
Asia, 5
assimilation, 9; and allotment, 54, 55, 58, 61, 172; and blood quanta, 93; and education, 63, 66, 70–71, 73, 80, 87; failure of, 87; forced, 37, 43, 70; resistance to, 58, 171; and work, 76, 78, 79
Austin, Lula, 103, 125
authenticity, 87
automobile license tags, 113
autonomy, 24

Bacone College, 67
bands, 50, 54–55, 166
Baptiste, Jane, 46–47
Baptists, 98, 120, 121, 125, 137–38, 139; churches of, 119, 122, 124, 126, 137
Barbee, J. W., 74, 135–36
Barnes, Angie, 81–82
Barth, Frederik, 36
Bartlesville, Oklahoma, 81–82
Batt, Isaac, 40–41

JAMES HAMILL is a professor of anthropology at Miami University at Ohio. He is the author of *Ethno-Logic: The Anthropology of Human Reasoning.*

The University of Illinois Press
is a founding member of the
Association of American University Presses.

---

Composed in 9.5/12.5 Trump Mediaeval
at the University of Illinois Press
Manufactured by Thomson-Shore, Inc.

University of Illinois Press
1325 South Oak Street
Champaign, IL 61820-6903
www.press.uillinois.edu